InDesign Type

Professional Typography
with Adobe® InDesign®

SECOND EDITION

Type

Nigel French

InDesign Type: Professional Typography with Adobe® InDesign®, Second Edition

Nigel French

Copyright © 2010 Nigel French

Adobe Press books are published by Peachpit, a division of Pearson Education.
For the latest on Adobe Press books, go to www.adobepress.com. To report errors, please send a note to errata@peachpit.com.

Acquisitions Editor: Karen Reichstein
Project Editor: Rebecca Freed
Development Editor: Kim Saccio-Kent
Production Editor: Lisa Brazieal
Technical Editor: Kate Godfrey
Copyeditor: Susan Festa
Compositor: Kim Scott, Bumpy Design
Indexer: Karin Arrigoni
Cover Design: Aren Howell
Interior Design: Charlene Charles-Will and Kim Scott

Printed and bound in the United States of America

ISBN-13: 978-0-321-68536-0
ISBN-10:   0-321-68536-9

9 8 7 6 5 4 3 2 1

Acknowledgments

I'm grateful to the following folks for their help (and patience): My fabulous editor Kim Saccio-Kent, superhero technical editor Kate Godfrey, and the lovely folks at Peachpit: Karen Reichstein, Rebecca Freed, Charlene Charles-Will, Scout Festa, Lisa Brazieal, and Kim Scott. I'd also like to say a big thank you to Melanie Hobson, my brother Stephen, sister-in-law Debbie, and last but not least, my dear old Mum.

TABLE OF CONTENTS

Introduction

Today we are all typographers. Everyone knows what a font is, and most people have an opinion about the fonts they like and those they don't. Typography is no longer an arcane trade plied by curmudgeonly men with inky fingers, but rather a life skill. We make typographic decisions every day—the printed material we choose to read, the fonts we select for our correspondence, even the advertising we respond to, consciously or subconsciously.

This democratization of typography is empowering; anyone can participate. But to participate well it helps to know a thing or two—with power comes responsibility. If you are using InDesign, or plan to, then you have at your disposal state-of-the-art software for creating typographic layouts of any length and complexity. It's worth bearing in mind that the concepts behind InDesign didn't just arrive simultaneously with the program's launch in 1999. InDesign itself may be a mere pup, but the principles upon which it is built are part of a long tradition. InDesign is part of a continuum of technological advances going back to the fifteenth century with the invention of movable type and moving with a quantum leap through the mid 1980s with the development of the PostScript page-description software language. The terminology and typographic conventions around which InDesign is built have evolved over generations. The typefaces on our font menus—even the funky postmodern ones—are clearly related to the letter shapes chiseled into the Trajan Column nearly 2000 years ago.

Whether you are new to InDesign or a seasoned user, you've probably found yourself wondering: What are all these controls? Where did they come from? And, perhaps more important: How do I use them, and why? This book attempts to answer these questions. It is not just a book about working with InDesign. Because it is impossible to talk about InDesign without discussing typographic history and best practices, it is also a book about why certain type solutions work better than others.

It's an oft-repeated adage that good typography is "invisible," meaning that, rather than drawing attention to itself, typography should serve the words it represents. As Stanley Morison, who in the 1930s brought us Times (the font designed for The Times of London, although the newspaper no longer uses it), said: "For a new fount to be successful it has to be so good that only very few recognize its novelty."

This perhaps makes typography sound like a thankless task. Where's the fame? The glory? There are few celebrity typographers, and those few walk the streets in relative anonymity. Nonetheless, typography is a noble cause. If typefaces are the bricks and mortar of communication, then we, the typographers, are the architects. A simple and understated building may pass unnoticed by many, but everyone notices an ugly one. Likewise with typography: Good designs serve their purpose and may not elicit comment, but we can all spot bad typography, even though we may not be able to say why it's bad. This book is about avoiding ugly and thoughtless type—a major step in the direction of creating beautiful type.

Who Should Read This Book?

This book deals almost exclusively with English-language typography—not because it is the most important, but because it is what I know. It focuses on print rather than online publishing, even though many of the techniques presented here apply equally to Web typography. It is primarily concerned with the typographic conventions of magazine and book publishing. The techniques in this book will help you create pages and layouts to a professional standard by following a certain set of typographic "rules." My approach is utilitarian rather than experimental. These rules are not intended to be stifling or limiting to creativity. Rather, they are intended as a starting point. Learn the rules. Then, if you choose, break them—but break them consciously, knowing why you do so. Whatever you do, don't ignore them.

I should also mention that although it was written specifically for Adobe InDesign CS5, most of the techniques in the book are applicable to earlier versions of InDesign. Where there is a keyboard shortcut for a command, I indicate the Macintosh shortcut first, followed by the Windows shortcut in parentheses. For example: Cmd+Option+W (Ctrl+Alt+W).

I hope that you enjoy *InDesign Type* and find it a useful addition to your typographic bookshelf. I'm keen to get your feedback, so please email me with any comments, corrections, or suggestions.

—Nigel French
nigel@nigelfrench.com

CHAPTER 1

Getting Started

WHEN IT COMES TO TYPE, we are wide-eyed kids in a candy store. Our font menus are expansive and seductive, spanning centuries of typeface history and reflecting the glorious typographic contributions of different cultures, art movements, mass transit systems, and eccentric individuals. However, with so many typefaces just a mouse click away, it's easy to feel more overwhelmed than empowered by such a treasure trove.

We've all felt intimidated at one time or another by the length of our font menus. If you're like me, you've probably frittered away the best part of a day experimenting with this or that enticingly named font chosen almost randomly from a cast of thousands, only to find yourself dissatisfied with the results but not really knowing why. I hope that this book will help keep such days to a minimum.

Typefaces are to the written word what different dialects are to different languages.
—Steven Heller

But before we get into the practical details of choosing type and working with it in InDesign, we need to become acquainted with some essential type terminology and conventions. To set good type in InDesign it's important to remind ourselves that InDesign is just a tool, and—breathtakingly brilliant tool though it is—unless we understand our raw material, all the power of InDesign won't amount to much. To use InDesign effectively we must understand how type works—and to understand how type works, we need to look at its history, how it is measured, how it is classified, and what messages our typeface choices may carry. And of course, we need to get comfortable with the InDesign interface. Specifically, we need to know where to find the type-related tools and preferences, how to navigate our documents smoothly, and how to set up an efficient type-oriented workflow.

Typography is two-dimensional architecture, based on experience and imagination, and guided by rules and readability.
—Hermann Zapf

Typefaces can be loaded—intentionally or otherwise—with symbolism and meaning. In Gary Hustwit's fantastic documentary film *Helvetica* (2007), graphic designer Paula Scher speaks of her negative connotations of the world's most ubiquitous font, Helvetica, calling it the "font of corporate America." She goes on, tongue firmly in cheek, to describe Helvetica as the font of the Vietnam War and the two Gulf Wars. Elsewhere in the movie, some of the leading lights of the type and design world extol the beauty and timelessness of Helvetica. Typefaces divide opinion.

Typography is a hidden tool of manipulation within society.
—Neville Brody

Taking Helvetica, or its now equally ubiquitous clone Arial, as a case in point, one might argue that their use screams "generic" because we see them as the "default" font, the choice that does not involve any conscious choice at all. But it's not just Helvetica that comes with cultural baggage. Anyone who's spent more than a few hours involved with type will have an opinion about why they love or hate this or that typeface; often it is through no fault of the typeface itself. To cite an extreme example, Fette Fraktur might now connote Nazism, even though similar Blackletter or Fraktur typefaces were used peaceably for hundreds of years before the National Socialists adopted them. Other typefaces, once fashionable, may be trapped in a historical period—great if you want to evoke that era, but a potential faux pas if you don't. Certain typefaces may have been co-opted by an overexposed advertising campaign and can't help but be associated with that product; others—like an overplayed song on the radio—may change from flavor of the month to fingernails-on-a-chalkboard irritation. What's more, there are many type geeks out there who relish the opportunity to point out the historical inappropriateness of using an English sans serif from the late 1920s for a book about a Russian art movement of the early 1920s.

If I exaggerate, it's not by much. The thing is, there's no way to predict how readers will react to our type choices, and, the bolder those choices, the more likely we are to upset someone. Therefore, it's a good idea to be armed with a robust knowledge of typographic history, a solid understanding of the typefaces you use most often, and an awareness of the connotations that certain typefaces carry. The bibliography at the end of this book lists many excellent resources for learning more about type.

My personal type aesthetic is a minimalist one, though perhaps this is just laziness: If less is more, then maybe I can get away with knowing fewer typefaces. Nevertheless, it's better to know and understand a few typefaces well than to have a font list a mile long and only a passing acquaintance with the fonts that are on it.

Typography is what language looks like.

—Ellen Lupton

There are now about as many different varieties of letters as there are different kinds of fools.

—Eric Gill

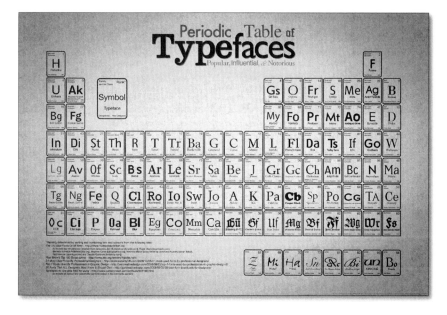

FIGURE 1.3 The whimsical Periodic Table of Typefaces poster available at www.squidspot.com.

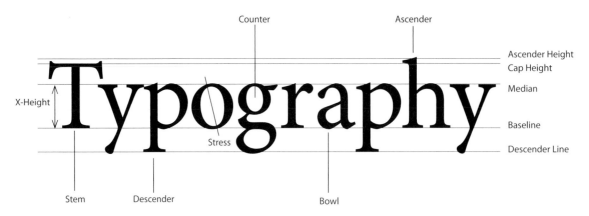

FIGURE 1.1 The parts of the letterform.

Stem: The main part of the letterform that is straight.

Descender: The portion of the lowercase characters *g, j, p, q,* and *y* that projects below the baseline.

Stress: The orientation of the letterform's curved strokes, from thin to thick.

Counter: The interior "negative" space of the letter. *A, a, B, b, D, d, e, g, O, o, P, p, Q, q* all have closed counters.

Bowl: The rounded part of the letterform.

Ascender: The part of the lowercase characters *b, d, f, h, k, l,* and *t* that extends above the x-height.

Cap Height: The height of the uppercase letters.

Median: The imaginary line defining the x-height.

Baseline: The implied line upon which the characters sit.

X-Height: The height of the main body of the lowercase characters. The letter *x* is chosen because the letter's strokes end at—rather than overshoot—this line of measurement.

Choosing a typeface is about enhancing the meaning of the text you are working with. It's also about meeting the expectations and matching the tastes of your client. In a perfect world, we'd all read and thoroughly digest the text documents we are given to work with as raw materials. Depending on the length of your documents, that may or may not be possible, but you should at least have an understanding of the intended message.

Type Anatomy and Classification

To talk meaningfully about type, we need to share a common vocabulary. FIGURE 1.1 is a simple diagram deconstructing letter shapes into their constituent parts.

Typography is necessarily pedantic and relies heavily on small details. Let's clarify some terms we'll be using frequently. A *typeface* is a complete alphabet including letters, numerals, punctuation, and accents. A *font* is a specific size and style of that typeface. For example, Adobe Garamond Pro is a typeface; Adobe Garamond Pro Regular 10 point is a font. These terms are frequently used interchangeably, but typographers love to split hairs, and I guess I'm no exception.

The broadest distinction we can make between typefaces is the distinction between *serif* and *sans serif.* Most typefaces fall into one or the other broad category.

Serifs are the small "ticks" at the end of the letter strokes. Sans serif typefaces do not have these ticks, *sans* meaning "without" in French.

FIGURE 1.2 The distinction between serif and sans serif, and examples of the different types of serif.

Serif
Adobe Garamond Pro

Sans Serif
Myriad Pro

Bracketed Serif
Hoefler Text

Unbracketed Serif
Chaparral Pro

Hairline Serif
Bauer Bodoni

Once we're familiar with this basic difference we'll want to drill down deeper in classifying our type. There is no single recognized standard for classifying typefaces; rather there are several overlapping standards. For our purposes I'm going to use a simplified version of Adobe's type classification, showing examples of each category.

Venetian Oldstyle

Venetian Oldstyle typefaces are named after the letterforms used by the scholars and scribes of northern Italy in the 14th and 15th centuries. Distinguishing features:

- Sloping cross stroke on the lowercase e
- Stress that approximates that of a broad-nibbed pen held at an angle to the page
- Little contrast between thick and thin strokes
- Examples: Adobe Jenson, Berkeley Oldstyle, Centaur

FIGURE 1.4 Venetian Oldstyle

Garalde Oldstyle

Garalde typefaces represent the late Renaissance evolution from the earlier Venetian style, and include some of the most enduring typefaces in use today. Distinguishing features:

- Horizontal cross stroke on the lowercase e
- A slightly greater contrast between thick and thin strokes than Venetian types
- Stress that is inclined to the left
- Bracketed serifs
- Examples: Adobe Garamond, Bembo, Minion Pro

FIGURE 1.5 Garalde Oldstyle

FIGURE 1.6 Script

Script

Script typefaces mimic handwriting by joining letters with connecting lines. For this reason, scripts require extra attention to the kerning of their letters and should never be set in all caps. Historically, the problem with script typefaces is that their "personal" nature is antithetical to their digital manufacture. In handwriting, which script typefaces mimic, no two "a"s would be exactly alike, but in a font, of course, they are. Recently, however, a number of beautiful scripts have been released with a wide range of alternate characters for specific letter combinations, allowing you to create unique and personal type treatments. See Chapter 6, "Small (but Important) Details."

- Examples: Bickham Script Pro, Champion Script Pro, Raniscript

FIGURE 1.7 Transitional

Transitional

A move away from letter shapes based on handwriting, transitional types were the first typefaces to be drawn as shapes in their own right. They represent a *transition* between Garalde and Didone (Modern) typefaces, and contain aspects of both. Distinguishing features:

- A vertical, or near vertical, stress
- Pronounced contrast between hairlines and main strokes
- Serifs are thin, flat, and bracketed
- Examples: Baskerville, Perpetua, Stone Serif

FIGURE 1.8 Didone (Modern)

Didone (Modern)

Named after Firmin Didot (1764–1836) and Giambattista Bodoni (1740–1813), Didone typefaces were a response to improvements in late 18th-century paper production, composition, printing, and binding, which made it possible to develop typefaces with strong vertical emphasis and fine hairlines. Distinguishing features:

- Strong contrast between thick and thin strokes
- Vertical stress
- Mechanical appearance—constructed rather than drawn
- Hairline serifs
- Examples: Bodoni, Didot, Fenice

Slab Serif

Until the late 18th century, type was used primarily for books. With the Industrial Revolution came the increased use of posters, billboards, and other forms of advertising, and the need for bolder, more in-your-face typefaces that stood out from the competition. Slab serif typefaces were originally called "Egyptians," reflecting the public's enthusiasm for the archeological discoveries of the time. Distinguishing features:

- Heavy, squared-off serifs
- Relatively consistent stroke weight
- Sturdy
- Examples: Clarendon, Memphis, Chaparral Pro

FIGURE 1.9 Slab Serif

Sans Serif

William Caslon IV (the great, great grandson of William Caslon) issued the first sans serif typeface in 1816, but it wasn't until the end of the 19th century that sans serifs became widely used.

This category can be subdivided into Grotesques (Helvetica, for example), relatively monoweight and noted for their plain or neutral appearance; Geometric (Futura), where the letterforms are geometric or near-geometric and the strokes monoweight; and Humanist (Gill Sans) where the letterforms are based on Roman proportions and the strokes are modulated.

- Examples: Futura, Helvetica, Gill Sans

FIGURE 1.10 Sans Serif

Decorative & Display

This is a catchall category for those typefaces whose primary purpose is to grab the reader's attention. They are most effective when used in large sizes for headlines, titles, and signage. Because they are so expressive and tend to evoke a particular fashion or moment in time, they can have a short shelf life.

- Examples: Arnold Böcklin, Rosewood, Industria

FIGURE 1.11 Decorative

Manuscript Abbey Metal Demon News Head banger Biere

FIGURE 1.12   Blackletter

Retro Typewriter Bank Charges Low-Fi Machine Default

FIGURE 1.13   Monospaced

FIGURE 1.14   Ornaments

Blackletter

These types are called Blackletter because they look so dark on the page. They are also sometimes referred to as Old English or Gothic; in Germany they are referred to as Fraktur. They may suggest a traditional newspaper masthead and the authority that entails. However, Fette Fraktur, a typeface designed in the mid-19th century, was unfortunate enough to be adopted by the Nazis in preference to the "non-Germanic" sans serif faces favored by the Bauhaus and other radical art movements of the time. In an interesting twist, the Third Reich discontinued the use of Blackletter typefaces in 1941, after allegations of Jewish contributions in the development of these faces, but it's still hard to see these letterforms without their negative baggage.

- Examples: Fette Fraktur, Goudy Text, Lucida Blackletter

Monospaced

Although most typefaces have proportionally spaced characters, all of the characters in a monospaced typeface have the same width. Monospaced typefaces are sometimes used when setting text on forms where exact spacing is necessary, or when differentiating a line of computer code in an instructional manual (although a proportionally spaced "techie looking" font like Letter Gothic is a good alternative). Courier is also used to indicate a missing font. InDesign can usually simulate the look of a missing font on screen, but it can't do the same in print. Printing a document that contains missing fonts results in Courier being substituted for the missing font. This convention has been adopted by all page layout applications because Courier looks so wrong that you can't miss it—you will presumably feel compelled to fix it.

- Examples: Courier, OCR A, Letter Gothic

Ornaments

Ornament typefaces contain decorative elements that can be used to embellish documents. Some OpenType fonts include ornaments as part of their extended character set.

- Examples: Minion Pro Ornaments, Adobe Caslon Ornaments, Adobe Wood Type Ornaments

Symbol, Dingbat, or Pi

There exists a parallel universe of typefaces that aren't letters at all, but pictograms. These picture fonts can be playful as well as practical, with such useful devices as bullets, ballot boxes, check marks, stars, and navigational arrows. As well as extending the range of your typical character set, they are used for musical notation, map making, mathematics, crosswords, and puzzle publishing. David Carson, enfant terrible of grunge typography in the 1990s, famously set an article—an interview with Bryan Ferry—for *Raygun* magazine in Zapf Dingbats. "It's not worth reading—why not do it in Zapf Dingbats?"

- Examples: Symbol, Zapf Dingbats, Carta

FIGURE 1.15 Symbol, Dingbat, or Pi

Why Some Fonts Look Bigger than Others

Take a selection of fonts, set them in the same point size, and you'll find that some look bigger than others. This is a legacy from the days of metal type when point size referred to the size of the metal block on which the type was cast. Some typefaces occupied more space within their blocks than others. Today, point size refers not to the size of a metal block, but to the size of its digital equivalent: the bounding box that surrounds each letter. We measure the space in which the type lives, not the letter itself; some fonts occupy relatively more of that space than others. For this reason, let your eye guide you, not the point size.

Here's an obvious point, but one still worth making: It's hard to correctly evaluate the size (and other aspects) of your type exclusively on screen. Unless you're creating type that is intended for screen reading only, print your test pages rather than rely on what you see on your monitor.

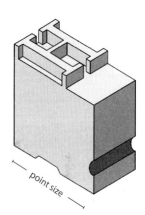

point size

FIGURE 1.16 A sample type block. The size of the type (point size) refers to the vertical height of the block itself, not the letterform within the block.

What's in a Name?

Many typeface names are in the public domain, and many of the typefaces we work with are revivals or interpretations of the originals. Anyone with font editing software can create a typeface and call it "Garamond"—just because something is called Garamond, doesn't mean it's going to look the same as somebody else's Garamond. Sometimes interpretations of a typeface can be dramatically different from each other in much the same way as interpretations of the same song may be more notable for how unlike they are rather than how similar. For this reason, be specific about which Garamond you're using and what vendor supplied it.

FIGURE 1.17 The same passage of text at the same point size and leading showing how some fonts look bigger than others.

Myriad Pro 9/11
One morning, when Gregor Samsa woke from troubled dreams, he found himself transformed in his bed into a horrible vermin. He lay on his armour-like back, and if he lifted his head a little he could see his brown belly, slightly domed and divided by arches into stiff sections. The bedding was hardly able to cover it and seemed ready to slide off any moment. His many legs, pitifully thin compared with the size of the rest of him, waved about helplessly as he looked.

Stone Serif 9/11
One morning, when Gregor Samsa woke from troubled dreams, he found himself transformed in his bed into a horrible vermin. He lay on his armour-like back, and if he lifted his head a little he could see his brown belly, slightly domed and divided by arches into stiff sections. The bedding was hardly able to cover it and seemed ready to slide off any moment. His many legs, pitifully thin compared with the size of the rest of him, waved about helplessly as he looked.

FIGURE 1.18 A selection of "Garamonds," all at 30 point (right), and a comparison of the differences found in a single character.

uncopywritable
Adobe Garamond Pro

uncopywritable
ITC Garamond

uncopywritable
Simoncini Garamond

aaaaa

uncopywritable
Garamond

uncopywritable
Stempel Garamond

TIP: You can view your menu items in alphabetical order by holding down Cmd+Shift+Option (Ctrl+Shift+Alt) when you choose the menu. This is handy when you're searching for that pesky menu item you can't find but you know is there. It may be a small thing, perhaps a feature you'll never use, but it's nice to know it's there.

An InDesign Type Map:
Where to Find the Type Stuff

Everything in InDesign relates to type in one way or another, but here I want to point out the most frequently used type-related menu and panel options. I'll also discuss InDesign preferences that control how type behaves. As with any of the big-hitter design applications these days, there's usually more than one way to do something. Sometimes, it's merely a matter of preference. Other times, new features have been added that improve on old features—and so that veteran users aren't alienated, the old menu options remain. We all work differently, and InDesign encourages customization.

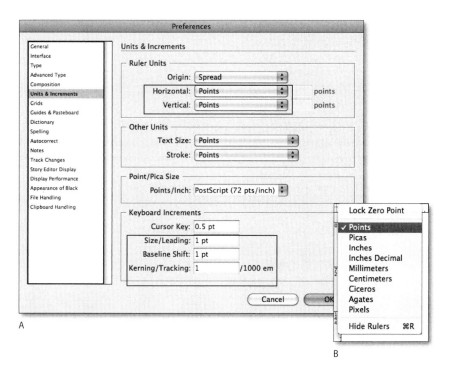

FIGURE 1.19 Units & Increments Preferences (**A**) **Ruler Units (circled):** Points are a typographic standard. Wouldn't you rather have an indent of 12 points (or 1 pica) than 4.233 millimeters? **Keyboard Increments (circled):** Size/Leading determines the increment when sizing type with keyboard shortcuts. A smaller increment allows more control, especially when sizing small type. To size in bigger increments, add the Option (Alt) key to the keyboard shortcut to increase that increment fivefold. **Baseline Shift:** The keyboard shortcut to adjust the baseline shift is Shift+Alt+Up Arrow or Shift+Alt+Down Arrow. It's not one you use often, but you may as well change this preference, too. **Kerning/Tracking (circled):** This value determines the increment used when custom tracking or kerning is applied through keyboard shortcuts: Option+Left Arrow (Alt+Left Arrow) to reduce the space or Option+ Right Arrow (Alt+Right Arrow) to increase the space. For fine (read: better) control, change this to the lowest increment possible, 1/1000 em. For bigger increments, add in the Cmd (Ctrl) key to increase that increment fivefold. You can easily change the measurement system on the fly by right-clicking where the rulers intersect (**B**).

There are several preferences relating to type; for now, I just want to point out where they are and suggest a couple of changes to the factory default settings. I'll deal with each preference specifically in the relevant chapter.

When you make a change to InDesign's preferences, you affect only the document you are working on. If you want to change the preferences for every document you create from this point on, make sure you have no InDesign document open so that your changes become application preferences. The following preferences become application-wide when you change them with no document open: General, Interface, Type, Advanced Type, Composition, Units & Increments, Grids, and Guides & Pasteboard.

If you're serious about type, I suggest you get used to working in points (or picas, of which points are a subdivision). Points are a typographic unit of measurement originated in the early 18th century. They're arcane and nondecimal, but there's still good reason to use them. Since type is rarely expressed in anything but points, it's helpful to have distances that relate to type, such as leading (space between the lines), indents, paragraph spacing, and gutter (inter-column) spacing also expressed in points. In the U.S., margin sizes and column widths are typically expressed in picas; in Europe they are more commonly expressed in millimeters.

Picas and Points In a Nutshell

6 picas = 1 inch or 25.4 millimeters
12 points = 1 pica
72 points = 1 inch
1 pica and 6 points = 1p6. Alternatively, this could be expressed as 0p18 or 18 pt.
6 points = 0p6, p6, or 6 pt.

TIP: Regardless of your chosen measurement system, you can express values in any of InDesign's supported measurement systems so long as you are explicit. For example, if you are using points but want a frame that is 50 millimeters square, select the frame and type *50 mm* in the height and width fields of the Control Panel. InDesign will convert this to its equivalent in points.

Typography also has relative units, two commonly used examples being the *em space* (the size of your type—if you're working with 10-point type, then an em space is 10 points) and the *en space* (half the size of the em space). Another relative unit is the 1/1000 em, which is used for kerning and tracking. To understand kerning and tracking units, it helps to know that each character of a typeface is designed within an em square of 1000 units. The character occupies a certain *set width* of that em square according to its shape; for example, an *m* will necessarily be wider than an *i*. The widest character in the typeface will likely be the em dash, which occupies nearly the full 1000 units. Kerning and tracking involve the adjustment of these relative amounts of space, either to create the "illusion" of perfect spacing or, in the case of tracking, to give the type a denser or airier feel.

FIGURE 1.20 Three screen captures from FontLab Studio, a typeface creation application, showing the different set widths of the characters within a 1000-unit em square.

The Tools Panel

There are two tools we use most of the time: the Selection Tool and the Type Tool. The Selection Tool is used for (among other things) moving, resizing, and threading text frames. The Type Tool is used for formatting and editing the text *inside* those frames. You move back and forth between these tools a lot, so it's handy that there's a way to toggle between them.

To work with text frames while the Type Tool is selected, hold down Cmd (Ctrl) to switch to the Selection Tool. With the key held down, you can drag the frame to move it, or drag any of the frame handles to resize it. When you release the key, you're back in the Type Tool.

When you're using your Selection Tool, you can double-click a text frame and your cursor changes to the Type Tool, inserted at the point where you double-clicked.

It's also worth memorizing the single-key shortcuts to access these tools: **T** for Type and the Esc key for the Selection Tool (**V** also works in other situations, but obviously not while you're in the Type Tool).

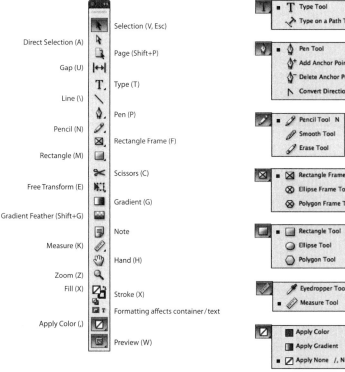

FIGURE 1.21 The Tools panel. To access the additional tools shown on the right, click and hold down on those tools that have a black triangle in their bottom-right corner.

TIP: When in any tool other than the Type Tool, pressing the spacebar temporarily switches the current tool to the Hand Tool; pressing "H" also works. However, if you are in the Type Tool, holding down the spacebar gets you a whole mess of spaces. This may appear to be an obvious point, but you'd be surprised how easy it is to make this mistake. If you are in the Type Tool, hold down the Option (Alt) key to temporarily access the Hand Tool. When working quickly it's easy to forget where you are and which key you need, so it's easier to standardize on Option+spacebar (Alt+spacebar), which works in all situations.

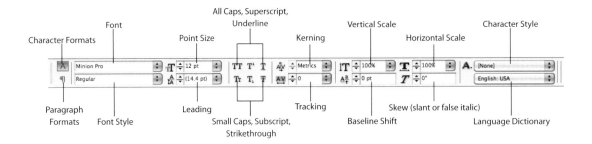

Character Formats
Font
Point Size
All Caps, Superscript, Underline
Kerning
Vertical Scale
Horizontal Scale
Character Style

Paragraph Formats
Font Style
Leading
Small Caps, Subscript, Strikethrough
Tracking
Baseline Shift
Skew (slant or false italic)
Language Dictionary

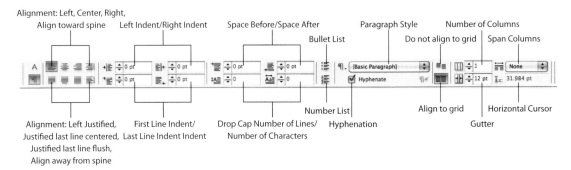

Alignment: Left, Center, Right,
Align toward spine
Left Indent/Right Indent
Space Before/Space After
Bullet List
Paragraph Style
Number of Columns
Do not align to grid
Span Columns

Alignment: Left Justified,
Justified last line centered, Last Line Indent Indent
Justified last line flush,
Align away from spine
First Line Indent/
Drop Cap Number of Lines/
Number of Characters
Number List
Hyphenation
Align to grid
Gutter
Horizontal Cursor

FIGURE 1.22 The Control Panel showing Character Formats (top) and Paragraph Formats (directly below). You can toggle between these two views by pressing Cmd+Option+7 (Ctrl+Alt+7). Click on the icon at the right of the Control Panel (circled) for more options (bottom left). Note that it's possible to customize the appearance of the Control Panel (bottom right).

Press the Tab key to move from one field to the next, or press Shift+Tab to move backward through the fields. Once in a field, press the Up or Down arrow to increase or decrease the values.

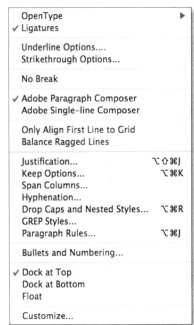

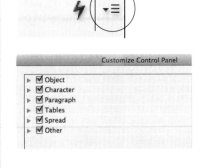

The Control Panel

The Control Panel is a chameleon, changing its appearance according to what you have selected. When you are using the Type Tool, the Control Panel has two views: Character Formatting Controls and Paragraph Formatting Controls. If your monitor is big enough, a digested list of Paragraph formats is displayed to the right of the Character formats in Character Formats view; this is reversed in Paragraph Formats view.

Note that it's possible to customize the Control Panel. If you don't see the options you expect—particularly if you are sharing your computer with another user—check the current options by choosing Customize from the bottom of the Control Panel menu.

Viewing Your Page

There are several ways to view and navigate your InDesign documents—some are better than others. Although you have myriad options, you can do most everything you need with just three shortcuts.

1. **Zooming In: Cmd+spacebar (Ctrl+spacebar).** If you value your eyesight, get in big when editing text. There's no point squinting at a page you can barely read. You could choose the Zoom Tool (Q) from the Tools panel, but save yourself the trouble. Instead, access the Zoom Tool by holding down Cmd+spacebar (Ctrl+spacebar); your cursor changes to a magnifying glass. Now, rather than click to increase your view percentage, click and drag a marquee around the portion of your layout you want enlarged. The defined portion then fills your window. If you want to zoom out incrementally, press Cmd+Option+spacebar (Ctrl+Alt+spacebar) and click.

2. **Moving Around: Option+spacebar (Alt+spacebar).** Once at an enlarged view, you'll likely want to move around. Press Option+spacebar (Alt+spacebar) and drag with the Hand Tool (🖐) to move your page or spread around within the document window. You can also use the Hand Tool at reduced view sizes to move vertically through pages. Don't bother with the scroll bars; it's hard to estimate their sensitivity and you'll waste a lot of time getting to exactly where you want to be.

TIP: If your type looks bitmapped on screen, it's probably because you have switched to the Fast Display mode, InDesign's low-resolution, quick screen redraw option. Choose View > Display Performance and switch to Typical or High Quality. If you have a fast computer, choose High Quality to ensure that your images are always rendered on screen at full resolution (note that Display Performance has no bearing on how your documents print). To make this an application preference, change the settings in Preferences > Display Performance, while no document is open.

3. **Zooming Out: Cmd+Option+0 (Ctrl+Alt+0).** Use this key combination to fit your spread (or page) in the window. Having zoomed in and made your changes at a comfortable view size, zoom out again to get an overall perspective on your page or spread.

A valid alternative to this triumvirate of view shortcuts is Power Zoom: At any view size press Option+spacebar (Alt+spacebar) to access the Hand Tool, then pause for a fraction of a second. A red magnification rectangle appears that you can reposition to view a different part of your page or spread. To change the size of the zoom rectangle, continue to hold down Option-spacebar (Alt-spacebar) while you press the Up or Down arrow to increase or decrease its size—the smaller the rectangle the bigger the magnification, and vice versa.

When editing type, Cmd+2 (Ctrl+2) and Cmd+4 (Ctrl+4) are useful shortcuts for zooming in to 200 percent and 400 percent, respectively.

Moving Between Pages

For documents consisting of only a few pages or spreads, you can navigate from one page to the next with the Hand Tool. For longer documents, use the Pages panel, the Pages pop-up menu at the bottom left of your document window, or the options under the Layout menu.

When using the Pages panel to navigate between spreads with facing pages, double-clicking the page numbers includes both pages of the spread in the window, whereas double-clicking the page icon fits that specific page in the window.

Creating a Typography Workspace

TIP: Press the Tab key to hide and show all your panels. Press Shift+Tab to hide or show all panels except Tools and the Control Panel.

InDesign panels are so numerous you would swear they breed like rabbits when your back is turned. A great many of these panels you'll seldom or never use, no matter how illustrious your InDesign career. Thankfully, InDesign gives you unprecedented control of your workspace, allowing you to save—and recall at any time—the visibility, positions, and groupings of your panels. The names of workspaces appear in the Workspace picker on the Application Bar or in the Workspace submenu of the Window menu. You can make a custom keyboard shortcut to switch to your workspace with a specified key combination.

First, arrange your panels the way you want them. Create groupings that make sense to you; close those panels you think you'll seldom or never use (if you

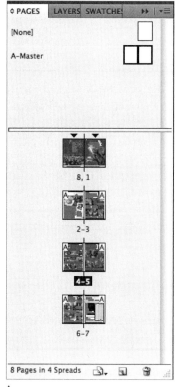

A

B

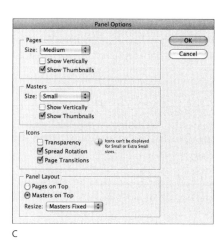

C

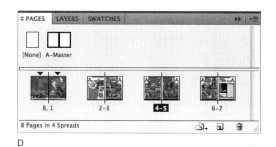

D

E

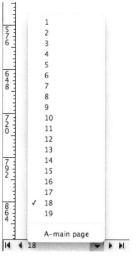

F

FIGURE 1.23 The Pages Panel in its familiar orientation showing thumbnails for an eight-page, facing-pages document (**A**). Some users prefer to change the Panel Options to have the thumbnails display horizontally, a more economical use of screen real estate (**B**), (**C**), (**D**). You can also navigate your document using the Layout menu (**E**), keyboard shortcuts, or the Pages drop-down at the bottom left of the document window (**F**).

TIP: You can make a keyboard shortcut to load your custom workspace from the Edit > Keyboard Shortcuts menu. Because you can't overwrite the default shortcut set, click New Set. For Product Area, choose Window Menu. You'll get a long list of all the commands on the window menu—scroll down to Workspace: Load 1st User Workspace. Click into the New Shortcut field, press the keys for your new keyboard shortcut. I use Ctrl+F12—Ctrl being the fourth, seldom used, modifier on the Mac. (Leave the Context list set to Default so that the shortcut functions in all situations.) Click Assign to create the new shortcut.

need them later, you can find them under the Window menu); then float or dock those you want, where you want them. From the Workspace picker choose New Workspace and give your workspace a name.

InDesign comes with a selection of predefined workspaces. The Typography workspace is a good starting point. To this I like to add the following: Object Styles, Info, Links, Scripts, and Align. I close the Paragraph and Character panels because their offerings are also available on the Control Panel.

Having saved your workspace, you can load it at any time by choosing it from the Workspace picker (located next to the search field, upper right). If you've made changes to the workspace and want to revert it to its previously saved state, choose Reset. If you'd like those changes to overwrite the workspace, choose New Workspace and choose the same name (you'll be asked to confirm that you want to overwrite the existing workspace).

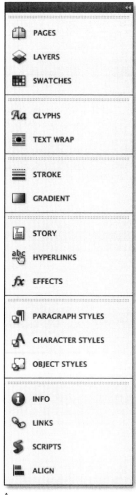

A

B

C

D

FIGURE 1.24 Setting a typography workspace: My preferred workspace (**A**), a modified version of the predefined Typography Workspace. You can also create a keyboard shortcut to quickly load your workspace (**B**, **C**), or just choose it from the Workspace picker (**D**).

CHAPTER 2

Getting Type on Your Page

TYPOGRAPHY BEGINS with a single character, and putting type on your page is about as fundamental as InDesign skills get. There are several different approaches to getting type on the page. You'll use all of them at one time or another. Let's begin with the most elemental.

Creating Text Frames

TIP: The appearance of your type cursor is a visual cue: If the cursor has a square, dotted line around it, you can click and drag to create a new text frame. When you move over an empty frame, the type cursor bulges to indicate you are about to insert into that frame.

In InDesign, text frames hold your type. Each independent section of text is referred to as a *story*. A story can contain a single character or hundreds of pages of connected, or "threaded," text. An InDesign document typically contains multiple stories, as would a newspaper or magazine. You can create a text frame in any of the following ways:

- Draw one using either a Frame Tool or a Shape Tool. Select the Type Tool and click within the object to activate it as a text frame.

- Create one on the fly by clicking and dragging on the page or pasteboard with the Type Tool to define the width and height of the frame. When you release the mouse button, a flashing type cursor appears in the top left of the frame and you're ready to start typing.

TIP: The Smart Cursor displays the width and height of the frame as you drag it out. Alternatively, you can specify the size of your frame, once drawn, using the Width and Height fields on the Control Panel.

- Choose File > Place or press Cmd/Ctrl+D to import a text document. You will see a loaded text cursor. Click on the page to flow the text and you automatically create a text frame that is the width of the column.

Unless you've redefined the [Basic Paragraph] Paragraph Style, the default font will be Minion Pro Regular 12 point. Since you'll be applying formats to the type, it doesn't really matter how it starts out. But if you want to change the default font, here's how: Open the Paragraph Styles panel, right-click [Basic Paragraph], and choose Edit. From the list of options on the left choose Basic Character Formats and change the font, point size, and so on. While you're in Paragraph Style Options you can also change any other attributes, like the alignment, indents, or hyphenation. Realistically, though, nothing ends up as [Basic Paragraph]. It is just the point from which you start your text formatting.

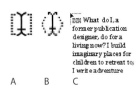

FIGURE 2.1 The Text Cursor: A dotted square around the cursor indicates you can drag to create a text frame (**A**). The cursor bulges (**B**) you are over an empty frame. When you import—or "place"—text, the cursor appears "loaded." (**C**)

FIGURE 2.2 The Smart Cursor indicates the dimensions of the frame you are drawing.

FIGURE 2.3 To change the default font, edit the [Basic Paragraph] definition.

FIGURE 2.4 Aligning the Type cursor to a guide.

Text Flow

While it's possible to compose your text in InDesign, most of the time the writing is done in a dedicated word processing application like Microsoft Word, or possibly in InDesign's editorial cousin, Adobe InCopy. For example, I'm writing this book in Word (it's not my choice, but my editors insisted). Arguably, when documents need to go back and forth in a review cycle it's easier to use Word for its editorial features like Comments and Track Changes. (A moot point, you might argue, now that InDesign also has a Track Changes feature.)

It's our job as designers to import the prepared text into InDesign, where—juxtaposed with imagery and flowed from column to column and from page to page—we make it look beautiful.

To import—or "place"—a text file, choose File > Place or Cmd-D/Ctrl-D, navigate to the file you're after, and click Open. Your loaded type cursor displays the first few words of the text file in a thumbnail.

You can either click the loaded cursor inside a frame or create a frame by clicking on a blank area of your page. The point at which you click becomes the top of the text frame; the width of the frame is determined by the page's column and margin settings. To align the top of the text frame with the top margin (or a ruler guide you have drawn), hover over the guide until the arrow that is part of the loaded cursor icon changes from black to white, indicating that the text frame will "snap" to that guide.

TIP: When dragging out a text frame with the Type Tool, work with your guides on so that you can size your text frames accurately. Align the horizontal tick on the Type cursor to the top margin or horizontal guide. To see your nonprinting guides, make sure you are in Normal Screen Mode and, if necessary press Cmd-; (Ctrl-;) to show the guides.

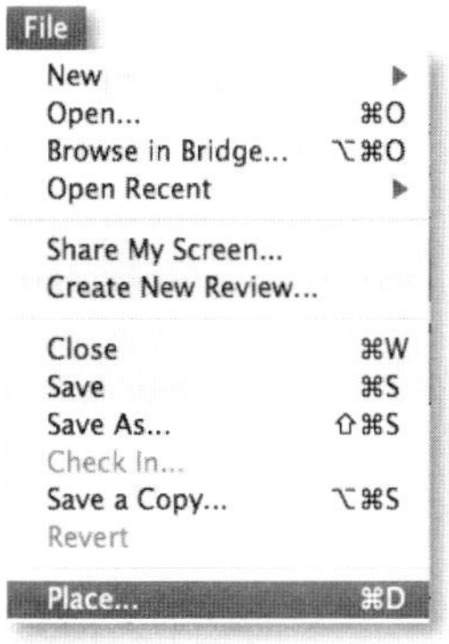

FIGURE 2.5 The Place selection on the File menu.

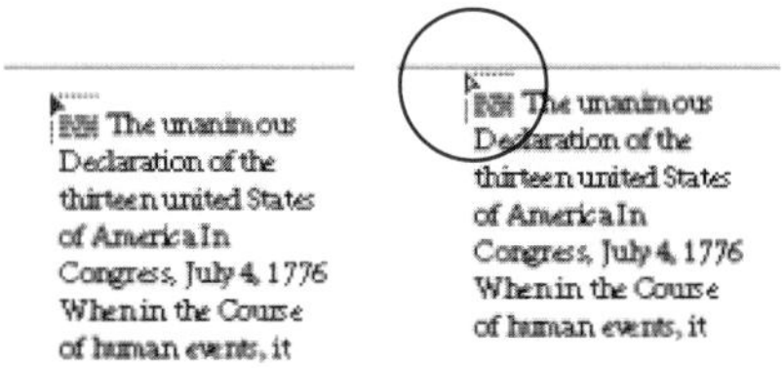

FIGURE 2.6 Aligning the loaded Text Cursor to the top margin. The white arrow indicates that the top of the text frame will "snap" to the guide.

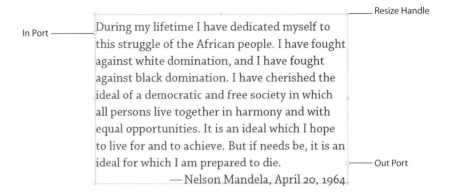

FIGURE 2.7 The anatomy of a text frame.

In Port

Resize Handle

Out Port

> During my lifetime I have dedicated myself to this struggle of the African people. I have fought against white domination, and I have fought against black domination. I have cherished the ideal of a democratic and free society in which all persons live together in harmony and with equal opportunities. It is an ideal which I hope to live for and to achieve. But if needs be, it is an ideal for which I am prepared to die.
>
> — Nelson Mandela, April 20, 1964

Each text frame contains an In port and an Out port, which are used to make connections to other text frames. An empty In port or Out port indicates the beginning or end of a story, respectively. A blue arrow in either indicates that the frame is linked to another frame. A red plus sign (+) in an Out port indicates that there is overset text—more text than will fit in the current text frame(s). To flow the overset text, select the frame with the Selection Tool, click the red plus sign to "reload" your cursor, move to where you want to continue the text flow, and click at the top of a new column or page, or inside a text frame.

Alternatively, click and drag the loaded type cursor to the size you want. When you release the mouse button, text will flow into the area defined.

What to Watch for When Flowing Text

'Replace Selected Item' option in the Place dialog box: If this is checked and you have a text frame selected with the Selection Tool, the text file you choose will replace the current contents of that frame. If your Type Tool is in a text frame, the new story will be flowed from that point in the story. These are both useful techniques, but if the results aren't what you expect, press Cmd+Z (Ctrl+Z) to restore the selected text frame to its original state. This will also return you to a loaded type cursor. Of course, you can just make sure this option isn't selected in the first place.

Canceling a loaded text cursor: If you decide you are not ready to flow the text, press Esc to "unload" the cursor.

If you have the Selection Tool selected and want to edit type within a text frame, double-click in the frame to switch to the Type Tool. You can toggle between the Type Tool and the Selection Tool by holding down Cmd (Ctrl). When you let up the Cmd (Ctrl) key, you're back in the Type Tool.

To move a text frame, select it with the Selection Tool and click and drag from within the frame. To resize a text frame, select it with the Selection Tool and pull from one of its handles.

Types of Text Flow

Manual Text Flow adds text one frame at a time. The text flow stops at the bottom of a text frame, or at the last of a series of linked frames. You'll need to reload the Type cursor to continue the text flow. Manual text flow is most appropriate for short bodies of text. This is the default option.

Manual

Autoflow (Shift) flows all the text, adding pages and frames as necessary. Autoflow functions best when working with single-column documents containing one main story—like a novel, a short story, or a journal article. Autoflow isn't much use when you are working with multiple columns and images because it flows text indiscriminately into all columns, regardless of whether those columns contain other content.

Autoflow

Semi-Autoflow (Option/Alt) works like Manual Text Flow, except that your cursor is reloaded automatically at the end of each frame, which saves you from having to click the red plus. You then continue the text flow by clicking to create a new text frame or clicking an empty text frame to add it to the text thread. If you click and drag you can span your text across multiple columns. Semi-Autoflow is most appropriate when working with magazine or newspaper articles.

Semi-Autoflow

Fixed-Page Autoflow (Shift+Option or Shift+Alt) flows as much text as will fit without adding pages, which is useful if your document has a fixed number of pages.

Fixed-Page Autoflow

FIGURE 2.8 The Text flow cursors.

Smart Text Reflow automatically adds or deletes pages as your text grows or shrinks. To use Smart Text Reflow, choose Preferences > Type and remove the check mark for the Limit to Master Text Frames option. New pages will be added to the document based on the Master Page applied to the current last page. Check Delete Empty Pages and any pages that no longer have any content will disappear. Note that Smart Text Reflow requires you to have at least two threaded text frames over at least two pages.

Live Preflight

InDesign's Live Preflight indicates potential errors in your document, including overset text. To open the Preflight Panel, double-click the red error dot that appears in the lower left of the document window. Click the disclosure triangle to the left of the listed error for more information, then click the hyperlinked number to jump to the problem.

FIGURE 2.9 The Preflight notification area (top) and the Preflight Panel showing overset text.

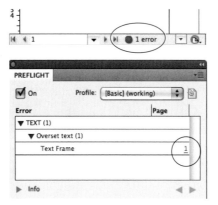

Dragging and Dropping Text Files

In addition to placing text files using the File > Place command, it's possible to drag and drop text files into InDesign from the Mac OS X Finder, from Windows Explorer, or from Bridge, the all-around Swiss Army knife–type application that comes with InDesign. Depending on the size of your monitor (this approach works best when you have a lot of screen real estate), this may be a faster, more fluid way of working. If you're lucky enough to have a dual monitor setup, you can park your Bridge window on the second display and drag content to your InDesign page as needed, speeding workflow massively. If you don't have a second monitor, you can set the Bridge view to Compact mode so that its Content window remains in front of InDesign—or, with CS5, use the Mini Bridge panel, which functions as an integral file browser within InDesign itself. Either option lets you drag text and pictures into your layout with such ease that your pages take form almost instantaneously.

For documents like newsletters, magazines, and newspapers that are made up of multiple stories, the ability to simultaneously place multiple text and/or image files is a huge time saver. In earlier versions of InDesign, this meant dragging and dropping multiple files from Bridge, and in CS5 you can continue to do this, but it's slightly more convenient to use Mini Bridge, which is now incorporated into the InDesign interface.

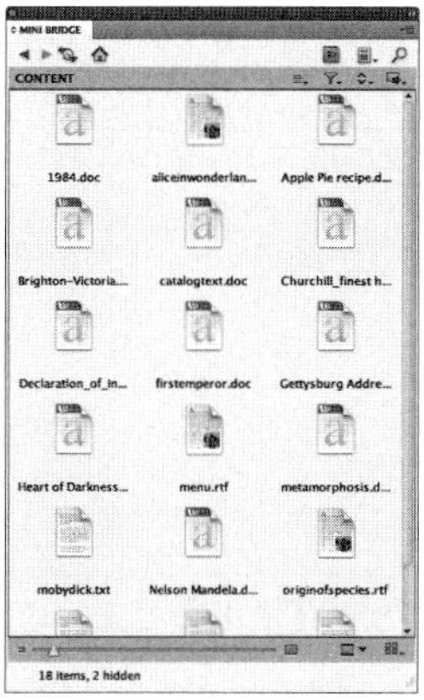

The Mini Bridge panel is found under the Window menu. Once it's open, you can use Mini Bridge to browse folders and adjust the size of the thumbnails using the slider at the bottom left of the panel. For multiple files, hold down the Shift key to make a continuous selection, or use the Cmd/Ctrl key to make a noncontinuous selection of the files. When you drag from the thumbnail of any one of the selected files into your InDesign document, a loaded text cursor (or picture cursor, if you're dragging pictures) displays in parentheses the number of files that are queued. To cycle through queued files on your cursor, press the Left/Right or Up/Down arrows.

FIGURE 2.10 Browsing a folder of text files in Mini Bridge.

If you use pencil sketches to plan the text flow, or pre-establish the text threads for a range of empty text frames, a multiple place can transform a document from foundation to near-complete dwelling with just a few mouse clicks. As when creating new text on the page, pay attention to the shape of your loaded cursor—if the document cursor is surrounded by parentheses the text will go into an existing frame; if it's surrounded by a square you'll create a new text frame.

Threading Text Frames

Continuing the text flow from one frame to another is called *threading*. Here are some typical threading techniques:

FIGURE 2.11 The Text Cursor loaded with multiple files.

Creating a thread. Select a frame containing overset text with the Selection Tool, then reload your Type cursor by clicking its In port or Out port—it's more likely you'd click the Out port since you usually want to continue from where the text stopped. Move to the next column or page and click or drag to create a new text frame, or click inside an empty frame. The text will flow from one frame to the next.

Deleting a frame from a text thread. Select the frame, then press the Delete key. Don't worry about losing the text—you are deleting the container, not the content.

Breaking a thread. Double-click the In port of the frame you want to remove from the thread. The frame remains, but the text is removed from it—though not deleted from the document.

Showing Text Threads

Want an overview of how the text in your document flows from one text frame to another? Choose Show Text Threads from the View > Extras menu. Arrows indicate the flow of the text for your selected story. Text threads are not always obvious, especially in a newspaper or magazine layout when a story jumps from one page to a noncontinuous page.

Mary had a little lamb, whose fleece was pure as snow.

And everywhere that Mary went, the lamb was sure to go.

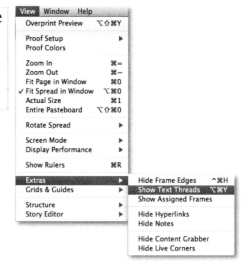

FIGURE 2.12 Text threads indicate how one text frame is connected to another.

Threading frames that are not part of the same story. If a story occupies multiple text frames, it's usually preferable to keep those frames threaded, rather than chop the text up into unthreaded text frames. Threaded text frames can be selected, spell checked, and viewed in the Story Editor as one story. You can also, if necessary, export the story as one file to be repurposed, perhaps for the Web, rather than having to piece it together from separate text frames. There may be times when you want to put back together parts of a story that have become unthreaded, or perhaps join two stories together. To do this, click the Out port on the last frame of the first story, then click inside the frame of the second story. This may cause the text to reflow as the type from what had been the second story moves into any available space in the previous text frame.

Making a headline span multiple columns. The Span Columns feature (see more on this feature on page 31), new to CS5, saves you from needing to manually span a headline across multiple columns. However, it's still a useful technique if you wish to span text over multiple columns, where one of those columns is used as a white space or caption column.

To make a headline span multiple columns (without using Span Columns), click the In port to load text from the beginning of the story, then follow these steps:

1. Pull down a guide from the Horizontal Ruler to where the first paragraph will begin.

2. Resize the top of each text frame to this guide.

3. Load your Text cursor from the In port at the top left of the text frame.

4. Click and drag to create a text frame that spans the width of the columns and is at the estimated height of the headline. The headline of the story (or as much of it as will fit) will flow into this text frame. If necessary, adjust the height of this frame afterwards.

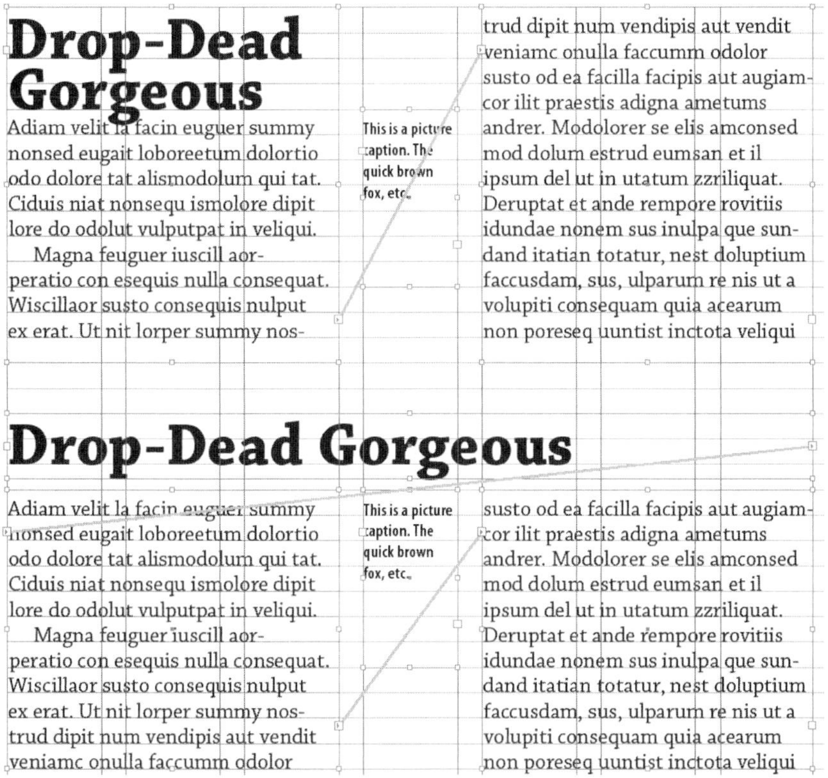

Drop-Dead Gorgeous

Adiam velit la facin euguer summy nonsed eugait loboreetum dolortio odo dolore tat alismodolum qui tat. Ciduis niat nonsequ ismolore dipit lore do odolut vulputpat in veliqui.
    Magna feuguer iuscill aorperatio con esequis nulla consequat. Wiscillaor susto consequis nulput ex erat. Ut nit lorper summy nos-

This is a picture caption. The quick brown fox, etc.

trud dipit num vendipis aut vendit veniamc onulla faccumm odolor susto od ea facilla facipis aut augiamcor ilit praestis adigna ametums andrer. Modolorer se elis amconsed mod dolum estrud eumsan et il ipsum del ut in utatum zzriliquat. Deruptat et ande rempore rovitiis idundae nonem sus inulpa que sundand itatian totatur, nest doluptium faccusdam, sus, ulparum re nis ut a volupiti consequam quia acearum non poreseq uuntist inctota veliqui

Drop-Dead Gorgeous

Adiam velit la facin euguer summy nonsed eugait loboreetum dolortio odo dolore tat alismodolum qui tat. Ciduis niat nonsequ ismolore dipit lore do odolut vulputpat in veliqui.
    Magna feuguer iuscill aorperatio con esequis nulla consequat. Wiscillaor susto consequis nulput ex erat. Ut nit lorper summy nostrud dipit num vendipis aut vendit veniamc onulla faccumm odolor

This is a picture caption. The quick brown fox, etc.

susto od ea facilla facipis aut augiamcor ilit praestis adigna ametums andrer. Modolorer se elis amconsed mod dolum estrud eumsan et il ipsum del ut in utatum zzriliquat. Deruptat et ande rempore rovitiis idundae nonem sus inulpa que sundand itatian totatur, nest doluptium faccusdam, sus, ulparum re nis ut a volupiti consequam quia acearum non poreseq uuntist inctota veliqui

FIGURE 2.13 Threading a headline across columns. Despite the new Span Columns feature, this is still a useful technique when working with an irregular number of columns and multiple threaded text frames. Top, before threading the headline across columns; bottom, a threaded headline.

Individual or Multiple-Column Text Frames?

Let's say you want a three-column layout. You can approach this in two ways. (1) You can draw a single text frame and divide it into three columns. Or (2) you can create three threaded text frames of one column each. Your choice affects how you edit your layout. A single frame divided into three columns lets you control the tops and bottoms of the three columns at once—and now with the Span Columns feature it is possible to have a heading straddle multiple columns within a single text frame. With three individual columns, however, you can control the columns independently—which can be useful if you want the columns to start or end at different positions on your page.

FIGURE 2.14 The example on the left shows two text frames threaded together; on the right a single text frame is divided into two columns.

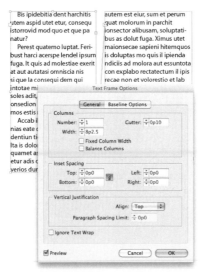

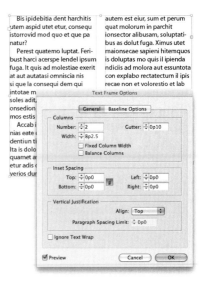

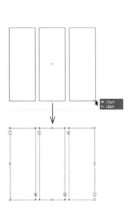

FIGURE 2.15 Adding columns (CS5 only). Create additional text frames as you drag the cursor by pressing the right arrow. To remove frames as you drag, press the left arrow.

Threading empty text frames. Some people prefer to draw text frames and thread them before the text content is ready, to create a "wire frame" of the document. To create a series of linked empty text frames, draw your frames with the Rectangle Frame Tool, and then click the first frame with your Type Tool to designate it a text frame. Click the text frame's Out port to "load" the text cursor (even though there is no actual text) and then click inside the next frame to thread it to the first frame. Repeat as necessary, threading frame 2 to 3, frame 3 to 4, and so on. Holding down Option (Alt) as you do so "reloads" the Type cursor, allowing you to continue threading without reselecting each new frame To mock up your layout you can fill the text frames with placeholder text.

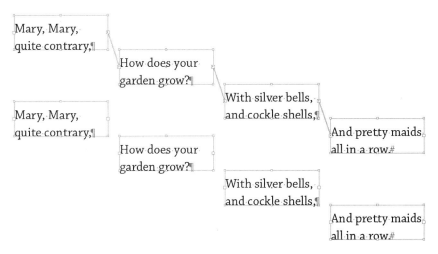

FIGURE 2.16 The SplitStory script used to unthread a story.

Now, with CS5, you can create multiple threaded text frames on the fly with the Type Tool. As you click and drag out a text frame, press the Right Arrow to create additional columns or the Left Arrow to remove columns. When you release the mouse the multiple columns are threaded.

Splitting a threaded story into separate text frames. You can "unthread" a story with the SplitStory script. Select the frames of the story you wish to unthread and choose Windows > Utilities > Scripts to access the Scripts Panel. Expand the Application folder, then the Samples folder, then the JavaScript folder. Double-click the SplitStory.jsx script to convert your story to a series of unconnected text frames.

Spanning and Splitting Columns

When working with a multicolumn text frame it's easy to have a headline span or straddle two or more columns. You can choose Span Columns from the Paragraph panel menu or the Control Panel menu, or use the widget on the Control Panel (though this has fewer options).

If you want to break two or more paragraphs into subcolumns, you can split them, which is perfect for lists in a wide text column.

The instructions to span and split columns can both be incorporated into a paragraph style definition; see Chapter 12, "Global Formatting with Styles."

TIP: To see the bounding boxes for your text frames, even if they have nothing in them, make sure View > Extras > Show Frame Edges or press Cmd+H (Ctrl+H) is checked.

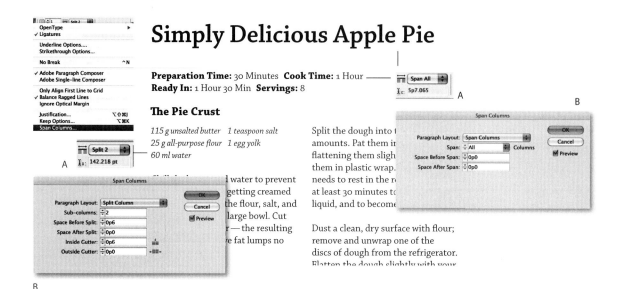

FIGURE 2.17 Spanning
and splitting columns. The
example shows two work
styles: using the Control Panel
widget (**A**) and using the Span
Columns dialog box (**B**).

TIP: You can create custom
placeholder text by making
a text file with the text you
want to use and naming it
"placeholder.txt." Save the
file in the InDesign application folder and thereafter
that's what you'll get when
you choose Fill with
Placeholder Text. If you're
a traditionalist and want
to return to Lorem Ipsum,
visit lipsum.com, where you
can generate a passage of
Lorem Ipsum of whatever
length your require—as well
as read about the venerable
history of this grandfather
of all dummy texts.

Using Placeholder Text

Using placeholder or dummy text when mocking up a layout is a time-honored tradition. Traditionally designers have used a piece of Latin text called *Lorem Ipsum*. This text is based on Cicero's "The Extremes of Good and Evil," written in 45 BC, but its word and sentence lengths have been tweaked to approximate those of an "average" article. Dummy text is used so that clients, when approving design concepts, don't get hung up on the meaning of the text content but rather concentrate on the overall visual impression. Ironically, using Lorem Ipsum sometimes requires designers to explain to their clients why the text is written in Latin.

InDesign has its own random text generator, which creates placeholder text similar to, but different from, Lorem Ipsum. To use placeholder text, insert your Type Tool into a text frame, or click and drag with the Type Tool to create one, then select Type > Fill with Placeholder Text. The frame (or threaded frames) is filled with dummy text. If you make your font smaller and need more placeholder text, you can return to the Fill with Placeholder Text menu to fill the frame.

Working with Thumbnails

Before you start working in InDesign, it's often desirable to make thumbnail sketches of your layout, rather than getting stuck immediately on the computer. No matter how quick on the draw you are with keyboard shortcuts, you're faster (and more free to explore) with pencil and paper. Thumbnails help to instantly

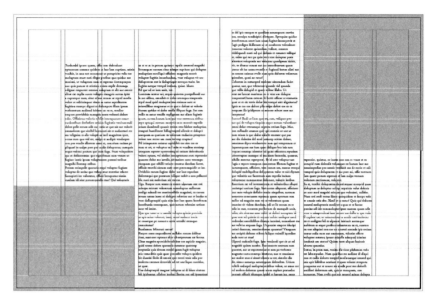

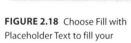

FIGURE 2.18 Choose Fill with Placeholder Text to fill your text frame(s) with dummy text.

FIGURE 2.19 A two-page spread "mocked up" with placeholder text and placeholder picture frames.

eliminate those daft ideas that we all have from time to time—and often need to work through before we can get to the good ideas. Based upon your sketches you can construct a "wire frame" of text and picture frames, threading the text frames together and filling them with placeholder text until the real copy is available. To help organize your content, put the text frames and picture frames on separate layers (see Chapter 14, "Pages, Margins, Columns, and Baseline Grids.")—that way you'll be able to tell which are which at a glance, based on the color of the frame.

Pasting Text

Another method for getting text into an InDesign document is to copy and paste it from another application. Using the regular Paste keyboard short-cut of Cmd+V (Ctrl+V) brings in the text; whether the formats come with it depends on how you have your Clipboard Handling Preferences set up. Choose All Information to include the styles and formatting of the incoming text. You can override this preference on a case-by-case basis by choosing Edit > Paste Without Formatting or pressing Cmd+Shift+V (Ctrl+Shift+V). The pasted text will be added seamlessly to the text already in your document, at the location of your text cursor.

TIP: As a starting point for your sketches, print out blank thumbnails of your pages with margins and column guides shown. In the Print dialog box General settings, check Print Blank Pages and Show Visible Guides and Grids. In Setup choose Thumbnails and a suitable grid: 2x2, 3x3, 4x4, and so on.

While copying and pasting—with or without formatting—usually works fine, it sometimes causes strange things to happen to special characters. It's preferable to place text rather than use copy and paste. Pasting is only necessary if you're copying small chunks from a larger whole, possibly from the body of an email message or a PDF document.

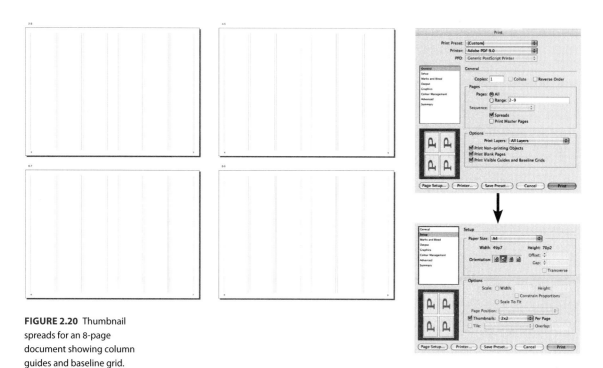

FIGURE 2.20 Thumbnail spreads for an 8-page document showing column guides and baseline grid.

FIGURE 2.21 Paste Without Formatting strips out formats from the incoming text.

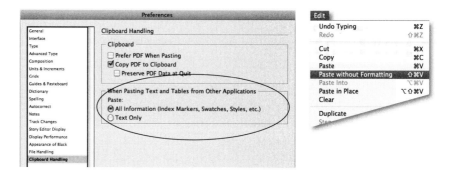

Rectangles and Rectangle Frames: What's the Difference?

There are two tools that do essentially the same thing: the Rectangle Tool (and its associated tools Ellipse and Polygon) and the Rectangle Frame Tool (along with the Ellipse Frame and the Polygon Frame). What's the difference? Not much. Shapes drawn with the Frame tools appear with an "X" inside them. Presumably you are going to put content into them. The Rectangle, Ellipse, or Polygon (the Shape tools), however, have no "X" and are intended as graphic elements in their own right. That said, there's nothing stopping you from putting text or a graphic inside a shape: Click in the frame with the Type Tool, and the object becomes a text frame. Likewise, there's nothing compelling you to put content into frames. Some people prefer their text frames to be text frames and their graphic frames to be graphic frames, so there is a Type preference you can change to prevent graphic frames from being converted to text frames with the Type tool.

If you need to change the shape of any object, for example from a rectangle to an ellipse or vice versa, choose Object > Convert Shape.

FIGURE 2.22 Unchecking Type Tool Converts Frames prevents graphic frames from being inadvertently converted to text frames.

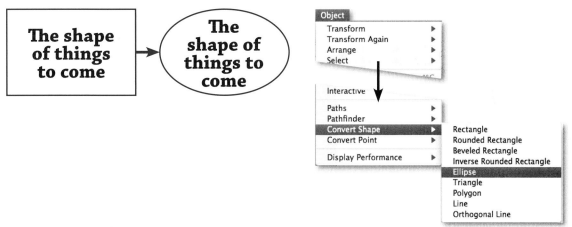

FIGURE 2.23 Use Convert Shape to change the shape of a text frame.

Importing Word Text

When placing a Microsoft Word or Rich Text Format (RTF) file, you can control how the text is imported into InDesign. Choose File > Place (Cmd+D or Ctrl+D). A dialog box appears asking for file location. At the bottom of this window are several check boxes. Select the file to import, check Show Import Options, and click Open, and you are taken to the Microsoft Word Import Options dialog box. Here, you can choose whether or not to import Word-created footnotes, endnotes, table of contents text, and index text. If you choose Preserve Styles and Formatting from Text and Tables, any paragraph and character styles in the Word document will be imported. Depending on how those Word styles were set up and implemented, this could be a blessing or a curse. In the best-case scenario, if the names of the Word styles are identical to the InDesign style names, the InDesign styles will take precedence, your text formatting is done, and you get to go home early. For information on how to map specific Word paragraph and character styles to their chosen equivalents in InDesign, see Chapter 12, "Global Formatting with Styles."

FIGURE 2.24 You can use the Word Import Options dialog box to control what formats from the Word document are imported into InDesign.

Using the Story Editor

InDesign offers an alternative to viewing the type on the page. In the Story Editor, text is displayed in one continuous column, all in the same font and all at the same size. To view text in the Story Editor, select a text frame with your Type Tool or Selection Tool and choose Edit > Edit in Story Editor, or press Cmd+Y (Ctrl+Y).

There are several reasons for using the Story Editor, chief among them the fact that editing text, especially long blocks of text, is quicker without the visual distractions of graphics, column breaks, and formatting. You don't have to worry about zooming in and out or navigating from column to column or from page to page. It's pure content. Any changes made in the Story Editor are automatically reflected in the layout and vice versa. You can not only edit text but also quickly apply paragraph and character styles.

If you don't see the left column with the style names as shown in the figure on the next page, choose View > Story Editor > Show Style Name Column. The Depth Ruler (View > Story Editor > Show Depth Ruler) is a vertical ruler on the left side of the Story Editor that displays the length of the story in column inches (or whatever measurement system you're using). When you're ready to return to Layout view, press Cmd+W (Ctrl+W).

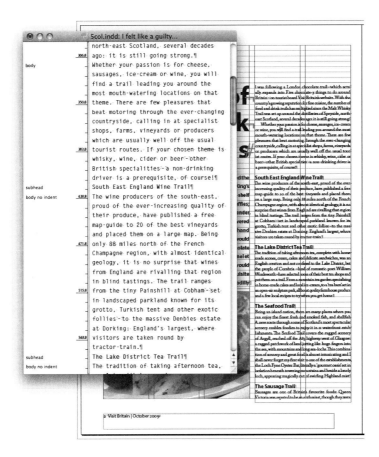

FIGURE 2.25 A story viewed in the Story Editor (left); the same story in Layout view with guides turned on (right).

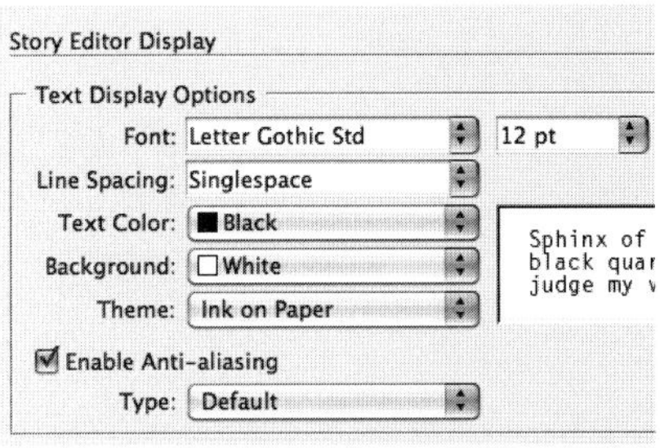

FIGURE 2.26 The Story Editor Preferences determine the appearance of your text in the Story Editor; they have no effect on how the text appears in Layout View, or on how it prints.

To change the appearance of your text in the Story Editor, choose Preferences > Story Editor Display.

Using the Story Editor is like getting under the hood to view the engine. You can see and more easily access things here that are hidden or hard to see in Layout View: markers for inline graphics and anchored objects, text variables, hyperlinks, nonprinting Notes, cross references, index markers, and XML tags. You can also edit overset text, including overset text in table cells. The Overset Text Indicator "redlines" the overset text, making it easier to write to fit the available space. And because the Story Editor reveals things Layout View does not, it's also useful for troubleshooting text composition problems, like mysterious line breaks or spacing gaps. Want to get to the text that mysteriously keeps falling out of the text frame (probably due to some inappropriate Keep Options setting)? Use the Story Editor.

Cleaning Up Text

Having placed a text file, the first thing to do—before you start formatting the text—is clean it up. Designers commonly work with text files that have been created by someone else. In a perfect world, these files would be as lean as a cheetah and as minimalist as a piece of Bauhaus furniture. This is rarely, if ever, the case. People clutter up their text files with all kinds of junk, often in the misguided notion that they're helping you out by doing the formatting. Extra carriage returns, multiple tabs, multiple spaces (in some cases used to justify lines of type) will all need to be removed. Of course, communication with your client can go a long way: Tell them what you want and you might even get it. But even with stellar communication and the best of intentions, you're still going to need to clean your text files—even if you created them in the first place. Thankfully, it's fast and easy to whip your stories into shape. A good place to start is with the predefined GREP Queries.

FIGURE 2.27 Using a predefined GREP Query to purge any unnecessary spaces from a document.

The simplest way to clean up text is the FindChangeByList script. An InDesign Script is a defined sequence of steps that you can play back with a single click. You can write your own with JavaScript (or AppleScript or Visual Basic) but thankfully, you don't need to know scripting languages to use the InDesign sample scripts.

Once you've located the Scripts panel (Window > Automation > Scripts), expand the Application folder, then the Samples folder, then the JavaScript folder. Scroll down to FindChangeByList and double-click that entry. In a blink of an eye, this little gem performs a sequence of Find/Change routines on your selection, your story, or your document. If you want to see exactly what it's doing—and customize how it performs—open the FindChangeSupport folder beneath the script on the Scripts panel, right-click the FindChangeList.txt file, and choose Show in Finder/Show in Explorer. You can open the text file in a text editor and edit its list of Find/Change routines. The easiest way to do this is to copy and paste an existing routine and then adjust the find and change criteria as necessary.

FIGURE 2.28 The FindChangeByList script—the quickest way to purge unwanted spacing from your story or document.

Even if you're not feeling intrepid enough to customize this script, just using it off the shelf to banish egregious spacing will save loads of precious time. A word of caution that applies to using any script: If you try using Undo after running a script you'll find yourself needing to press Cmd+Z (Ctrl+Z) numerous times to restore things to the way they were. This is because a script is a sequence of steps, and Undo undoes only a single step in that sequence at a time. To play it safe, save your work before you run the script. You can then use Revert to get your document to the previously saved version if you don't like the results.

```
77
grep  {findWhat:" +"}      {changeTo:" "} {includeFootnotes:true, includeMasterPages:true,
includeHiddenLayers:true, wholeWord:false}      Find all double spaces and replace with single spaces.
grep  {findWhat:"\r "}      {changeTo:"\r"} {includeFootnotes:true, includeMasterPages:true,
includeHiddenLayers:true, wholeWord:false}      Find all returns followed by a space And replace with single returns.
grep  {findWhat:" \r"}      {changeTo:"\r"} {includeFootnotes:true, includeMasterPages:true,
includeHiddenLayers:true, wholeWord:false}      Find all returns followed by a space and replace with single returns.
grep  {findWhat:"\t\t+"}      {changeTo:"\t"} {includeFootnotes:true, includeMasterPages:true,
includeHiddenLayers:true, wholeWord:false}      Find all double tab characters and replace with single tab characters.
grep  {findWhat:"\r\t"}      {changeTo:"\r"} {includeFootnotes:true, includeMasterPages:true,
includeHiddenLayers:true, wholeWord:false}      Find all returns followed by a tab character and replace with single
returns.
grep  {findWhat:"\t\r"}      {changeTo:"\r"} {includeFootnotes:true, includeMasterPages:true,
includeHiddenLayers:true, wholeWord:false}      Find all returns followed by a tab character and replace with single
returns.
grep  {findWhat:"\r\r+"}      {changeTo:"\r"} {includeFootnotes:true, includeMasterPages:true,
includeHiddenLayers:true, wholeWord:false}      Find all double returns and replace with single returns.
text  {findWhat:" - "}      {changeTo:"^="} {includeFootnotes:true, includeMasterPages:true,
includeHiddenLayers:true, wholeWord:false}      Find all space-dash-space and replace with an en dash.
text  {findWhat:"--"} {changeTo:"^_"} {includeFootnotes:true, includeMasterPages:true, includeHiddenLayers:true,
wholeWord:false}      Find all dash-dash and replace with an em dash.
```

FIGURE 2.29 The find and change queries that the FindChangeByList script runs on your story or document. You can add your own queries or remove queries from the list.

· space

¶ carriage return

¬ line break

» tab

⫟ right indent tab

— em space

⁻ en space

˘ thin space

† indent to here

FIGURE 2.30 Some common hidden characters.

Show Hidden Characters

Working with hidden characters visible is a good way to troubleshoot potential composition problems because you can see any forced line breaks, tabs, and multiple spaces that may have crept into your text. You can toggle this view option on and off by choosing Type > Show Hidden Characters, by choosing Hidden Character from View Options on the Application Bar, or by pressing Cmd+Option/Alt+I (Ctrl+Option/Alt+I).

CHAPTER 3

Character Formats

A WEALTH OF OPTIONS ARE available on InDesign's Control Panel, some of them obvious, some far so less so. Their arrangement reflects how they have evolved from predigital typesetting, and to get the best results from these options, we need to be aware of the conventions for using them. Starting out with the Character Formatting controls, we'll look beyond the buttons to the historical precedents and the aesthetic considerations of using these options.

Text Selection Methods

Before we can format type, we must first select it. Here's a list of useful short-cuts for selecting text and moving within stories:

- Select one word: Double-click word

- Select one line: Triple-click line (depending on Text Preferences setting)

- Select to beginning of line: Cmd+Shift+Up Arrow (Ctrl+Shift+Up Arrow)

- Select to end of line: Cmd+Shift+Down Arrow (Ctrl+Shift+Down Arrow)

- Delete one word to left of cursor: Cmd+Delete (Ctrl+Backspace)

- Delete one word to right of cursor: Cmd+Fn+Delete (Ctrl+Delete)

- Move to start or end of story: Cmd+Fn+Left Arrow or Right Arrow (Ctrl+Home or End)

- Select from the point of the cursor to the start or end of story: Cmd+ Shift+Home or End (Ctrl+ Shift+Home or End)

- Move to beginning of line: Fn+Left Arrow (Ctrl+Up Arrow)

- Move to end of line: Fn+Right Arrow (Ctrl+Down Arrow)

- Move one word to the right: Cmd+Right Arrow (Ctrl+Right Arrow)

- Move one word to the left: Cmd+Left Arrow (Ctrl+Left Arrow)

- Move to beginning of next paragraph: Cmd+Down Arrow (Ctrl+Down Arrow)

- Move to beginning of previous paragraph: Cmd+Up Arrow (Ctrl+Up Arrow)

Character Formatting Options

This section looks at the basic options available in the Character Formatting panel.

Font

To change the font of a selected range of text, use the Font field on the Control Panel. To jump to the Font field when Character formats are active, press Cmd+6 (Ctrl+6). From there, type the first few letters of the font name that you want to jump to, or at least the name of a font close to it on the font menu. To move through the fonts on your menu, applying them to your selected text, press the Up or Down arrows. This is, of course, no substitute for having a type specimen book like *FontBook: Digital Typeface Compendium* (FontShop International). Alternatively, you can browse type specimens in the Adobe Type Library at http://store.adobe.com/type.

The following icons are used to indicate different kinds of fonts:

O OpenType

a Type 1

Tr TrueType

You can turn off the preview feature or change the point size of the font names or font samples in Type Preferences.

TIP: If you see a typeface you like and you need to find out what it is, you can upload a scanned type sample to MyFonts's handy Web tool WhatTheFont, at http://new.myfonts.com/ WhatTheFont. If the automatic recognition doesn't work, you can submit the image to the WhatTheFont Forum, where forum members will identify the type. There's even a WhatTheFont iPhone app.

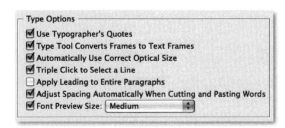

FIGURE 3.1 The Font Preview Size option in Type Preferences.

FIGURE 3.2 The WhatTheFont online tool (http://new.myfonts.com/ WhatTheFont)—a useful resource for typeface identification.

FIGURE 3.3 Adrian Frutiger's Univers.

Font Style

A choice of different type styles—like bold or italic, for instance—within the same typeface family lets you indicate hierarchy and emphasis, while at the same time maintaining stylistic continuity. InDesign won't allow you to apply "faux" bold or italic font styles: There's no B or I button to make the text heavier or slanted. Instead, you need to choose the italic or bold weights of that typeface from the Font Style menu—or use the shortcuts: Cmd+Shift+I (Ctrl+Shift+I) or Cmd+Shift+B (Ctrl+Shift+B).

Numerous terms are used to describe the styles within a typeface. Type that doesn't slant is referred to as *roman*. This "normal" style is usually called *regular,* but in certain typefaces may be called *book* or *medium*. The terms *italic* and *oblique* both refer to slanted type, the latter employed in some sans serif typefaces. Terms like *light, semibold, bold,* or *black* refer to the font weight and are self-explanatory; other lesser-used terms to describe font weight are *heavy* and *extra bold*. The terms *condensed* and *extended* refer to character width. Another way of describing the weights and widths within a typeface is to give the styles a number prefix. The first typeface to use this naming convention was Univers, designed by Adrian Frutiger in 1957. The higher the number, the heavier the weight. Odd numbers are roman, even numbers oblique—although in recent issues of Univers, the slanted versions are identified as "obliques" rather than by number.

Italics

Italic type styles—so named because they evolved in Italy—are designed to complement their roman siblings. Most fonts come with a matching italic. The company that developed InDesign's predecessor, PageMaker, took the name Aldus after Aldus Manutius (c. 1449–1515), a Venetian printer who was the first to use italic type in the early 16th century.

Italics are separate fonts in their own right, not just slanted versions of the roman. When they were first used, they were considered distinct from the roman forms. Over time, printers began pairing italics with romans of the same weight and x-height, but italics retain their identity through narrower proportions and unique letterforms.

Italics can have the following uses:

- Emphasis

- Foreign language words or phrases, except where those words are in such common usage as to not require distinguishing: for example, cliché, elite, genre. Such conventions shift over time; a good rule of thumb is to check to see if the word in question is in the dictionary.

- The titles of films, books, magazines, or works of art

- In written dialogue to indicate that the conversation is thought by the character(s), rather than said.

Common wisdom advises against setting long passages in italics. The calligraphic flow of italics makes the type look hurried; or perhaps the characters, being more decorative, attract too much attention. If overused, the uniqueness of italics is lost. It may be that italics are harder to read in long passages simply because we're not used to doing so.

How razorback-jumping frogs can level six piqued gymnasts!   Italic (Chaparral Pro)

How razorback-jumping frogs can level six piqued gymnasts!   Fake Italics (Chaparral Pro)

How razorback-jumping frogs can level six piqued gymnasts!   Oblique (Helvetica)

FIGURE 3.4 Italics, fake italics (note the different letter shapes), and oblique.

Bold

Bold weights are typically applied to headings and subheads to establish hierarchy. It's also common in newspapers and magazines to distinguish supporting text like sidebars, captions, and pull quotes by using a bold or semibold weight for the body text.

Ag **Ag**
Ag **Ag**
Ag **Ag**

FIGURE 3.5 Combining different weights within a typeface family. From top to bottom: regular with bold, light with semibold, regular with semibold. In the top two options the weights are clearly differentiated; in the last option, they are too similar.

There are numerous ways to give *emphasis*. Making words **bold** *or italic* are the most common, but using color or a highlight can also be effective. Whichever method you choose, you need only *one way* to signify difference. For example, it is *redundant* to use ***bold and italic***, or **bold and a color**.

FIGURE 3.6 Different approaches to giving emphasis.

In larger typeface families there may be relative weights of boldface with names like semibold, black, extra bold, and super. Given the option of several weights within the same family (as listed on the Font Style menu), it's preferable to differentiate by two weights to achieve the desired contrast. For example, pair regular with bold, or light with semibold; a regular paired with a semibold may not provide sufficient contrast.

The use of bold as opposed to italics for emphasis in body text is a style issue. If you are using bold, do so sparingly. If everything is emphasized, then nothing is emphasized. Bold text breaks up the continuity of the type and gives your text an overly didactic tone. The eye will jump to text called out in bold rather than discover the emphasis as part of the reading as with italics, which blend in more harmoniously with the roman type.

From a historical perspective the use of boldface may undermine the authenticity of your page, since prior to the 19th century there was no such thing as bold roman type, printers relying instead on small caps or italics for emphasis. As Robert Bringhurst puts it in his landmark book *The Elements of Typographic Style*, inappropriate use of boldface can "create unintentional anachronisms, something like adding a steam engine or fax machine to the stage set for *King Lear*."

Font Size

As well as sizing type using the Control Panel, you can use keyboard shortcuts: Cmd+Shift+ > (Ctrl+Shift+ >) increases the point size by the increment specified in the Units and Increments preferences for Size/Leading. Cmd+Shift+ < (Ctrl+Shift+ <) reduces the type size by the same increment. Add Option (Alt) to this key combination and you can increase or decrease your point size by five times the specified increment.

Leaving out the Shift key and just pressing Cmd (Ctrl) plus the > or < keys scales both the text frame and the type at the same time. This scales the type relative to the text frame, rather than by increment specified in the Units & Increments preferences.

If you're working with a single word or single line of display type, it's often easier to scale the type and the text frame together. To do this, drag out a text frame with your Type Tool, then type your text. If your text frame is bigger than necessary to accommodate the text, click the Fit Frame to Content icon ▦ in the Control Panel, or press Cmd+Option+C (Ctrl+Option+C). This fits your frame snugly around your text. To scale the text by eye, hold down Cmd+Option+C (Ctrl+Shift) as you drag from one of the corners of the text frame to size the type while maintaining its proportions. You can also use the Scale Tool to size the text frame and its contents.

Font Size in Parentheses

By default, when you change the scale of a text frame, the text inside the frame is also scaled. For example, when you double the size of a text frame, the text also doubles in size, so 20-point text increases to 40 points, for example.

There is an ill-advised preference that changes this behavior. If you change the preference option from Apply to Content to Adjust Scaling Percentage, the Font Size field displays both the original and the scaled size of the text, such as "20 pt (40)."

By default, with Apply to Content selected, scaling values display at 100% after a text is scaled. If you select Adjust Scaling Percentage, the scaling values reflect the scaled frame, so doubling the scale of a frame displays as 200%.

The Adjust Scaling Percentage option is there so the user can monitor scale changes to frames—which is useful if you have to revert a frame and the text inside it to their original size. In practice, however, it just confuses people.

If you inherit a document with font sizes in parentheses and want to set them to display their "real" sizes, choose Redefine Scaling as 100% from the Control Panel menu. Choosing this option doesn't change the appearance of the scaled frame.

FIGURE 3.7 Use a type scale to maintain harmony between different sizes of type.

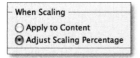

A

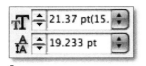

B

C

FIGURE 3.8 Choosing Adjust Scaling Percentage in General Preferences (**A**) results in type sizes in parentheses, if you scale a text frame, and is apt to cause confusion. (**B**) If you inherit a document where this option has been applied, select the text frame and choose Redefine Scaling as 100% to see the real type size. (**C**)

Common Text Sizes (and the Terms Used to Describe Them)

Body text or body copy is the type (typically in sizes between 8 and 12 points) that makes up the majority of a book or article and carries the bulk of the message. When choosing the size of your body text, you can probably go smaller than you think. Text that is too large looks amateurish and clunky. While 12-point type is InDesign's default type size—and looks about right on screen—chances are it will look too big in print. Start out with 10 point, then increase or decrease the size as necessary according to the characteristics of the font (and the needs of your audience).

Display type is the big type (typically 18 points and above) whose primary purpose is to be seen, the bait that lures the reader. While size usually indicates the type's intent, this is not always the case. For example, an understated headline can sometimes attract attention by being unexpected.

Subheads allow a story to be broken down into bite-size chunks that are more visually enticing than a mass of undifferentiated paragraphs. They provide visual relief and interest as well as acting as signposts throughout a book or article. Subheads may be the same size as the body text but distinguished by a different font or weight, or they may be a point or two bigger.

Captions help interpret an image and are usually set a point or two smaller than the body text. In our media-saturated world, it's the captions that the tentative or busy reader reads first before engaging fully with the body copy or moving on.

Headline
Subhead
Body text
Caption

FIGURE 3.9 Common sizes set in Chaparral Pro: Headline bold 24 point, Subhead bold 12 point, Body text regular 10 point, Caption semibold 8 point.

Casing

While our capital letters evolved from the Romans, it wasn't until the end of the 8th century that anything like lowercase letters were used. Credit for their invention goes to Alcuin of York, Charlemagne's leading adviser on ecclesiastical and educational affairs, who oversaw the standardization of ecclesiastical texts. With the invention of the printing press in Europe around 1450 (though it existed earlier in both China and Korea), the terms *uppercase* and *lowercase* came from the wooden type cases used to hold the movable type. The top case was for the majuscules, the bottom case for the minuscules. Today, most fonts come with both uppercase and lowercase letters, but some are *unicase* or *unicameral*. Trajan by Carol Twombly (1959–), for example, comes only in uppercase, while Herbert Bayer's Universal (1900–1985) comes only in lowercase—in fact, Bayer, a leading figure in the Bauhaus, advanced the idea of doing away with uppercase letters altogether.

THE
GREATEST
SHOW ON
EARTH

graphic design
architecture
interior design

FIGURE 3.10 Trajan and Universal, two examples of a unicase typeface.

Continuous text set in unicase can be challenging to read. Text set in all caps, for example, is less readable than text in uppercase and lowercase because the word shapes all look alike and are differentiated only by their length. We recognize words as shapes—the descenders and ascenders of lowercase text help us to instantly identify letters. Also, text set in all caps tends to look disproportionately large when set among upper- and lowercase text; hence the need for small caps. Just as shouting doesn't make your message any clearer, setting text in all caps doesn't make your message any more compelling. At the other extreme, continuous text set all in lowercase makes it harder for the reader to distinguish one sentence from another and is really only appropriate if you are k.d. lang, bell hooks, or e. e. cummings.

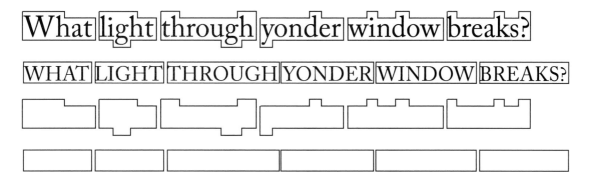

During my lifetime I have dedicated myself to this struggle of the African people. I have fought against white domination, and I have fought against black domination. I have cherished the ideal of a democratic and free society in which all persons live together in harmony and with equal opportunities. It is an ideal which I hope to live for and to achieve. But if needs be, it is an ideal for which I am prepared to die.
    —Nelson Mandela, April 20, 1964

DURING MY LIFETIME I HAVE DEDICATED MYSELF TO THIS STRUGGLE OF THE AFRICAN PEOPLE. I HAVE FOUGHT AGAINST WHITE DOMINATION, AND I HAVE FOUGHT AGAINST BLACK DOMINATION. I HAVE CHERISHED THE IDEAL OF A DEMOCRATIC AND FREE SOCIETY IN WHICH ALL PERSONS LIVE TOGETHER IN HARMONY AND WITH

FIGURE 3.11 The word shapes made by the ascenders and descenders of upper- and lowercase type make the text more identifiable, whereas text in all caps makes word shapes that are basically identical (top). The same text set in all caps is a more challenging read—and of course takes up much more space (left).

Nonetheless, all caps can be effective in headlines and subheads. Because there are no descenders, however, you should tighten the leading. With a serif font, you may want to loosen the letterspacing for a sophisticated and understated look, or tighten the letterspacing on a sans serif typeface for a denser, more solid look.

FIGURE 3.12 An uppercase headline with Auto Leading applied (top) and with negative leading (bottom).

ONE SMALL STEP FOR MAN;
ONE GIANT LEAP FOR MANKIND

ONE SMALL STEP FOR MAN;
ONE GIANT LEAP FOR MANKIND

If your text has been typed in lowercase or sentence case, you can easily convert it to all caps by using the **TT** icon on the Control Panel, pressing the shortcut Cmd+Shift+K (Ctrl+Shift+K), or choosing Type > Change Case. Unfortunately, converting text that has been typed with Caps Lock toggled on is a bit hit-and-miss if you want to convert to sentence casing: InDesign interprets any period, question mark, or exclamation point as the end of a sentence. This causes unexpected case changes when these characters are used in other ways, as in abbreviations, file names, or URLs. In addition, proper names will become lowercase when they should be uppercase.

FIGURE 3.13 The Change Case options and an example of how easily fooled they are when changing text that was originally typed with Caps Lock on.

House styles vary when it comes to the casing of chapter headings, headlines, and subheads. Up Style, in which every major word is capitalized, is the most common approach. With Down Style, only the initial cap and proper nouns are capitalized. This style, more popular in Europe than the U.S., has the obvious editorial appeal that no one has to agonize over whether a word is a "major" word and thus needs to be capitalized. Another advantage is that since more words appear in lowercase, there are more familiar word shapes. (It's somewhat ironic, given my preference for Down Style, that this book uses Up Style heads.) A third approach, not used for heads or subheads but more for product names, is CamelCase, in which compound words or phrases are written without spaces and the first letter of each compound is capped, for example PlayStation, MySpace, and of course … InDesign.

Small Caps

Small caps are as tall as the x-height and so do not, like regular caps, overwhelm the upper- and lowercase type they appear with. Small caps are mainly associated with serif typefaces and are nearly always roman. Small caps have the following uses:

- Acronyms, initialisms, and historical designations such as BC and AD—preferably without periods, though house styles differ

- As a transition from a drop cap to the regular body text size

- For abbreviations like AM and PM—with no letter spaces or periods, though it's more contemporary to use lowercase: 3pm, 7pm, etc.

- The names of speakers in plays

Unless you are using an OpenType font or an Expert Set (a font of supplementary characters), your small caps will be scaled down to the percentage specified in the Advanced Type preferences. These software-generated or "fake" small caps are regular caps reduced in size, rather than distinct characters designed to work in proportion with the upper- and lowercase text. Because the weight of their stroke has been reduced, they appear too light when set alongside other text at the same size. Real small caps, on the other hand, are distinct characters that have been designed with their weights the same as the full-size text.

When working with OpenType fonts, there is also the option of using all small caps (rather than the first character of each word being a full-size cap).

FIGURE 3.14 Small caps: The top example shows "fake" small caps at 70% of the full capitals. Notice the lighter stroke weight compared to the real OpenType small caps, below.

THE CONSTITUTION OF THE UNITED STATES OF AMERICA
Fake Small Caps

THE CONSTITUTION OF THE UNITED STATES OF AMERICA
Real Small Caps

FIGURE 3.15 The use of small caps for acronyms, initialisms, dates, and times.

The BBC and CNN reported the decision by the IMF and the World Bank to cancel all debts as of 8 A.M. on October 4, 2010. Poverty, AIDS, malnutrition, and illiteracy will be significantly reduced by 2015.

The BBC and CNN reported the decision by the IMF and the World Bank to cancel all debts as of 8 AM on October 4, 2010. Poverty, AIDS, malnutrition, and illiteracy will be significantly reduced by 2015.

FIGURE 3.16 OpenType All Small Caps (bottom), as compared to using full-size caps and small caps together (top).

SMALL CAPS
SMALL CAPS

NOTE: Working with equations? If there are just a few, you can use a typeface like Mathematical Pi in conjunction with baseline shift and tabs. If it's something you'll be doing on a regular basis, consider a third-party plug-in like InMath or MathMagic Pro. The InDesign Secrets Web site has an interesting discussion of different approaches (http://indesignsecrets. com/typesetting-math-in-indesign.php).

Superscript and Subscript

Superscript is typically used for ordinals in numbers or for footnotes. Subscript is used for scientific notation. With OpenType typefaces, rather than use the Superscript and Subscript buttons on the Control Panel, choose Superior/ Superior or Subscript/Inferior from the OpenType flyout menu. In most cases, ordinals and superscript/superior are the same thing. These are distinct glyphs with a stroke weight the same as that of the upper- and lowercase text. If you don't have this luxury, you'll need to fake your superscript and subscript characters, which will unavoidably result in them looking too light next to the main text. In Text Preferences, you can change the size of superscripts and subscripts relative to the point size of the text. For best results, set the Super/ Subscript size to 60. See Chapter 6, "Small (but Important) Details," for a way to use superscript and subscript characters to create fractions.

April 1st H$_2$O

Superscript

Subscript
(position 20%)

FIGURE 3.17 Superscript
compared with OpenType
Superior (left), and subscript
compared with OpenType
Inferior (right).

April 1st H$_2$O

OpenType
Superior

OpenType
Inferior

Underlining

In days of yore, when records came on vinyl and people typed on machines
called *typewriters,* underlining was de rigueur for adding emphasis—but that
was only because typewriters couldn't do it any other way. Underlining, as every
type manual will tell you, should never be used for emphasis. The underline
is too heavy and collides with the descenders. If you're using underlining to
indicate hyperlinks, be sure to change the weight, the offset, and possibly the
color of the line in Underline Options—it will still look ugly, but you can make
it slightly less so.

groovy

Underline slices
through descenders

FIGURE 3.18 Underline
Options on the Control Panel
menu and some different
approaches to underlining.

groovy

Text is stroked
with white (Paper)

groovy

Underline is offset,
Line Style wavy.

Charles Robert Darwin FRS (12 February
1809–19 April 1882) was an <u>English naturalist</u>
who realised and presented compelling evidence
that all <u>species</u> of life have <u>evolved</u> over time
from <u>common ancestors</u>, through the process he
called <u>natural selection</u>.

FIGURE 3.19 Underlining
applied as a Character Style to
indicate hyperlinks.

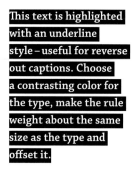

FIGURE 3.20 Underlining applied as a highlight.

FIGURE 3.21 An overprinted Strikethrough combined with a heavy underline that is offset behind the text.

By adjusting the weight, offset, and color of the underline, it's possible to make a Character Style to apply "highlighting" to text. (See Chapter 12, "Global Formatting with Styles," for more on creating Character Styles.)

Strikethrough

Strikethrough is used to indicate which text will be deleted as a document moves through revision cycles. If you tweak the Strikethrough Options, the strikethrough could potentially be used as a second underline.

Baseline Shift

Baseline shift, (Option+Shift+Up or Down Arrow or Alt+Shift+Up or Down Arrow), is used to vertically shift certain characters relative to the baseline of the type. It should never be used to adjust interparagraph spacing, which is a function of leading and paragraph spacing.

Baseline shift can be used for the following:

- Adjusting the position of bullets, ornaments, inline graphics, and symbols like $, ®, ©, ™

- Adjusting the position of a decorative drop cap

- Manual fractions, although it's preferable to use a fraction script or, better still, an OpenType Pro font with real fractions

- Monetary amounts where the size of the currency symbol is reduced

- Mathematical or chemical formulas

- Adjusting the position of parentheses, braces, and brackets—all of which center on the lowercase x-height, relative to the type they enclose. When used with all caps, they should center on the cap height. (OpenType fonts make using baseline shift unnecessary because of their ability to glyph shift, that is, adjust the position of certain characters, like opening and closing parentheses according to whether they are preceded or followed by an upper or lowercase character—see "Glyph Positioning.")

- Creating type that looks like the thing it is describing

FIGURE 3.22 Some uses of baseline shift.

(415) (415)

Parentheses shifted up, right.

glyph (SHIFT) glyph (SHIFT)

Glyph Shifting with OpenType font, right.

$10.99 $10⁹⁹

Superscript Superior and Baseline Shift applied, right.

b^ump

Interpreting a word.

*C*all me Ishmael. Some years ago—never mind how long precisely—having little or no money in my purse, and nothing particular to interest me on shore, I thought I would sail about a little

*C*all me Ishmael. Some years ago—never mind how long precisely—having little or no money in my purse, and nothing particular to interest me on shore, I thought I would sail about a little

Drop Cap baseline shifted up to avoid collision

Glyph Positioning

With display type in all caps, the positioning of hyphens, dashes, and parentheses requires adjustment. Hyphens are centered on the x-height, which is appropriate for lowercase letters, but too low for capitals. Hyphens, dashes, and parentheses may need to be adjusted with baseline shift.

The beauty of OpenType fonts—and InDesign's support of them—is that this glyph positioning happens automatically. If you format an OpenType font as all caps, the surrounding hyphens, dashes, parentheses, braces, and brackets all shift vertically. Note, however, that this happens only when you choose all caps character formats, not when you key in text with Caps Lock on.

Condensed and Extended Type

Larger typeface families may include condensed or extended versions. Condensed type can be useful if you have a lot of text to fit into a finite space, whereas extended type may be appropriate if you want to fill a defined space with a relatively small amount of text. Choose a real condensed or real expanded typeface rather than try to fake this effect by adjusting the horizontal or vertical scale. Scale your type nonproportionally and you're trampling roughshod over the life's work of some of the world's finest artisans. Faking a condensed typeface (squeezing the horizontal scale) or an expanded typeface (stretching the horizontal scale) will make the character shapes look puny and the overall effect amateurish. Get caught using these options, and the Design Police will come knocking on your door (www.design-police.org). However, every rule can be broken creatively. Just make sure that if you break the rules, you're breaking them consciously—and not because you don't know better.

Condensed faces are useful for headlines, where because the letterforms are narrower, you can increase the point size and still have the headline fit the allotted space.

Condensed faces are also useful for tabular material and captions.

Extended faces are more typically used for display instead of body type, and are more likely to be sans serif—like Helvetica Neue Expanded or Univers Extended.

FIGURE 3.23 The Design Police (www.design-police.org): Don't give them reason to cite you!

Ag Ag

Squeezed   Condensed

We quickly seized the black axle and just saved it from going past him

Squeezed (72%)

We quickly seized the black axle and just saved it from going past him

Condensed

FIGURE 3.24 Squeezed type: "fake condensed" compared with real condensed.

Man Bites Dog

Helvetica Neue Black 44 pt

Man Bites Dog

Helvetica Neue Condensed Black 56 pt

Man Bites Dog

Helvetica Ultra Compressed 100 pt

FIGURE 3.25 Condensed typefaces can have more impact within the same horizontal space.

FIGURE 3.26 Some examples of extended typefaces: Wide Latin and Blackoak (top) and Univers Extra Black Extended (bottom).

Readability

Readability refers to the ease with which we comprehend text by recognizing words and phrases as shapes. For a designer, readability means putting the reader first and leaving your ego behind—or at least confining it to your early drafts. Good typography is said to be "invisible": You don't even notice it. Instead, the type is a conduit for the message of the text. This might make the designer sound undervalued, but while your readers may not notice good typography, they will certainly know when it's bad. As the acclaimed German typographer and book designer Jan Tschichold (1902–1974) put it in his work *The Form of the Book*: "To remain nameless and without specific appreciation, yet to have been of service to a valuable work and to the small number of visually sensitive readers—this, as a rule, is the only compensation for the long, and indeed never-ending, indenture of the typographer."

However, not all type is intended to be readable: A cynic might cite legal small print or terms and conditions text as examples of typography where readability is a low priority. At the other end of the typographic scale, some decorative typefaces are deliberately challenging in terms of readability, but are arguably more, not less, recognizable for that. Type can be *legible* without necessarily being easily readable.

Serif vs. Sans Serif

The conventional wisdom is that serif typefaces are more readable than sans serif faces. Explanations for this vary. Perhaps it is because the serifs function like rails, guiding your eye along the line. Perhaps we perceive serif typefaces as more "human" because the transition of their strokes resembles calligraphy. Perhaps sans serif typefaces are less readable because the letters are inherently more like each other, it being hard to distinguish between an uppercase *I* and a lowercase *l*, for example.

Or perhaps—and my money's on this one—the explanation is self-fulfilling. We read serif type more easily because we're more used to reading serif type. In the words of Zuzana Licko (1961–), co-founder of Émigré Graphics: "You read best what you read most."

We could get used to anything, but we've been reading serif type for centuries and the habit is in our DNA. Sans serif typefaces are the new kids on the block, relatively speaking—they weren't invented until the early 19th century and were not in common usage until much later. That said, 15 plus years into the Web, we are becoming more accustomed to sans serif type for reading online.

Readability is more nuanced than applying a list of dos and don'ts. It depends not just on a choice of one class of typeface over another, but on how the many variables of setting type are handled. In the right hands, there's no reason why a sans serif typeface can't be every bit as readable as a serif typeface. To put it another way, choosing a serif typeface is no guarantee that your type will be readable.

Readability is a lesser concern when it comes to display type. Because it is set in short bursts rather than long passages, it doesn't try to be invisible, but rather to draw attention to itself. For headlines, it is as important to be attention-grabbing as it is to be readable.

One morning, when Gregor Samsa woke from troubled dreams, he found himself transformed in his bed into a horrible vermin. He lay on his armour-like back, and if he lifted his head a little he could see his brown belly, slightly domed and divided by arches into stiff sections. The bedding was hardly able to cover it and seemed ready to slide off any moment. His many legs, pitifully thin compared with the size of the rest of him, waved about helplessly as he looked.

Adobe Jenson Pro

One morning, when Gregor Samsa woke from troubled dreams, he found himself transformed in his bed into a horrible vermin. He lay on his armour-like back, and if he lifted his head a little he could see his brown belly, slightly domed and divided by arches into stiff sections. The bedding was hardly able to cover it and seemed ready to slide off any moment. His many legs, pitifully thin compared with the size of the rest of him, waved about helplessly as he looked.

Gotham Book

FIGURE 3.27 The 15th century (Jenson) versus the 21st (Gotham). Is one more readable than the other?

Other Readability Factors

Your choice of font is just one of several factors that work in sync to create readable type. Other factors include but, as they say in legalese, are not limited to:

- Leading

- Column measure (the ratio of type size to column width)

- Alignment

- Margins

- Printing conditions (if, that is, the piece will be printed): What kind of paper stock will the document be printed on?

- Reading conditions: This is an enormous variable over which you, the typographer, have no control. There's no way you can know whether your audience will be reading by candlelight, while standing on a busy commuter train, or while in the bath. Depending on the type of document you're creating, however, you may be able to speculate. For example, if you're designing a bus timetable, you'll want to forgo challenging postmodern typography in favor of a straightforward, get-your-message-across approach.

CHAPTER 4

Leading

LEADING (pronounced "ledding") is the space between lines of type, sometimes referred to as *line spacing*. The term comes from the days of hot-metal typesetting when thin strips of lead, known as *reglets*, were inserted by hand between the lines of type to add vertical space. Lines of type without these strips of lead were—and still are—referred to as "set solid." Leading plays a big part in the readability of your text. Body text is usually made more readable by a positive amount of leading (a leading value greater than the point size of the type). Headlines and display type, however, may benefit from negative leading (a leading value less than the point size of the type).

Getting the Lead Out

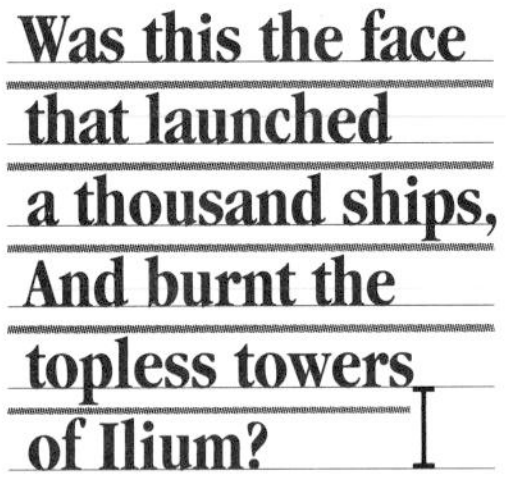

**Was this the face
that launched
a thousand ships,
And burnt the
topless towers
of Ilium?**

FIGURE 4.1 Leading is indicated by the red strips between the lines. The total leading is measured from the baseline of one line to the baseline of the next.

When it comes to leading there is no "one size fits all." On one hand, tight leading increases the density of the type and gives your type authority. On the other, if you go too tight your type looks claustrophobic, and the descenders of one line may collide with the ascenders of the next. On one hand, loose leading can create a luxurious look. On the other, if the leading is too loose, the lines of type look like individual strips that don't belong together as paragraphs. This is especially true if the leading value is greater than the size of the space between the paragraphs.

Leading is measured in points from one baseline to the next. The leading value includes the point size of the typeface and the actual space between the lines. Thus, 10-point type with 12 points of leading really means two points of space between each line. This is written 10/12, spoken as "10 on 12." Other common type size and leading combinations for body text are 9/11, 11/13, and 12/15.

How Much Is Enough?

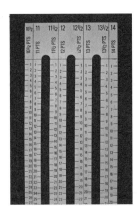

FIGURE 4.2 You can measure the leading value used on a printed piece with a leading gauge.

Bad leading makes your text harder to read because the eye has trouble locating the next line of type. Getting the leading just right depends on several variables:

- **The nature of the text.** While text intended for continuous reading benefits from some breathing space, a short burst of advertising copy or a title might be more effective if the lines are tightly leaded.

- **Type size.** As type point size increases, you will want proportionally less leading. With display sizes, the same relative amount of space between the lines appears larger, so much so that it's common to use negative leading for display type.

- **The width of the column.** Increase leading as you increase column width. Increasing the leading anywhere from 0.5 point to 2 points improves readability by keeping the lines distinct and preventing the eye from dropping off to the line below or doubling back to reread the same line.

- **The width of the column gutters.** Leading, like all type attributes, needs to work in harmony with everything else on the page. The width of the column gutters should be the same as the leading value or a multiple thereof. If the gutters are too small there will be a tendency to read across the columns; too large and the separate columns will look unconnected.

Pour and drink; and according to your choice of goblet, I shall
know whether or not you are a connoisseur of wine. For if you
have no feelings about wine one way or the other, you will want
the sensation of drinking the stuff out of a vessel that may have
cost thousands of pounds; but if you are a member of that vanish-
ing tribe, the amateurs of fine vintages, you will choose the
crystal, because everything about it is calculated to reveal rather
than hide the beautiful thing which it was meant to contain.   Perpetua 9/11

Pour and drink; and according to your choice of goblet, I shall
know whether or not you are a connoisseur of wine. For if you
have no feelings about wine one way or the other, you will want
the sensation of drinking the stuff out of a vessel that may have
cost thousands of pounds; but if you are a member of that vanish-
ing tribe, the amateurs of fine vintages, you will choose the
crystal, because everything about it is calculated to reveal rather
than hide the beautiful thing which it was meant to contain.   10/12

Pour and drink; and according to your choice of goblet, I shall
know whether or not you are a connoisseur of wine. For if you
have no feelings about wine one way or the other, you will want
the sensation of drinking the stuff out of a vessel that may have
cost thousands of pounds; but if you are a member of that vanish-
ing tribe, the amateurs of fine vintages, you will choose the
crystal, because everything about it is calculated to reveal rather
than hide the beautiful thing which it was meant to contain.   11/13

Pour and drink; and according to your choice of goblet, I shall
know whether or not you are a connoisseur of wine. For if you
have no feelings about wine one way or the other, you will want
the sensation of drinking the stuff out of a vessel that may have
cost thousands of pounds; but if you are a member of that vanish-
ing tribe, the amateurs of fine vintages, you will choose the
crystal, because everything about it is calculated to reveal rather
than hide the beautiful thing which it was meant to contain.   12/15

FIGURE 4.3 An excerpt from Beatrice Ward's influential 1932 essay on typography *The Crystal Goblet,*
showing common leading and type size combinations.

I told you that you knew the answer already. Everyone knows it. The thing that is in Room 101 is the worst thing in the world.

Hoefler Text 9.5/Auto (11.4)

The thing that is in Room 101 is the worst thing in the world.

Hoefler Text 17/Auto (21.6)

The thing that is in Room 101 is the worst thing in the world.

Hoefler Text 17/18

FIGURE 4.4 Positive leading works OK for body text sizes (**A**), but as the type gets bigger (**B**), proportionally less leading is needed (**C**).

FIGURE 4.5 Leading and column width. In the top example the leading is too tight; below, the leading has been increased to compensate for the wide column.

How will the struggle for existence, briefly discussed in the last chapter, act in regard to variation? Can the principle of selection, which we have seen is so potent in the hands of man, apply under nature? I think we shall see that it can act most efficiently. Let the endless number of slight variations and individual differences occurring in our domestic productions, and, in a lesser degree, in those under nature, be borne in mind; as well as the strength of the hereditary tendency. Under domestication, it may be truly said that the whole organisation becomes in some

How will the struggle for existence, briefly discussed in the last chapter, act in regard to variation? Can the principle of selection, which we have seen is so potent in the hands of man, apply under nature? I think we shall see that it can act most efficiently. Let the endless number of slight variations and individual differences occurring in our domestic productions, and, in a lesser degree, in those under

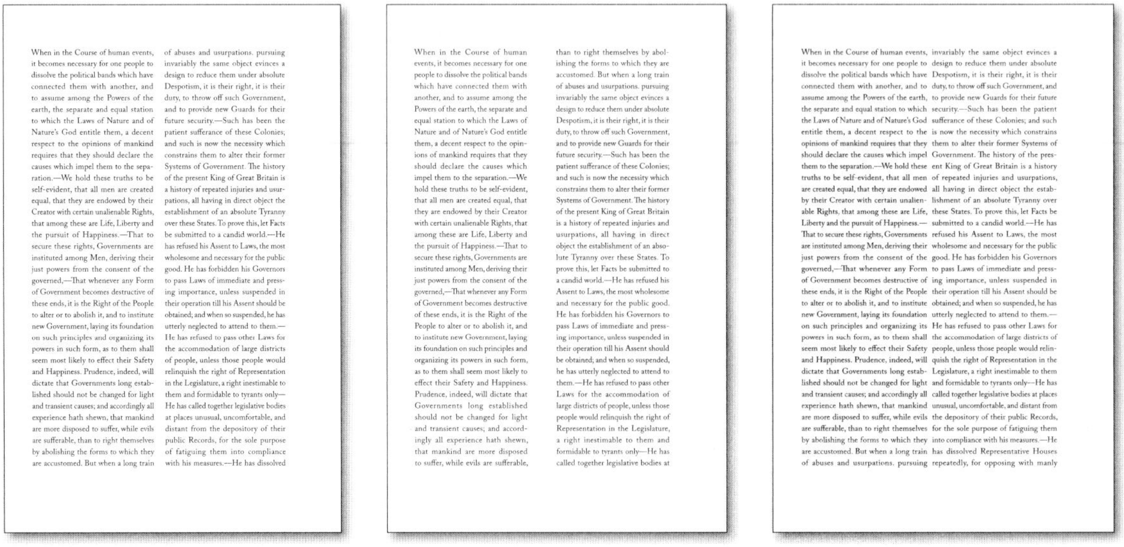

When in the Course of human events, it becomes necessary for one people to dissolve the political bands which have connected them with another, and to assume among the Powers of the earth, the separate and equal station to which the Laws of Nature and of Nature's God entitle them, a decent respect to the opinions of mankind requires that they should declare the causes which impel them to the separation.—We hold these truths to be self-evident, that all men are created equal, that they are endowed by their Creator with certain unalienable Rights, that among these are Life, Liberty and the pursuit of Happiness.—That to secure these rights, Governments are instituted among Men, deriving their just powers from the consent of the governed,—That whenever any Form of Government becomes destructive of these ends, it is the Right of the People to alter or to abolish it, and to institute new Government, laying its foundation on such principles and organizing its powers in such form, as to them shall seem most likely to effect their Safety and Happiness. Prudence, indeed, will dictate that Governments long established should not be changed for light and transient causes; and accordingly all experience hath shewn, that mankind are more disposed to suffer, while evils are sufferable, than to right themselves by abolishing the forms to which they are accustomed. But when a long train of abuses and usurpations. pursuing invariably the same object evinces a design to reduce them under absolute Despotism, it is their right, it is their duty, to throw off such Government, and to provide new Guards for their future security.—Such has been the patient sufferance of these Colonies; and such is now the necessity which constrains them to alter their former Systems of Government. The history of the present King of Great Britain is a history of repeated injuries and usurpations, all having in direct object the establishment of an absolute Tyranny over these States. To prove this, let Facts be submitted to a candid world.—He has refused his Assent to Laws, the most wholesome and necessary for the public good. He has forbidden his Governors to pass Laws of immediate and pressing importance, unless suspended in their operation till his Assent should be obtained; and when so suspended, he has utterly neglected to attend to them.—He has refused to pass other Laws for the accommodation of large districts of people, unless those people would relinquish the right of Representation in the Legislature, a right inestimable to them and formidable to tyrants only—He has called together legislative bodies at places unusual, uncomfortable, and distant from the depository of their public Records, for the sole purpose of fatiguing them into compliance with his measures.—He has dissolved

When in the Course of human events, it becomes necessary for one people to dissolve the political bands which have connected them with another, and to assume among the Powers of the earth, the separate and equal station to which the Laws of Nature and of Nature's God entitle them, a decent respect to the opinions of mankind requires that they should declare the causes which impel them to the separation.—We hold these truths to be self-evident, that all men are created equal, that they are endowed by their Creator with certain unalienable Rights, that among these are Life, Liberty and the pursuit of Happiness.—That to secure these rights, Governments are instituted among Men, deriving their just powers from the consent of the governed,—That whenever any Form of Government becomes destructive of these ends, it is the Right of the People to alter or to abolish it, and to institute new Government, laying its foundation on such principles and organizing its powers in such form, as to them shall seem most likely to effect their Safety and Happiness. Prudence, indeed, will dictate that Governments long established should not be changed for light and transient causes; and accordingly all experience hath shewn, that mankind are more disposed to suffer, while evils are sufferable, than to right themselves by abolishing the forms to which they are accustomed. But when a long train of abuses and usurpations. pursuing invariably the same object evinces a design to reduce them under absolute Despotism, it is their right, it is their duty, to throw off such Government, and to provide new Guards for their future security.—Such has been the patient sufferance of these Colonies; and such is now the necessity which constrains them to alter their former Systems of Government. The history of the present King of Great Britain is a history of repeated injuries and usurpations, all having in direct object the establishment of an absolute Tyranny over these States. To prove this, let Facts be submitted to a candid world.—He has refused his Assent to Laws, the most wholesome and necessary for the public good. He has forbidden his Governors to pass Laws of immediate and pressing importance, unless suspended in their operation till his Assent should be obtained; and when so suspended, he has utterly neglected to attend to them.—He has refused to pass other Laws for the accommodation of large districts of people, unless those people would relinquish the right of Representation in the Legislature, a right inestimable to them and formidable to tyrants only—He has called together legislative bodies at

When in the Course of human events, it becomes necessary for one people to dissolve the political bands which have connected them with another, and to assume among the Powers of the earth, the separate and equal station to which the Laws of Nature and of Nature's God entitle them, a decent respect to the opinions of mankind requires that they should declare the causes which impel them to the separation.—We hold these truths to be self-evident, that all men are created equal, that they are endowed by their Creator with certain unalienable Rights, that among these are Life, Liberty and the pursuit of Happiness.—That to secure these rights, Governments are instituted among Men, deriving their just powers from the consent of the governed,—That whenever any Form of Government becomes destructive of these ends, it is the Right of the People to alter or to abolish it, and to institute new Government, laying its foundation on such principles and organizing its powers in such form, as to them shall seem most likely to effect their Safety and Happiness. Prudence, indeed, will dictate that Governments long established should not be changed for light and transient causes; and accordingly all experience hath shewn, that mankind are more disposed to suffer, while evils are sufferable, than to right themselves by abolishing the forms to which they are accustomed. But when a long train of abuses and usurpations. pursuing invariably the same object evinces a design to reduce them under absolute Despotism, it is their right, it is their duty, to throw off such Government, and to provide new Guards for their future security.—Such has been the patient sufferance of these Colonies; and such is now the necessity which constrains them to alter their former Systems of Government. The history of the present King of Great Britain is a history of repeated injuries and usurpations, all having in direct object the establishment of an absolute Tyranny over these States. To prove this, let Facts be submitted to a candid world.—He has refused his Assent to Laws, the most wholesome and necessary for the public good. He has forbidden his Governors to pass Laws of immediate and pressing importance, unless suspended in their operation till his Assent should be obtained; and when so suspended, he has utterly neglected to attend to them.—He has refused to pass other Laws for the accommodation of large districts of people, unless those people would relinquish the right of Representation in the Legislature, a right inestimable to them and formidable to tyrants only.—He has called together legislative bodies at places unusual, uncomfortable, and distant from the depository of their public Records, for the sole purpose of fatiguing them into compliance with his measures.—He has dissolved Representative Houses repeatedly, for opposing with manly

FIGURE 4.6 In the example on the left, the gutter width is the same as the leading value. In the center, the gutter width is too big and the columns lose their visual relationship to each other. On the right, the gutter is too small so that the two columns look almost like a single line.

■ **The size of the word spaces.** Justified type in narrow columns, such as in newspapers, may result in word spaces that are larger than the leading size. This causes the eye to jump to the next line rather than to the next word. In such situations, adding extra leading ensures that the space between the lines is at least as wide as the space between the words. Better still, don't set justified type in narrow columns.

■ **The color of the background.** Because we're used to reading black type on white paper, when we use the opposite, we're guaranteed to get attention. However, reversed type tends to "sparkle," making it hard to read. A slight increase in leading—as well as avoiding fonts with delicate serifs—can compensate.

TIP: A convenient rule of thumb for determining leading is to take the width of a column in picas and divide it by the type point size, then round the result to the nearest half point. For example, if I have 10-point type on a 24-pica measure my leading is 2.4, rounded up to 2.5 and expressed as 12.5 (the lead added to the point size).

Leading Shortcuts

The keyboard shortcuts for changing the leading of a selected range of text are Option+Up Arrow (Alt+Up Arrow) to tighten the leading and Option+Down Arrow (Alt+Down Arrow) to loosen the leading. The amount is determined by the value in the Size/Leading field in the Units & Increments Preferences. To increase or decrease the leading value by five times this amount, press Cmd+Option+Up Arrow (Ctrl+Alt+Up Arrow) or Cmd+Option+Down Arrow (Ctrl+Alt+Down Arrow).

How will the struggle for existence, briefly discussed in the last chapter, act in regard to variation? Can the principle of selection, which we have seen is so potent in the hands of man, apply under nature? I think we shall see that it can act most efficiently. Let the endless number of slight variations and individual differences occurring in our domestic productions, and, in a lesser degree, in those under nature, be borne in mind; as well as the strength of the hereditary tendency. Under domestication,

How will the struggle for existence, briefly discussed in the last chapter, act in regard to variation? Can the principle of selection, which we have seen is so potent in the hands of man, apply under nature? I think we shall see that it can act most efficiently. Let the endless number of slight variations and individual differences occurring in our domestic productions, and, in a lesser degree, in those under nature, be borne in mind; as well

FIGURE 4.7 With justified type on a narrow measure, it helps to increase the leading to ensure that the space between the lines is not less than the space between the words.

One of London's most loved landmarks, Battersea Power Station now faces an uncertain future. Admired for it's majestic four-chimney skyline silhouette, Battersea Power Station supplied London with electricity between 1933 and 1983. Designed by Sir Giles Gilbert Scott, whose other design credits include Waterloo Bridge and the red telephone box,

One of London's most loved landmarks, Battersea Power Station now faces an uncertain future. Admired for it's majestic four-chimney skyline silhouette, Battersea Power Station supplied London with electricity between 1933 and 1983. Designed by Sir Giles Gilbert Scott, whose other design credits include Waterloo

FIGURE 4.8 Type that reverses out of a solid color benefits from increased leading (right).

■ **The characteristics of the typeface.** Typefaces with larger x-heights, such as Helvetica, are perceived as bigger than other typefaces at equivalent sizes. The lowercase letters are large relative to the size of the overall character, and thus require more leading.

Didone (also called Modern) typefaces, like Bodoni, that have a strong vertical stress guide the eye down the page rather than across the line. Adding more leading with these typefaces keeps the eye tracking horizontally rather than vertically.

FIGURE 4.9 Typefaces with a large x-height, like Helvetica, require more leading. Didone or Modern typefaces, like Bodoni, that have a strong vertical stress require more leading to keep the eye moving along the line, rather than down the page.

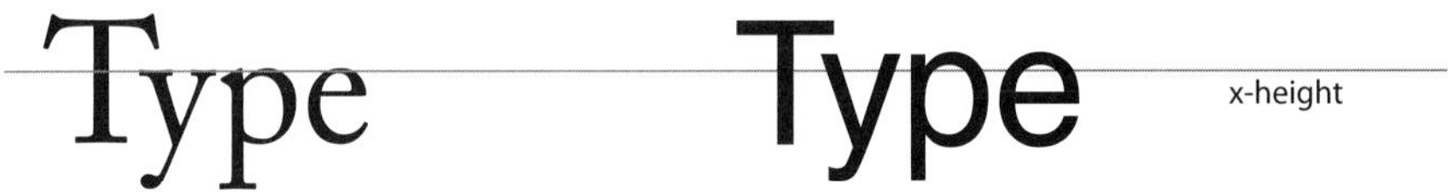

Type

x-height

Type

If books are printed in order to be read, we must distinguish readability from what the optician would call legibility. A page set in 14-pt Bold Sans is, according to the laboratory tests, more *legible* than one set in 11-pt Baskerville. A public speaker is more *audible* in that sense when he bellows. But a good speaking voice is one which is inaudible as a voice. It is the transparent goblet again!

Adobe Caslon Pro 10/12

If books are printed in order to be read, we must distinguish readability from what the optician would call legibility. A page set in 14-pt Bold Sans is, according to the laboratory tests, more legible than one set in 11-pt Baskerville. A public speaker is more audible in that sense when he bellows. But a good speaking voice is one which

Helvetica 10/13

If books are printed in order to be read, we must distinguish readability from what the optician would call legibility. A page set in 14-pt Bold Sans is, according to the laboratory tests, more *legible* than one set in 11-pt Baskerville. A public speaker is more *audible* in that sense when he bellows. But a good speaking voice is one which is inaudible as a voice. It is the transparent goblet again!

Adobe Caslon Pro 10/12

If books are printed in order to be read, we must distinguish readability from what the optician would call legibility. A page set in 14-pt Bold Sans is, according to the laboratory tests, more legible than one set in 11-pt Baskerville. A public speaker is more audible in that sense when he bellows. But a good speaking voice is one which is inaudible as a voice. It is the transparent goblet again!

Bodoni 10/12.5

Top Hat,
White Tie
& Tails
Top Hat,
White Tie
& Tails

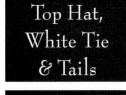

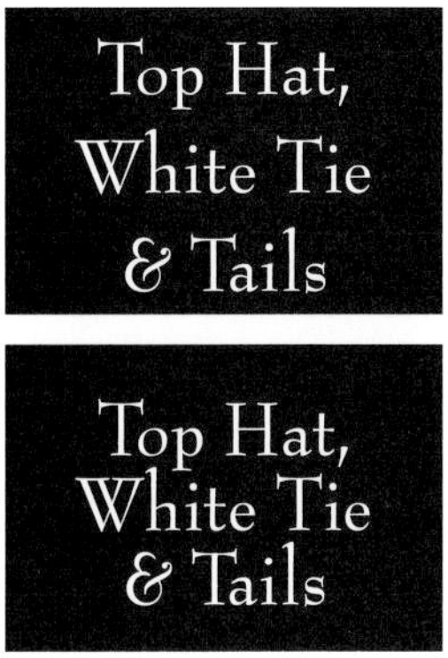

FIGURE 4.10 Even though Bernhard Modern has elongated ascenders, it has a low x-height and short descenders, and so can be leaded tightly (bottom).

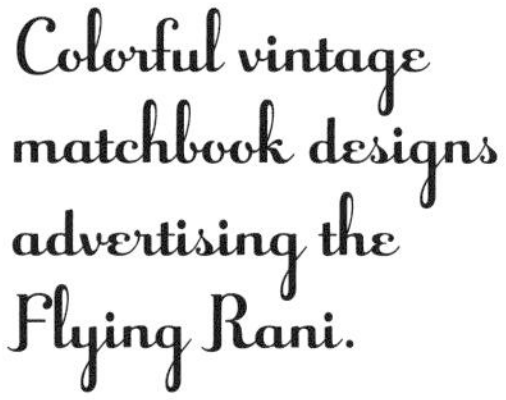

Colorful vintage
matchbook designs
advertising the
Flying Rani.

FIGURE 4.11 Raniscript has elongated ascenders and descenders, but its low x-height means it looks good tightly leaded.

Typefaces that combine a low x-height with particularly tall ascenders require special treatment. The low x-height begs for tighter leading, but tighter leading might lead to the ascenders and descenders colliding. Much depends on the characters themselves. If you're working on display type, rewording—if you have editorial license—might make all the difference. Let common sense prevail—and be open to the possibility that colliding ascenders and descenders might even look good in certain situations.

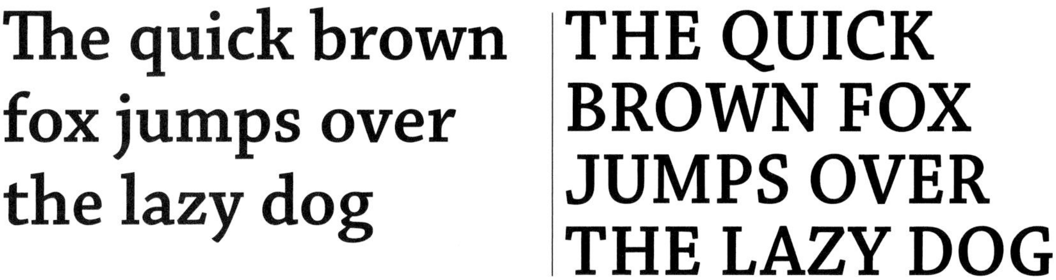

TIP: The paragraph mark, or pilcrow, at the end of every paragraph carries the text formats. Not including it in a selection can result in inconsistent leading. To select the whole paragraph, click four times in the paragraph rather than swiping across it with the Type Tool—and make sure your Hidden Characters are shown.

Bold and Semibold typefaces benefit from extra leading to prevent the *type color*—the darkness or blackness of the letterforms as a block—appearing too dense.

Typefaces with small x-heights, like Garamond, appear to have more horizontal space between lines and thus require less leading.

Type set in all caps requires less leading because the lack of descenders makes the lines appear farther apart.

The quick brown
fox jumps over
the lazy dog
THE QUICK
BROWN FOX
JUMPS OVER
THE LAZY DOG

Chaparral Pro Semibold 28/31

Chaparral Pro Semibold 28/27

FIGURE 4.12 The same headline in all caps needs less leading because there are no descenders.

FIGURE 4.13 Stacked all caps with negative leading to create a wall of type.

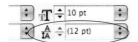

When you work in points, there's an easy way to determine the leading value for a specific number of lines in your type area. First, draw a rectangle between the top and bottom margins of a page. Then, insert your cursor in the Control Panel after the height value of the rectangle and type /N (where N is the desired number of lines). Press the Tab key to divide the height of the rectangle by the number of lines. The new height of the rectangle is your desired leading value. You can now delete the rectangle.

(Not) Using Auto Leading

FIGURE 4.14 By default the Auto Leading value is 120% of the point size of the type. When Auto Leading is chosen the value appears in parentheses on the Control Panel.

Auto Leading is a relatively new concept, emerging with desktop publishing in the mid-1980s. Auto Leading allows InDesign to assign a leading value based on the type's point size. By default, Auto Leading is 120 percent of the type size, although you can change this in your Justification options. Leading values in parentheses indicate Auto Leading.

The best thing you can say about Auto Leading is that it's convenient. You can change your text size as often as you like and your type will always be readable. As your font size increases or decreases, so does your leading.

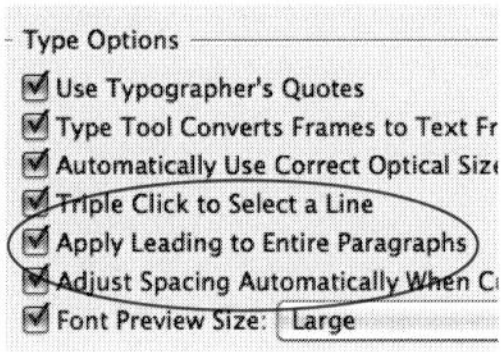

The largest leading value in a line of type determines the leading for the whole line, which means that the leading will be inconsistent if you inadvertently make one character bigger than the rest of the text. You can change this behavior in your Type preferences by selecting the Apply Leading to Entire Paragraphs option. This ensures that only one leading value can be applied to any given paragraph. Changing this setting does not affect the leading in existing frames. This may be a worthwhile "safety" feature, but strangely, it does not apply to paragraphs with Auto Leading applied. The problem with having this preference turned on is that when you apply optical leading, you need to apply more than one leading value within a paragraph.

FIGURE 4.15 The Apply Leading to Entire Paragraphs option keeps your leading within a paragraph consistent. However, it doesn't work with Auto Leading.

Auto Leading is useful when you're experimenting with type sizes, but when you decide upon the size, convert the leading value to an absolute number—even if it is the same as the Auto Leading value. Here's why you shouldn't use auto leading:

- Auto Leading is proportional to your type size—but specific to the biggest piece of type in the paragraph. This means that if you have one word larger than the rest of the paragraph, your leading value will be 120 percent of the largest word or character.

- Auto Leading doesn't give you the control that you need. Sure, if you're using 10-point type, Auto Leading is 12 points, a nice easy number to work with. However, if you're working with 11-point type, then your leading value is 13.2, which is difficult to calculate in multiples if you intend to work with a baseline grid.

- While Auto Leading works fine for body text, it can look terrible when applied to display type, which generally requires less leading.

Auto Leading and Inline Graphics

Auto Leading does have a legitimate use: when you're using inline graphics—picture frames that are pasted into a blank paragraph in the text frame and thereafter move with the flow of text. If the text makes specific reference to figures above or below, these figures are candidates to be made inline graphics, so that the relationship between text and graphic is never disrupted by edits to the text. Inline graphics are a hybrid of text and graphics: You control the spacing of inline graphics using leading. Auto Leading ensures there's always enough space for the graphic on the line, since the leading value increases or decreases according to the height of the graphic. When you're working with inline graphics, make a paragraph style with the leading value set to Auto (you may wish to adjust the actual percentage of the Auto Leading) and apply this to the blank-line paragraphs into which the graphics are placed or pasted.

Keep It Consistent, Except …

Leading, like so much in typography, is about rhythm—and as with a piece of music, you want your rhythm to be steady and unfaltering. The best way to achieve this is to set the leading values within Paragraph Styles. Should you need to change the leading values, you can edit the style definition rather than work on the text locally.

We are met on a great battlefield of that war. We have come to dedicate a portion of that field, as a final resting place for those who here gave their lives that that nation might live. It is altogether fitting and proper that we should do this.

FIGURE 4.16 The problem with Auto Leading: 120% of what exactly? Because one character (a space at the end of line 5) is larger than the rest of the paragraph, the leading is inconsistent.

Sedit aut ut optaspitias dolorpor aut qui dolo. See picture below:

Blabor apero omnis renihit quos vel erio. Nam, atempori dolorae rferspe ligenditibus. See picture below:

Dunt quatusam quis aliquatis as quaspit, sinit quaeprem res opture.

FIGURE 4.17 Using Auto Leading for inline graphics ensures that the height of the line grows to accommodate the size of the graphic.

When it comes to fixing widows and orphans, don't mess with the leading. You have other tricks up your sleeve—rewriting, tracking, discretionary hyphens, forced line breaks—to fix such problems. Tempting though it may be to tighten the leading a little bit here and there, your document will suffer if you do. Always keep your body text leading consistent, otherwise the rhythm of your type will wander like the beat of a distracted drummer.

Also, don't be tempted to go for the quick 'n' dirty solution of using vertical alignment, which increases the leading in a short column to make it bottom out (i.e., end on the same baseline as other columns). While columns of uniform depth are usually preferable in continuous prose, InDesign CS5 can now achieve this with the Balance Columns feature, which will adjust the height of all columns, rather than just extend the shortest one.

FIGURE 4.18 Good leading gone bad: The columns are balanced, but at the expense of inconsistent leading across the two columns.

Olesequatie magna feu faci blam dolorem zzrit nosto euip ea adigna faccum velit autet lummod tem quametum quamcommod dolore molor sit, quat vent il et nonse commod tat iureet irit lortie dolorercin volobor peratueros nulput laor sed dolum ad magnim incilit wisi bla facipit. Endrem

illa feu feummy nibh ercillam iure digna faccum ing eniamet lore exer in etue modolore veliquat ipisl dolessequat. Put in ut alis ad molor sumsandigna feuipsu sciduisim acidunt nulla alis alisi. Perostrud tem eniametum quiscil. ■

Leading and Baseline Grids

If your text is aligned to a baseline grid, the grid increment will trump your leading value. For example, if you have a 12-point baseline grid and you increase the leading value of text that is aligned to that grid to 13 points, the leading will round up to the next grid increment of 24 points. See Chapter 15, Margins, Columns and Baseline Grids, for more details.

FIGURE 4.19 When using a baseline grid, the grid increment will trump the leading value, as in the right column. Any increase in the leading value causes the lines of the paragraph to snap to the next available grid increment.

Ebis deria aut porepuda consendae repuda simus, int maiorecto exerae velecab oreptur as ides est voluptam facerib usciis reserum fugit alibeario blaccus sitatem excesti atiissu ndipidus dolest

Memphis Medium 10/12, aligned to grid

Ebis deria aut porepuda

consendae repuda simus, int

maiorecto exerae velecab

oreptur as ides est voluptam

Memphis Medium 10/12.1, aligned to grid

Ultimately, it is our eyes we should trust and not the math. There may be times when you need to relax consistency in favor of optical leading and tweak the leading of individual lines to make the leading *appear* more consistent. Such a situation may arise in display type, for example, if one line doesn't have descenders.

<table>
<tr><td>

The only way
to get rid of a
TEMPTATION
is to yield to it.

—Oscar Wilde
The Picture of Dorian Gray

</td><td>

The only way
to get rid of a
TEMPTATION
is to yield to it.

—Oscar Wilde
The Picture of Dorian Gray

</td></tr>
</table>

FIGURE 4.20 Using optical leading: In the example on the right the leading for the fourth line has reduced to compensate for there being no descenders on the line above.

Skip by Leading

There's a (deservedly) overlooked preference that determines how leading is affected by a text wrap. Choose Preferences > Composition and select the Skip by Leading option to ensure that text below the wrap object is moved down to the next available leading increment. The purpose of this is to achieve cross alignment of your baseline of type. This sounds like a good idea, but Skip by Leading only works when the text goes over—not around—the wrap object. Also, if the wrap object is at the top of the column, the preference is ignored. While it won't do any harm to have Skip by Leading turned on, it doesn't do a whole lot of good either. You're better off using a baseline grid to achieve the same effect.

Skip by Leading Off

Skip by Leading On

FIGURE 4.21 The Skip by Leading option pushes the line after the graphic down to the next leading increment. However, if cross alignment of baselines is what you're after, you're better off aligning your text to a baseline grid (see Chapter 15).

CHAPTER 5

Letterspacing, Tracking, and Kerning

TYPE IS ABOUT NOT ONLY THE LETTERS, but also the space between the letters and the space between the words. Typography is not just black on white, but also white on black. Each letterform and each word inhabits a field of negative white space, and this space establishes the rhythm of the words.

You can put as much nationality in the spacing of a typeface as in the typeface itself.

—Danny van den Dungen of graphic design studio Experimental Jetset. [Quoted in Helvetica, *Dir. Gary Hustwit, 2007]*

The spacing of type is to some degree a matter of personal preference and typographic trend, but whether a tight or loose letter fit is favored, for the type to be readable and to communicate without interruption, the spacing should be even, the rhythm steady.

InDesign offers three distinct but related approaches to adjusting the space between words and letters. Letterspacing is the *overall* adjustment of space between letters and between words. Tracking is the adjustment of the space between the letters and words across a *range* of text. Kerning is the adjustment of space between *letter pairs*, to compensate for uneven spacing.

Letterspacing vs. Tracking

In InDesign, letterspacing adjustments are made using the Word Spacing and Letter Spacing options in the Justification dialog box. Letterspacing and tracking can both achieve the same results, but there is an important distinction: letterspacing is macro; tracking is local.

Use letterspacing to adjust the overall tightness or looseness of certain classes of paragraph as part of the paragraph style definition. This approach is preferable when you can predict the need for adjusting the spaces between characters, as in tightening headlines or loosening captions. I'll refer to Word Spacing and Letter Spacing options collectively as *letterspacing* throughout this chapter.

Use tracking for local adjustments to sections of text to fix composition problems (see the section "Widows, Orphans, and Runts," later in this chapter), or to adjust the space between the characters of a range of text within a paragraph.

In general, it isn't necessary to adjust the letterspacing of your body text. Doing so is like taking a musician's composition and playing it at a different tempo, overriding what the type designer considered the optimum figure-ground relationship for his or her typeface.

The Nellie, a cruising yawl, swung to her anchor without a flutter of
the sails, and was at rest. The flood had made, the wind was nearly
calm, and being bound down the river, the only thing for it was to come
to and wait for the turn of the tide.

FIGURE 5.1 The blue bars indicate Word Spacing (line 1) and Letter Spacing (line 3).

▣ Millennium Bridge
Foster And Partners, Anthony Caro, Arup, 2000-01
The first completely new pedestrian bridge to be built over the
Thames for a hundred years, the Millennium Bridge is a combination of art, design and technology. The three main contributors:
engineer, architect and sculptor, designed the bridge to be stream-
lined, using an innovative and complex structure to achieve a simple
form: a shallow suspension bridge that spans the river as an 'elegant

▣ Millennium Bridge
Foster And Partners, Anthony Caro, Arup, 2000-01
The first completely new pedestrian bridge to be built over the
Thames for a hundred years, the Millennium Bridge is a combination of art, design and technology. The three main contributors:
engineer, architect and sculptor, designed the bridge to be stream-
lined, using an innovative and complex structure to achieve a simple
form: a shallow suspension bridge that spans the river as an 'elegant

	Justification		
	Minimum	Desired	Maximum
Word Spacing:	85%	110%	115%
Letter Spacing:	10%	10%	10%
Glyph Scaling:	97%	100%	103%

When applying tighter letterspacing, pay careful attention to what happens to
pairs like rn; letterspaced too tight, these might look like an "m," ri might look
like an "n," and cl like a "d." If you find yourself reducing letterspacing often,
consider using a condensed typeface that was designed with the efficient use
of space in mind.

FIGURE 5.2 The first two lines in the example on the right have positive letterspacing applied as part of their paragraph style Justification options.

Increasing letterspacing for an airier feel has its own pitfalls. Go too far and you
disrupt the relationships between the letterforms so that they no longer form
familiar word and phrase shapes, but are merely a scattershot of disconnected
characters. Italic or script types with letterforms designed to almost or actually
connect with their neighbors should never be loosely tracked. Spacing your letters loosely might not seem like a big deal to the layperson, but typographers
get quite upset about such practices. The American typographer Frederic Goudy
(1865–1947) famously said, "Men who would letterspace lowercase would steal
sheep." Reputedly, that's the sanitized version of the quote.

That said, none of these admonitions are absolute. Sometimes we need to make
adjustments to the letterspacing of our type, and some designers feel that
tight letterspacing enhances readability and improves comprehension. Don't
take anything as gospel. Print your page and evaluate for yourself, getting a
second opinion if necessary.

Tight letterspacing might be useful in the following situations:

- In sans serif headlines, tight letterspacing can help the characters hold
  together better to form more easily recognized word shapes and create
  more density and impact.

- When using condensed typefaces, their vertical nature calls for a
  reduction in the spaces between letters. Too much "air" and the words
  lose their dynamism.

FIGURE 5.3 Tight letterspacing can cause certain letter pairs to look like other letters.

DRAMA COMEDY TRAGEDY

Letter Spacing 0%

DRAMA COMEDY TRAGEDY

Letter Spacing 50%

DRAMA COMEDY TRAGEDY

Letter Spacing -20

DRAMA COMEDY TRAGEDY

DRAMA COMEDY TRAGEDY

DRAMA COMEDY TRAGEDY

FIGURE 5.4 The effect of letterspacing on display type in all caps. Positive letterspacing gives the serif type (Trajan, top) an elegant look and feel, whereas negative letterspacing causes the serifs to collide. With the sans serif type (Verlag Bold, bottom), positive letterspacing causes the word shapes to lose their cohesion and the eye tracks vertically instead of horizontally, whereas negative letterspacing creates an effective, dense look and feel.

Loose letterspacing might be useful in these situations:

- In serif headlines set in all caps, extra letterspacing can yield a more elegant look.

- When reversing type out of a solid background, extra letterspacing can improve readability.

- When using small type, like captions or photo credits, loose letter-spacing can ensure that the individual letterforms are clearly identifiable.

Tracking vs. Kerning

A surefire way to raise the hackles of a purist typographer is to use the terms *tracking* and *kerning* interchangeably. While closely related, they are distinct. Here's the difference: With a range of characters selected, you are tracking; with the cursor inserted between a pair of characters, you are kerning. Both share the same keyboard shortcut (Option/Alt+Left Arrow for tighter, or Option/Alt+Right Arrow for looser). Tracking works in combination with your other type settings; if your Justification and Hyphenation settings are set appropriately, for example, there will be much less need for manual intervention in the form of tracking.

Widows, Orphans, and Runts

Given the drama of their names, the actual definitions of *widows, orphans,* and *runts* may be a little disappointing. Definitions vary depending on your source, but I define them as follows.

A **widow** is the last line of a paragraph, stranded at the top of a column or page. Widows should always be avoided.

An **orphan** is the first line of a paragraph that occurs at the bottom of a column or page. Orphans are not desirable.

A **runt** (a termed coined by InDesign guru David Blatner) is the last line of a paragraph that ends with a short word or, worse, a single syllable of a hyphen-ated word (which you can prevent with appropriate Hyphenation settings). A single word on the last line may not be a problem if it's a long word. Ideally, the last line of a paragraph should be about one fifth of the column measure.

To fix widows, orphans, and runts, select a range of text within the problem paragraph, possibly the last line or perhaps the whole paragraph, and apply tighter tracking with the keyboard shortcut (Option+Left Arrow or Alt+Left Arrow). Tracking is a flexible and fast way of improving the look of type, but it is a compromise: It goes against the golden rule of consistency. It's important that the reader not notice that the spacing between the words gets a little tighter here and there. The aim is to pull back a line by (imperceptibly) tightening the letterspacing across the range of words. Choose your battles wisely — certain paragraphs may be resistant to tracking. Forcing them too much will result in a cure worse than the original problem. Different publications have different standards of what's acceptable, but I suggest applying no more than –15/1000 em. More tracking than this and the reader may notice a concertina effect on the type.

Fixing widows and orphans should be one of the last stages in your workflow. There's no point in addressing these problems when the layout or the text itself isn't yet finalized. Here are some other things to consider when tracking to fix widows and orphans:

- Start at the beginning of your text flow and work methodically to the end. Don't flip back and forth from one page to the next or you'll find yourself fixing one problem only to create another.

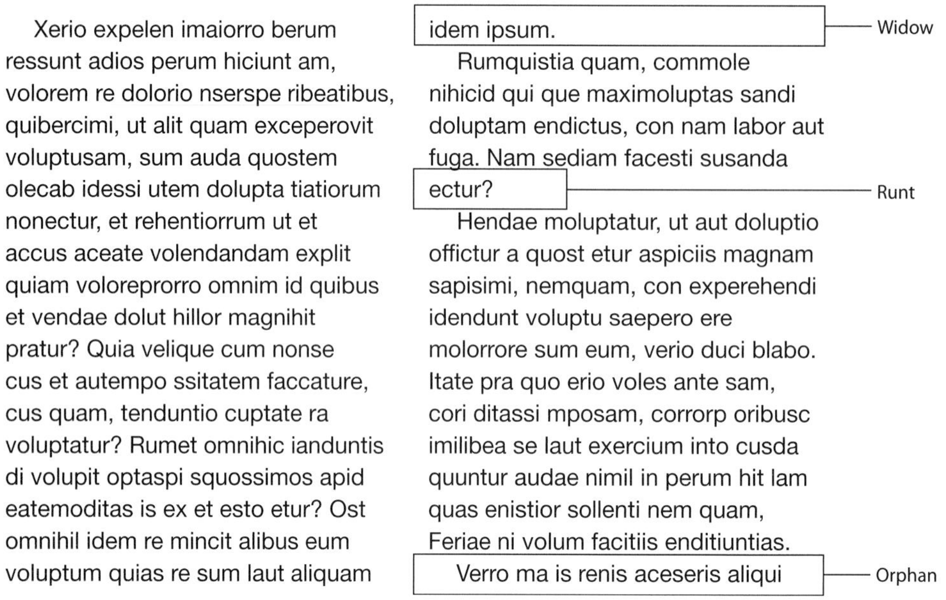

Xerio expelen imaiorro berum ressunt adios perum hiciunt am, volorem re dolorio nserspe ribeatibus, quibercimi, ut alit quam exceperovit voluptusam, sum auda quostem olecab idessi utem dolupta tiatiorum nonectur, et rehentiorrum ut et accus aceate volendandam explit quiam voloreprorro omnim id quibus et vendae dolut hillor magnihit pratur? Quia velique cum nonse cus et autempo ssitatem faccature, cus quam, tenduntio cuptate ra voluptatur? Rumet omnihic ianduntis di volupit optaspi squossimos apid eatemoditas is ex et esto etur? Ost omnihil idem re mincit alibus eum voluptum quias re sum laut aliquam

idem ipsum. ——— Widow

Rumquistia quam, commole nihicid qui que maximoluptas sandi doluptam endictus, con nam labor aut fuga. Nam sediam facesti susanda ectur? ——————————— Runt

Hendae moluptatur, ut aut doluptio offictur a quost etur aspiciis magnam sapisimi, nemquam, con experehendi idendunt voluptu saepero ere molorrore sum eum, verio duci blabo. Itate pra quo erio voles ante sam, cori ditassi mposam, corrorp oribusc imilibea se laut exercium into cusda quuntur audae nimil in perum hit lam quas enistior sollenti nem quam, Feriae ni volum facitiis enditiuntias.

Verro ma is renis aceseris aliqui ——— Orphan

FIGURE 5.5 Widow, orphan, and runt.

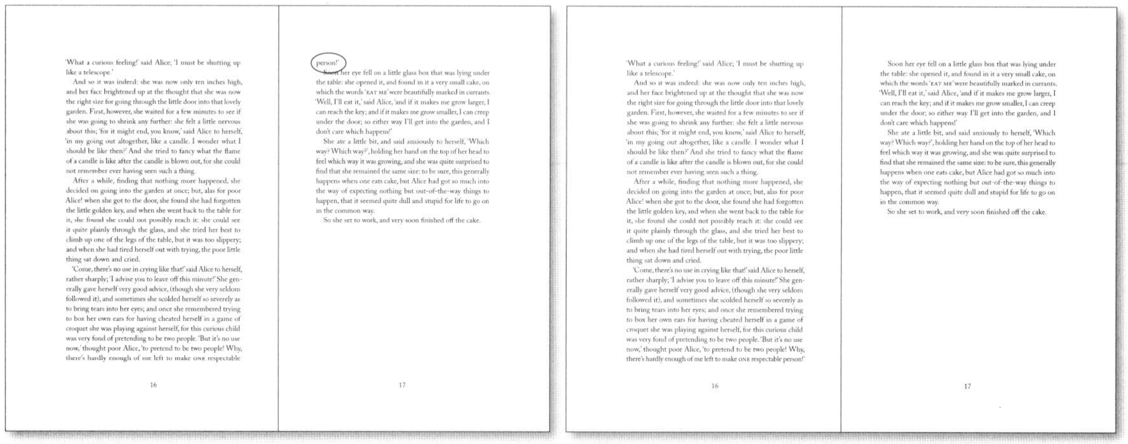

FIGURE 5.6 Tracking to fix a widow at the top of page 17 (left). The widow fixed by applying –4/1000 em tracking to the last paragraph on page 16 (right).

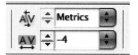

- It's sometimes easier to tighten up a paragraph that precedes the composition problem (rather than the problem paragraph itself), in the hope that this will have a positive secondary effect.

- A useful preference highlights in green any ranges of text that have been custom tracked or kerned. Any orange lines appearing within the overall green tracking areas show where single spaces have been customized further. To turn on this option, choose Preferences > Composition and select the Custom Tracking/Kerning check box. This is helpful if you have inherited a document and want to make sure that the text hasn't been overzealously tracked, or if the layout or text of a document is revised so that the tracking in certain areas is no longer necessary. This preference is the reason you don't want to apply tracking as part of a paragraph style definition: If it's been applied everywhere, you can't distinguish the exceptions.

Rivers

When you adjust tracking, stay alert to the color of the whole paragraph, not just the line, watching out for rivers — another composition problem that can spoil an even type color. In typographic terms, a river is a line or crack that runs vertically through your paragraph, caused by a random and unfortunate positioning of word spaces on successive lines. Rivers are most common in narrow columns of justified text, but can also occur when letters are spaced too tightly. If you're using an appropriate column measure and appropriate Hyphenation and Justification settings, rivers are unlikely to occur. Sometimes, however, you're unlucky, and applying tracking with a light touch may be the solution to the problem.

TIP: The best way to spot a river is to print a proof and turn your page upside down so that the negative space between the letters is abstracted. Any scars on the page will be more noticeable.

Other Ways to Fix Widows, Orphans, and Rivers

If the line is impervious to the charms of tracking, don't force it. Remove the tracking (Cmd+Option+Q or Ctrl+Alt+Q) and try one of the following options instead.

Adjust the word spacing. You can tighten or expand the word spacing across a range of characters without affecting the character spacing. Cmd/Ctrl+Option/Alt+Delete tightens the word spaces. Cmd/Ctrl+Option/Alt+Shift+Backslash increases the word spaces.

FIGURE 5.7 Horrible word spacing and rivers caused by justified text set in a narrow column. Applying a modest amount of tracking (–5/1000 em) to lines 4 and 5 does at least fix the rivers (right).

Oreo similiquid que consecto et escitat. Arit facearum, status quo omi mint. Ebistio rrovidis eiusae nam, sinverunt, nosame dolut abore, test repeliqui optatur aboribu int. Culpa des que volessi audae nos et verepre mporenis eniti net doluptiis evelici autem.

Oreo similiquid que consecto et escitat. Arit facearum, status quo omi mint. Ebistio rrovidis eiusae nam, sinverunt, nosame dolut abore, test repeliqui optatur aboribu int. Culpa des que volessi audae nos et verepre mporenis eniti net doluptiis evelici autem.

Tracking and the Paragraph Composer

The lines of paragraphs composed with the Adobe Paragraph Composer (the default composition method) don't always break as expected when tracked. This is because the lines are recomposed on a paragraph basis rather than line by line — every change you make to a paragraph causes InDesign to reconsider the line breaks of the whole paragraph, not just the line you are working on. While this can be frustrating for editors and proofreaders, using the Adobe Paragraph Composer rather than the Single-line Composer will result in better type color. See Chapter 7, "Alignment."

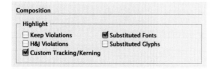

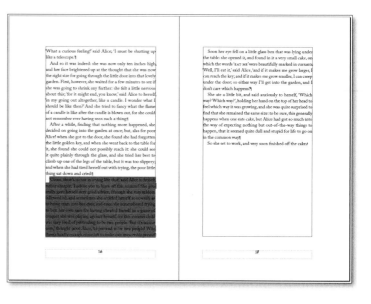

FIGURE 5.8 Turn on Custom Tracking/Kerning in Composition Preferences to highlight where custom tracking or kerning has been applied.

Use the No Break option. Adjusting the tracking and word spacing not doing the trick? Apply No Break to a range of text to prevent it from breaking across a line. You can apply this on a case-by-case basis by selecting the last two words of the paragraph and choosing No Break from the Control panel menu.

Revise the copy. This may not be an option, depending on the kind of document you're working with, but if you have license to rewrite, then go for it — often a subtle rewording will do the trick.

Employ the Keep Options. Keep Options is the umbrella term for different methods of controlling how paragraphs break — or don't break. The various options are: Keep With Previous, Keep With Next, Keep Lines Together, as well as Start Paragraph, which can force a page, frame, or column break. If you don't need your columns to "bottom out" (i.e., share the same last baseline), you can control how your paragraphs break by using Keep Options to specify a number of lines at the end of the paragraph be kept together. Beware: Overzealous use of Keep Options can cause your text to behave oddly, with paragraphs jumping from frame to frame as if they have a life of their own. That said, Keep With Next is useful for preventing headings and subheadings from being divorced from the text that follows them. See Chapter 9, "Breaking (and Not Breaking) Lines, Paragraphs, Columns, and Pages."

TIP: Other Uses of Tracking. Apply positive tracking, preferably as part of a character style, to acronyms (for example, NATO, AIDS, ASBO) or initialisms (FBI, USA, HTML), where it's more important to distinguish the individual characters than for them to be cohesive as word shapes.

TIP: Flipping through your pages at a small view percentage with the type greeked can often help to identify the problem areas.

Alice was beginning to get very tired of sitting by her sister on the bank, and of having nothing to do: once or twice she had peeped into the book her sister was reading, but it had no pictures or conversations in it, 'and what is the use of a book,' thought Alice 'without pictures or conversation?'

No tracking

Alice was beginning to get very tired of sitting by her sister on the bank, and of having nothing to do: once or twice she had peeped into the book her sister was reading, but it had no pictures or conversations in it, 'and what is the use of a book,' thought Alice 'without pictures or conversation?'

Word Spacing adjusted

Alice was beginning to get very tired of sitting by her sister on the bank, and of having nothing to do: once or twice she had peeped into the book her sister was reading, but it had no pictures or conversations in it, 'and what is the use of a book,' thought Alice 'without pictures or conversation?'

FIGURE 5.9 Adjusting word spacing to fix a runt line. Paragraph 2 shows the result of decreasing the space between the words only. Paragraph 3 shows the Composition preference Show Custom Tracking/Kerning turned on.

Using GREP Styles to Fix Runt Lines

You can use a GREP style to apply a No Break character style to the last two words of a paragraph. Doing this ensures that there are at least two words on the last line of every paragraph with a particular paragraph style applied to it. I'll be talking about GREP styles in Chapter 12, "Global Formatting with Styles," but because this application of a GREP style relates specifically to preventing composition problems, I'm going to give you the expression without getting into an explanation of how it works. This tip comes courtesy of InDesign expert Michael Murphy. I recommend you check out his "Learning GREP" title on Lynda.com.

Make a character style that incorporates the No Break attribute. Edit the paragraph style definition for paragraphs where you want to avoid runt lines. In the GREP Style section of Paragraph Style Options, choose No Break from the Apply Style menu. Type the following GREP expression into the To Text field: (?<=\w)\s(?=\w+[[:punct:]]+$)

FIGURE 5.10 You can apply No Break manually to keep two or more words together. Alternatively, you can use a GREP style to apply a No Break character style to the space between the last two words in a paragraph — automatically preventing the possibility of a runt line.

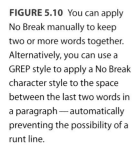

Kerning

TIP: The default kerning and tracking increment in Preferences > Units & Increments is 20/1000 of an em, which is too coarse. Do yourself a favor and change this increment to 1/1000 of an em with no InDesign document open so that it becomes an application Preference.

Kerning operates at the micro level of spacing adjustment. Its purpose is corrective: to compensate for the appearance of unequal spacing between certain pairs of letters, especially when one or both of those letters is angled or curved. For a better reading experience, it's necessary to use kerning to even out any inconsistent spacing. Typically, this involves reducing the space between the characters, although it might on occasion mean an increase in space. Inconsistently spaced type can destroy a page. While most readers won't be able to pinpoint poor kerning as the culprit, they will know intuitively that something is wrong.

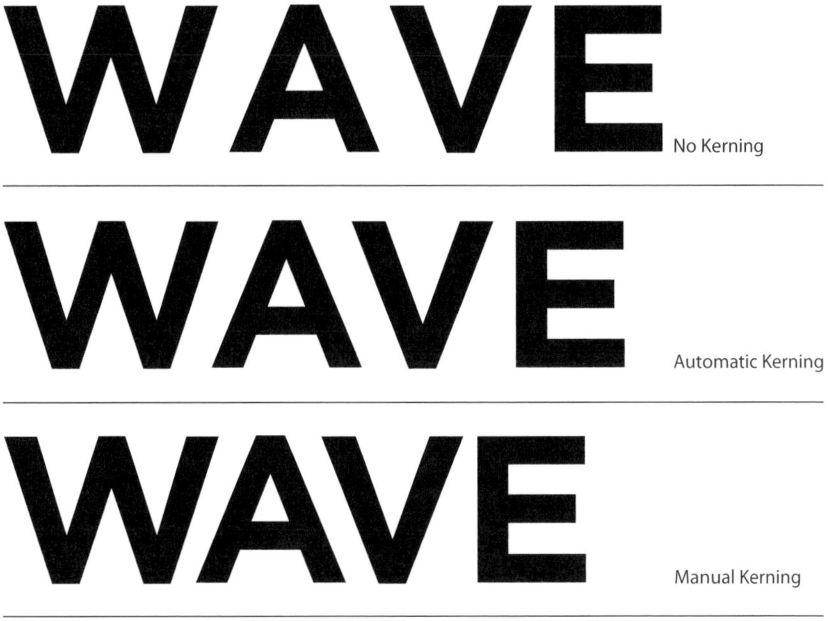

WAVE
No Kerning

WAVE
Automatic Kerning

WAVE
Manual Kerning

FIGURE 5.11 Display text without kerning, with automatic (Metrics) kerning, and with manual kerning.

Automatic Kerning

If adjusting the space between every pair of letters seems like an obsessive and ridiculously time-consuming endeavor, take heart: The majority of our kerning needs are addressed by InDesign's automatic kerning methods, so you don't need to drive yourself crazy finding troublesome letter pairs and manually adjusting their spacing. There are two automatic kerning methods, both of which are adequate for small type: Metrics (the default) and Optical. Regardless of the method you use, you can always add manual kerning as needed.

To see how much automatic kerning is applied to any given letter pair, insert your Type cursor between the characters; the Kerning field displays the amount in parentheses. Typefaces are designed in a 1,000-unit em square; InDesign kerns (and tracks) in these increments of thousandths of an em. Because these are relative units, a kerning and tracking adjustment made at one point size will scale along with the type and have proportionally the same effect at any other point size.

TIP: Quark users migrating to InDesign will need to multiply the old Quark kerning and tracking values by 5 for the equivalent InDesign values. In Quark terms, a kerning/tracking value of 1 equals 1/200th of an em; in InDesign, "1" equals 1/1000th of an em. For example, if you tracked text to 1 in Quark, you would need to track it to 5 in InDesign.

FIGURE 5.12 The em square.

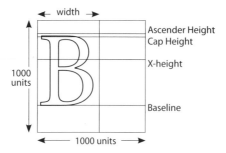

FIGURE 5.13 The same passage of text comparing InDesign's two automatic kerning methods.

One morning, when Gregor Samsa woke from troubled dreams, he found himself transformed in his bed into a horrible vermin. He lay on his armour-like back, and if he lifted his head a little he could see his brown belly, slightly domed and divided by arches into stiff sections. The bedding was hardly able to cover it and seemed ready to slide off any moment. His many legs, pitifully thin compared with the size of the rest of him, waved about helplessly as he looked.   Metrics Kerning

One morning, when Gregor Samsa woke from troubled dreams, he found himself transformed in his bed into a horrible vermin. He lay on his armour-like back, and if he lifted his head a little he could see his brown belly, slightly domed and divided by arches into stiff sections. The bedding was hardly able to cover it and seemed ready to slide off any moment. His many legs, pitifully thin compared with the size of the rest of him, waved about helplessly as he looked.   Optical Kerning

Metrics vs. Optical Kerning

Metrics kerning uses the metrics values that are built into most fonts. The values are instructions to adjust the spacing between particular letter combinations. They reflect the type designer's judgment about how the space should be spaced and make an important contribution to the quality of a typeface. Font creation software can automate the creation of kerning pairs, but most type designers prefer to create them manually — at least for those letter combinations that are known to be troublesome.

Optical kerning is a mathematical solution that ignores the metrics values within a font and instead adjusts the space within letter pairs according to their character shapes. Typically, Optical kerning yields a slightly tighter result. In addition, because it is a mathematical solution, it is more consistent. But does Optical kerning look better? Ultimately it depends on the quality of the metrics you are comparing it against. Kerning metrics are the subjective judgment of the type designer, and as any type designer will tell you, a good typeface is one that looks good to the eye — it's more an art than an exact science.

Here are some things to consider when choosing Metrics or Optical kerning:

- Theoretically, Optical kerning yields more consistent character spacing. Every character pair — even the most unlikely ones, such as zh, xw, or gk — is kerned based on its character shapes.

- If your font includes few or no built-in kerning pairs, you're better off with Optical kerning. Decorative and novelty fonts may have a limited number of kerning pairs.

- Use Optical kerning when combining typefaces in the same word (admittedly rare), since there will be no kerning metrics for letter pairs of different fonts. Kerning metrics are applied to two letters, and the result is the kerning pair. If you use one letter from one face and another letter from another typeface there will be no previously determined kerning pair for the new coupling.

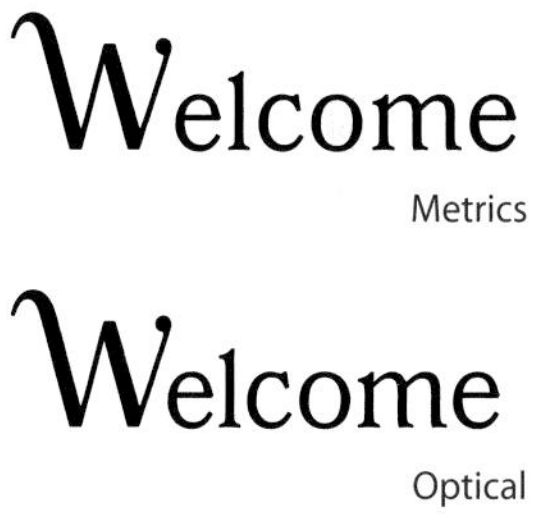

Manual Kerning

Manual kerning is not usually necessary for type at text sizes, but it plays an important role with display type. Because any spacing anomalies become more apparent as type size increases, the bigger the type, the more need there is to kern to achieve visually consistent spacing between the characters.

Possible candidates for manual adjustment include:

- Headlines and display type

- Drop caps where the large opening letter collides with the type that follows

- Combined fonts (especially roman-italic combinations)

- Script typefaces — to ensure that the connecting strokes touch the letters that follow them

NOTE: Kerning and tracking are cumulative; they don't cancel each other out. You can use tracking to adjust the overall look of your type, then use kerning to adjust particular letter combinations.

Welcome
Metrics

Welcome
Optical

FIGURE 5.14 Optical kerning is preferable when combining two fonts in the same word.

Approaches to Kerning Display Type

It takes time to develop an eye for kerning. Until you feel confident, be cautious and make only slight adjustments. Manual kerning needs to be approached carefully and thoughtfully or it becomes a giant (some say obsessive) time sink. Before you start adjusting the kerning on display type make sure you have the letterspacing and tracking the way you'd like them. Any fine tweaks to kerning pairs may be redundant should you later make a blanket change to the letterspacing.

FIGURE 5.15 Kerning display type (Helvetica Neue Bold Condensed 62 pt). The numbers indicate the amount of kerning adjustment applied between each letter pair.

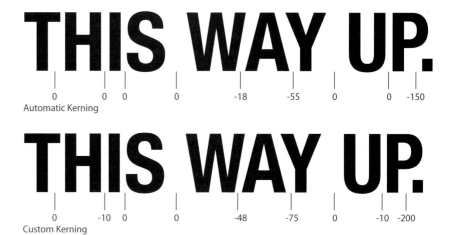

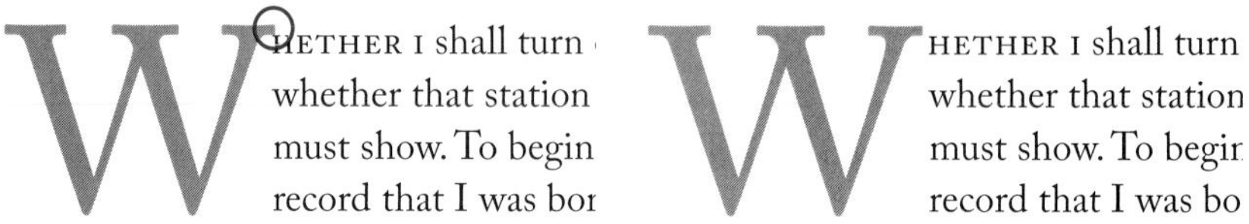

THIS WAY UP.

0   0   0   0   -18   -55   0   0   -150

Automatic Kerning

THIS WAY UP.

0   -10   0   0   -48   -75   0   -10 -200

Custom Kerning

FIGURE 5.16 A drop cap colliding with the first line of the text, fixed by applying positive kerning between the "W" and the "h."

FIGURE 5.17 Kerning script type.

Metrics Kerning   Manual Kerning

Manual kerning is not static, it's kinetic. Any changes you make to the kern of a particular letter pair will affect not just that pair, but all the letters in the text you're working on. For this reason you should fix the worst problem first and then let that kerning pair determine the spacing for the rest of the characters. Of course, if there are multiple instances of a letter pair in the text you're kerning, make sure you apply the same treatment to each.

Don't overdo it. Along with the ease of kerning comes a tendency to want to fix things that aren't broken in the first place. Most letter shapes fit well with nearly all their possible neighbors.

When making kerning adjustments, zoom in to a large enough view size to evaluate your results — and then zoom out again to 100 percent view to make sure your changes look appropriate. Be sure to evaluate the results on paper and not just onscreen.

FIGURE 5.18 The Kern Hoodie available at Veer.com.

Water
Rights

Metrics Kerning

Water
Rights

Custom Kerning

FIGURE 5.19 The biggest problem in the example on the left is the spacing between the "W" and the "a." That's where I started, then I tried to even out the spacing according to this letter pair. This meant increasing the space between the "R" and the "i."

A Kerning Anecdote

When I was a wee lad growing up in South London (and long before I cared about type), I spied the large neon sign of a new video store from a distance of about 100 yards. The name of the store was FLICKERS, set in all caps. The letters were very tightly spaced so that — from a distance — the LI combination looked like a U. It certainly grabbed my attention.

CHAPTER 6

Small (but Important) Details

TYPOGRAPHY IS ALL ABOUT THE DETAILS, and good typographers tend to be mildly obsessive by temperament. But this sweating the small stuff is more than just nitpicking; it's about clear communication. Attending to detail requires that we take charge of our computers so that they don't force us into making amateurish mistakes. All design programs have some dumb default settings, and InDesign is no exception. Avoiding bad default settings is no guarantee that your type will look good, but it helps guard against it looking bad. For good-looking typography we must take advantage of InDesign's many options for finessing our type—understanding the different widths and uses of the spacing characters, knowing the difference between em dashes and en dashes, and taking advantage of OpenType features. It's this attention to detail that sets your work apart from the crowd.

"Don't count the days, make the days count."

"Don't count the days, make the days count."
— *Muhammad Ali*

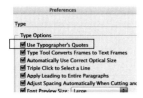

FIGURE 6.1 Typographer's quotes (top) versus inch marks (bottom).

«Plus ça change, plus c'est la même chose.»

FIGURE 6.2 Change the language in Dictionary Preferences to use the appropriate type of quote marks. Here, guillemets are used in place of typographer's double quotes.

NOTE: Non-French refers to guillemets used in an unofficial way without spaces. The official French style uses spaces.

Typographer's Quotes

No self-respecting typographer would be caught dead using straight quotation marks, or inch marks, instead of paired typographer's ("curly") quotes. By default, this preference is on. Using typographer's quotes is also an option in Word Import Options when you place text with the Show Import Options box checked. In American English, double quotation marks are used to set off a quote and single quotation marks are used for quotes within a quote. In British English, it is the other way around. In addition, American English requires commas and periods to go inside the quotation marks even if the punctuation is not part of the quoted sentence. Colons and semicolons, however, go outside the quotation marks. In British English, all punctuation goes outside the quotation marks, which perhaps makes more sense, but looks ugly.

Dictionary Preferences allows you to choose the appearance of your single and double quotes for specific languages.

‹ O › French single quotes

« O » French double quotes (guillemets)

«O» Non-French guillemets without space

‚O' German single quotes

„O" German double quotes

Straight quote marks are a legacy from when engineers (not typographers) translated typewriter keyboard layouts to ASCII codes. The misuse of straight quotes became common when desktop publishing programs empowered everyone with a computer to set their own type. If you need to convey feet or inch measurements, it is possible, though not recommended, to toggle to straight quotes by pressing Cmd+Option+Shift+' (Ctrl+Alt+Shift+'). A better option is to avoid straight (dumb) quotes altogether and use the prime (feet, minutes) and double prime (inches, seconds) characters instead. You can find these characters in the Symbol font and access them using the Glyphs panel—or you could add them to your own custom glyph set, as described in "Creating a Glyph Set" later in this chapter.

Apostrophes

An apostrophe is the same character as a single closing quote. Confusion can arise when InDesign second-guesses you and thinks you want a single opening quote rather than an apostrophe. This is most likely to occur in phrases where an apostrophe substitutes for missing letters or in dates where the apostrophe substitutes for missing numerals. To make sure you get an apostrophe rather than a single opening quote, type Shift+Option+] (Shift+Alt+]).

Punctuation

In running text, when a comma, period, or colon follows a word set in italic or bold, it should also be in italic or bold. Quote marks, question marks, and exclamation marks should be set in the same style as the rest of the sentence.

Punctuation (and hyphens) should hang outside the column measure—something that is easily achieved using Optical Margin Alignment, applied either locally through the Story Panel or globally as part of an Object Style definition (see Chapter 13, "Global Formatting with Styles"). The font size setting determines the amount of overhang. Usually this should be the same size as the text, but you'll want to eyeball it.

Punctuation in display type can look disproportionately large, so be prepared to reduce the size of your commas, periods, colons, and quote marks to compensate.

Max Headroom: 6' 11"
Bedroom One: 15' × 10'
Letter Size: 8 ½" × 11"
Quote Marks

Max Headroom: 6' 11"
Bedroom One: 15' × 10'
Letter Size: 8 ½" × 11"
Inch Marks

Max Headroom: 6' 11″
Bedroom One: 15′ × 10′
Letter Size: 8 ½″ × 11″
Prime Marks

FIGURE 6.3 Prime marks from the Symbol font compared to quote marks and inch marks.

Fish 'n' Chips
Rock 'n' Roll
'90s
Incorrect

Fish 'n' Chips
Rock 'n' Roll
'90s
Correct

FIGURE 6.4 Apostrophes versus single opening quote marks.

Choose a Style Guide

All publishers have their own style manual, which specifies the use of punctuation, em spaces, and other points. Many take as their starting point *The Chicago Manual of Style*. You can buy the style guides of large publishers like the *New York Times*, the *Guardian* (UK), and the Associated Press. Regardless of which style manual you follow, most important of all is to be consistent.

Frankenstein! If thou
: of revenge against me,
han in my destruction.
xtinction that I might
if yet, in some mode
STORY
Optical Margin Alignment
12 pt

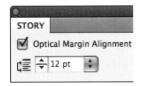

FIGURE 6.5 Use Optical Margin Alignment to make punctuation "hang" outside the text frame.

Optical Margin Alignment

Have you ever noticed how punctuation at the margin of a text frame can make the left or right sides of a column appear misaligned? When a line begins with punctuation, like an opening quotation mark, or ends with a comma, period, or hyphen, you get a visual hole.

Until recently, these shortcomings were regarded as part of the price of progress. After all, we could all do so much more with our page layout programs. At the end of the day, did it really matter that we had to forgo a few niceties? Along came InDesign to the rescue.

Optical Margin Alignment allows punctuation, as well as the edges of letters, to hang outside the text margin so that the column edge appears straighter. Surprisingly, some people don't like this look, preferring everything contained within the text block. But then, some people have become so accustomed to the taste of instant coffee that they prefer it to the real thing.

"One Small Step For Man,
One Giant Leap For Mankind"

"One Small Step For Man,
One Giant Leap For Mankind"

FIGURE 6.6 Adjusting the size of punctuation in headlines: No adjustment (top); punctuation reduced from 30 points to 24 points (bottom).

Dashes

There are three lengths of dash—five if you include the minus sign and the figure dash—and they all serve different functions.

The **hyphen** is the shortest dash, typically one-third the length of an em dash. Hyphens are used to break single words into syllables when hyphenation is turned on (soft hyphens), to join ordinarily separate words into compound words, or to link the words of a phrase that is used as an adjective. The hyphen does not require spaces on either side, except for suspended hyphens, which require a space after the hyphen. Suspended hyphens are used when hyphenated adjectives refer to a common basic element and this common element is shown only with the last term—such as upper- and lowercase, two- and four-wheel drive, pre- and post-war, and so on.

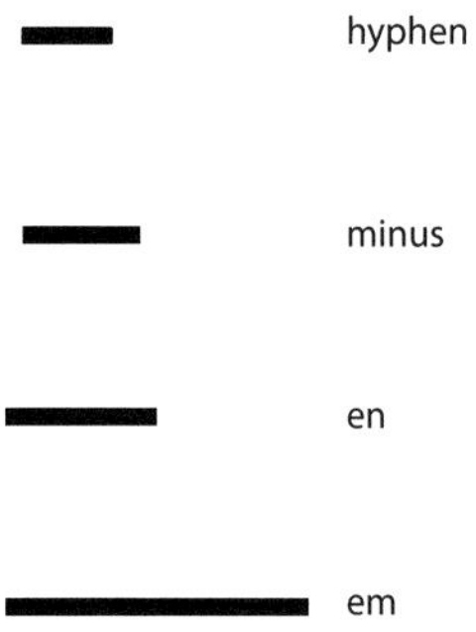

The **en dash** (Option+- or Alt+-) is used to indicate duration. If you would say "to" when reading the sentence out loud, then use an en dash. You would also use an en dash when you have a compound adjective, one part of which consists of two words or a hyphenated word. There is no space around the en dash.

The **em dash** (Shift+Option+- or Shift+Alt+-) is used to separate a parenthetical break in the sentence.

Em dashes should not touch the characters that precede or follow them. You can put a thin space (Cmd/Ctrl+Option/Alt+Shift+M) around em dashes to ensure they remain separate. A regular word space is too wide and in justified type will grow and shrink to achieve justification. A thin space is one-eighth the width of an em space, is nonbreaking (meaning that it prevents the dash from being separated from the words next to it), and will not change size in justified text.

Some people find the em dash too wide and choose instead to use an en dash as a phrase marker, or to use an em dash at 75–80 percent horizontal scale. If you opt for the latter, you can set up a GREP style (see Chapter 13) to automate the process. This was my preference for the em dashes, but the Peachpit style uses full em dashes.

FIGURE 6.7 Four different widths of dash (Adobe Caslon Pro, 60 pt).

Open 9-5
1914-1918
September-October

Incorrect

Open 9–5
1914–1918
September–October

Correct

FIGURE 6.8 The en dash is used here to separate times and dates.

Em dashes—also known as long dashes—are used to set off a phrase. They also indicate an abrupt change in thought—like this.

Em dashes with Thin Spaces before and after.

Em dashes—also known as long dashes—are used to set off a phrase. They also indicate an abrupt change in thought—like this.

Em dashes at 75% horizontal scale.

FIGURE 6.9 Correct usage of the em dash.

A ... Z

Three dots

A . . . Z

Ellipsis character
[Option-; / Alt-;]

A . . . Z

Dots separated by thin spaces
[Cmd-Shift-Option-M /
Ctrl-Shift-Alt-M]

...all men are created
equal...they are
endowed...with certain
unalienable Rights...
Life, Liberty and the
pursuit of Happiness.

Ellipsis Character

...all men are created
equal...they are
endowed...with certain
unalienable Rights...
Life, Liberty and the
pursuit of Happiness.

Custom Ellipsis

FIGURE 6.10 Different
approaches to the ellipsis.

On a typewriter, an em dash is conveyed with double hyphens. Because some people are resistant to unlearning this habit, you're likely to encounter this and all manner of other approximations of an em dash, which you'll need to find and change. See "Cleaning Up Text" in Chapter 2, "Getting Type on Your Page," for more about this.

OpenType fonts may also have a figure dash, which is the width of a lining numeral and is designed to work in concert with lining numerals, and a minus sign, which is slightly wider than a hyphen and may be slightly wider or narrower than the en dash, depending on the typeface.

Ellipses

An ellipsis indicates omission or rhetorical pause. When the omitted words are within a sentence, use a three-dot ellipsis preceded and followed by a space. When the omission occurs at the end of a sentence, add a period at the end of the sentence just before the ellipsis.

A three-dot ellipsis is included in most standard font sets (Option+; /Alt+0133). If you find the dots of the ellipsis character too tightly spaced, you can create your own ellipsis with dots separated by thin spaces. Use Find/Change to automatically replace any other ellipsis forms with your custom ellipsis or set up a GREP style to automate their conversion within the text.

End Marks

An end mark is a common device in magazines, newsletters, and journals to signify the end of an article, especially when the article spans several pages. The end mark can be a character taken from a picture font like the venerable Zapf Dingbats, or an inline graphic such as the logotype of the publication. End marks should be scaled so that they are no bigger than the cap height of the text; depending on the mark you're using you may want to size them to the x-height. They can be separated from the text with an en space (Cmd/Ctrl+Shift+N) or set flush right with the margin (Shift+Tab). To ensure consistency, create an End Mark character style.

Symbols

Frequently used special characters can be accessed by choosing Type > Insert Special Character > Symbols; all others can be accessed from the Glyphs panel. As with punctuation, as your text gets bigger, the symbols should become proportionately smaller.

White Space Characters

There are 12 other spacing characters in addition to the word space, and they can be accessed by choosing Type > Insert White Space, or by selecting Insert White Space from the Type Tool context menu (Ctrl-click or right-click).

Em Space

An em space (Cmd+Shift+M/Ctrl+Shift+M) is a relative unit, equal in width to the size of your type. In 12-point type, an em space is 12 points wide; in 72-point type, it is 72 points.

Em Space = size of the type (in this example 36 pt)

En Space

An en space (Cmd+Shift+N/Ctrl+Shift+N) is half the width of an em space.

En Space = ½ an em

Flush Space

A flush space can be useful to flush out a series of items across a column measure without increasing the word spacing within those items. Flush spaces work with Justify All Lines alignment only.

Third Space = ⅓ of an em

Hair Space

A hair space (Cmd+Option+Shift+I/Ctrl+Alt+Shift+I) is ¹⁄₂₄ the width of an em space. It can be used as an alternative to a thin space.

Quarter Space = ¼ of an em

Sixth Space = ⅙ of an em

and so, in conclusion, it's fair to say that the quick brown fox jumped over the lazy dog. ■

and so, in conclusion, it's fair to say that the quick brown fox jumped over the lazy dog.   ■

FIGURE 6.11 An end mark, sized to the x-height of the type and separated by an en space (left) or set flush right using Shift+Tab (right).

Thin Space = ⅛ of an em

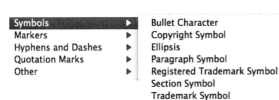

FIGURE 6.12 The special characters available in the Symbols menu—all others can be found in the Glyphs panel.

Hair Space = ¹⁄₂₄ of an em

FIGURE 6.13 The white space characters available on the Type > Insert White Space menu. Their relative sizes relate to the point size of the type.

FIGURE 6.14 Flush spaces are used to spread out items across the column measure without increasing the space between those items.

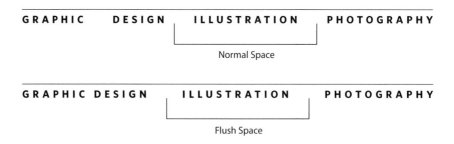

No Double Spaces, Please

There's never an excuse for having more than one consecutive word space anywhere in your text. But wait … I hear you say, surely … No. Never.

The convention of double spacing after a period is a holdover from the days of the typewriter when fonts were monospaced, that is, all characters had the same width regardless of the shape of the letter, so that an **i** occupied the same width as a **w**. The characters were so wide and so open that a single space wasn't enough between sentences.

These days our typefaces—unless you're aiming for a retro typewriter look—are proportionally spaced, which means that each character has a unique width corresponding to its character shape. The word spaces in pro-portionally spaced typefaces are designed to separate sentences perfectly. Putting two spaces after every period undermines the goal of even type color and looks amateurish.

These days you're more likely to see a typewriter displayed as a piece of retro art than a working typesetting tool, but the double spacing habit persists. Choose Edit > Find/Change, select Queries, and then choose Multiple Space to Single Space. This will zap any extra spaces in the blink of an eye.

Nonbreaking Space

TIP: Both Mac OS and Microsoft Windows support keyboard layouts for mul-tiple languages. Make sure you're using the appropriate one, so that you have ready access to the characters you need.

The same width as a word space, a nonbreaking space (Cmd+Option+X/ Ctrl+Alt+X) prevents two (or more) words, like a name for example, from being broken across a line. Using a nonbreaking space is preferable to a forced line break to fix a runt line. If the text is edited or reflowed, you won't end up with a break in the middle of your line. The Nonbreaking Space (Fixed Width) is used in justified type to prevent the space from varying with the other spaces on the line in order to achieve justification. Instead of using a nonbreaking space, however, you can apply No Break to a selected range of text. See Chapter 9, "Breaking (and Not Breaking) Lines, Paragraphs, Columns, and Pages."

Thin Space

A thin space (Cmd+Option+Shift+M/Ctrl+Alt+Shift+M) is one-eighth the width of an em space—a good choice on either side of an em dash or to separate the dots of an ellipsis.

Figure Space

A figure space is the same width as a figure in the typeface, if the typeface you are using is designed with Tabular Lining or Tabular Oldstyle figures, where each figure occupies the same set width. Figure spaces can be used to help align numbers in tables.

Figure Spaces

FIGURE 6.15 Figure spaces can be used to align numbers.

Punctuation Space

A punctuation space is the same width as an exclamation mark, period, or colon in the typeface.

What Are CID Fonts?

CID fonts are a form of Type 1 font developed by Adobe in the mid-1990s to support large character sets, particularly non-Roman character sets, like Chinese, Japanese, and Korean. The CID number refers to the identifier used to index and access the characters in the font.

The Glyphs Panel

To access the special characters, foreign accents, currency symbols, and diacritical marks that are not on an English keyboard, we have the Glyphs panel. To view the Glyphs panel, choose Type > Glyphs. The Glyphs panel is a less than perfect solution to finding specific glyphs, especially when working with typefaces that have big character sets. You can subset your view, sort by Unicode number (which is useful only if you know the Unicode number for the glyph you're after), and change the view size of the glyphs. These techniques notwithstanding, searching for a glyph can still seem like hunting for the proverbial needle in a haystack. When you find the glyph you want, make sure your Type Tool is inserted in a text frame, then double-click to insert the glyph into the text.

Characters and Glyphs: What's the Difference?

A glyph is a specific form of a character. Most characters correspond to a single glyph, but certain typefaces include characters that correspond to several glyphs—the Glyphs panel gives you access to these alternate forms.

Recently used Glyphs are listed on the top row

Filter your view to a subset of glyphs using the Show drop down menu.

Change the sort order of the glyphs from the Glyphs panel menu.

View alternate glyphs for the character by clicking and holding down on character boxes that have a triangle in their bottom right hand corner, or by choosing Alternates for Selection from the Show drop down menu.

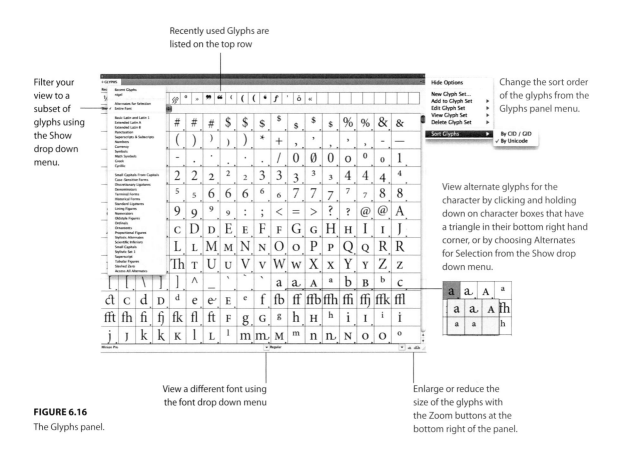

View a different font using the font drop down menu

Enlarge or reduce the size of the glyphs with the Zoom buttons at the bottom right of the panel.

FIGURE 6.16
The Glyphs panel.

Creating a Glyph Set

If you find yourself repeatedly using the same glyphs, making a glyph set saves hunting for them each time you need them.

1. Choose Type > Glyphs.

2. From the Glyphs panel menu, choose New Glyph Set, name your glyph set, and click OK.

3. Click on a glyph you want to add to your glyph set. Ctrl-click (right-click) and choose Add to Glyph Set from the context menu that appears.

Once you've made your glyph set, choose Edit Glyph Set from the Glyphs panel menu. As appropriate, deselect the option Remember Font with Glyph for those glyphs where you don't want to capture the specific font, but only the glyph itself. If the typeface you're working with doesn't have that particular character (for instance, an exclamation mark is not part of Zapf Dingbats), then the glyph will revert to its original typeface.

TIP: To download a list of all the characters in the Adobe Western 2 character set go to www.adobe.com/type/pdfs/AdobeWestern2.pdf. This list provides the Unicode value for each character as well as the keyboard commands to access the characters.

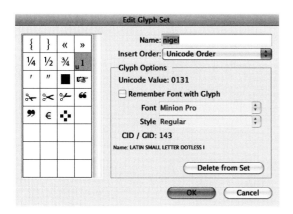

FIGURE 6.17 Editing a glyph set. When you deselect Remember Font with Glyph, a U appears in the lower-left corner of the character box.

Unicode

OpenType fonts are based on Unicode—an international, cross-platform standard that assigns numbers to the characters in a font. Before Unicode, the recognized standard was ASCII, which has a character set of 256 characters. The problem with ASCII is that Mac OS and Windows use different encoding schemes. While they agree on the first 128 characters, the next 128 numbers are specific to each platform. This means that specifying the characters you need requires different key combinations on the different platforms.

FIGURE 6.18 Loading a selected glyph into the Find dialog box.

Finding and Changing Glyphs

Problems can occur when working with non-Unicode fonts and special characters. Because older fonts don't use a standard encoding for their special characters, when you change from one font to another you may end up with a mess.

Switching to an OpenType font (based on Unicode) is part of the solution, but you'll also need to reassign the special characters to the correct Unicode glyph. Thereafter, you'll be able to switch the fonts without any problem.

You can use Find/Change to find any glyph from any font and replace it with any other glyph from any other font. To choose the glyph you want to find, select it, then Ctrl-click (right-click) and choose Load Selected Glyph in Find from the context menu.

Unicode, however, offers a character set of up to 65,000 — and to think, it used to be the boast of typographers that "with 26 soldiers of lead" they could conquer the world! In reality, no font comes close to having this many characters, but OpenType Pro fonts have expanded character sets that include a full range of Latin characters, accented characters to support central and Eastern European languages, such as Turkish and Polish, as well as Cyrillic and Greek characters. In addition to making multilingual typography easier, OpenType Pro fonts also give us all kinds of typographic delicacies — such as extra ligatures, real small caps, real fractions, and Oldstyle numerals — that we formerly had to switch to an "Expert Set" in order to access.

In Windows, you can type any glyph using Alt + the Unicode value. The same option exists in Mac OS, although it's a bit obscure. With the "Unicode Hex Input" keyboard selected in the Language & Text System Preferences — it's close to the bottom of the list of language keyboards — you can type Option + the Unicode value as you would in Windows. However, using the Hex Input keyboard does make using keyboard shortcuts that include the Option key nonfunctional, so it's something you'd only want to use on an as-needed basis.

Making Fractions

PostScript and TrueType fonts have the following fractions in their character set: ¼, ½, ¾. Certain OpenType Pro typefaces may also contain ⅛, ⅓, ⅔, ⅛, ⅜, ⅝, ⅞. More importantly, OpenType typefaces allow you to make custom fractions. Highlight the numbers you want to convert to fractions and choose Fractions from the OpenType menu on the Control Panel. Unfortunately, leaving this feature on will "fractionize" all numerals in your text, so it's necessary to apply it on an as-needed basis.

Finding Characters on the Mac

Both the Windows Character palette and the Mac OS Character Viewer show you the Unicode numbers of specific characters and allow you to search for characters by name. Mac OS's Character Viewer also shows which of your installed fonts contain a given character. The advantage of the Mac OS Character Viewer over InDesign's Glyphs panel is that you can more easily compare the same character in different fonts.

To access the Character Viewer, go to System Preferences > Language & Text, choose Input Sources, and select Keyboard & Character Viewer to add it to the menu bar. For example, if you're searching for a double prime you can type its Unicode value (but really, who's ever going to remember that?) or its name in the search field. You'll see a list of all the installed fonts that contain the glyph. This allows you to compare the same glyph in multiple fonts at the same time—something you can't do in InDesign's Glyphs panel. To insert the glyph into your InDesign document, make sure your Type cursor is inserted in a text frame and click Insert.

FIGURE 6.19 The Character Viewer in Mac OS 10.6 (**B**), accessed via the Language & Text system preferences (Unicode Hex Input chosen) (**A**).

A

B

FIGURE 6.20 The parts of a fraction (**A**). Making fractions (**B**): No treatment (top), non-OpenType fractions made either manually or using a fraction script (center), and Open Type fractions. The OpenType options (**C**) accessed via the Control Panel menu.

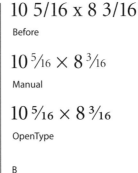

10 5/16 x 8 3/16

Before

$10\ ^{5}/_{16} \times 8\ ^{3}/_{16}$

Manual

$10\ ^{5}/_{16} \times 8\ ^{3}/_{16}$

OpenType

A B C

NOTE: A short-lived solution to the some of the limitations of Type 1 PostScript fonts was the multiple master, which allowed the user to generate different weights and widths of the typeface from a small number of master outlines. However, multiple masters didn't catch on, mainly because these fonts were expensive and confusing to use. Names like MyriadMM 215LT didn't exactly roll off the tongue. Multiple masters were discontinued in 2001, though they still show up on font menus.

If you're using PostScript Type 1 or TrueType fonts you can still make your own fractions without too much fuss. There are several fraction scripts, like Dan Rodney's Proper Fraction, that you can download for a nominal fee or for free from the Adobe Exchange Web site. These scripts convert the numerator to superscript, the denominator to subscript, and replace the slash or virgule with a fraction bar or solidus (Option/Alt+Shift+1). For best results, in Advanced Type Preferences set Super/Subscript size to 60%, the Superscript position to 33%, and the Subscript position to 0. No matter how you get your fraction, if it follows a whole number, no space is necessary before the fraction.

Multiplication Sign

The multiplication or dimension sign is its own character, more symmetrical than a lowercase x. It's available in the Symbol font or in OpenType fonts. To access the multiplication sign, filter your view in the Glyphs panel to show Math Symbols.

FIGURE 6.21
The multiplication sign (right) compared to a lowercase x (left).

The Euro Symbol

Fonts newer than 1998 should have the Euro symbol as part of the character set: Option+Shift+2 (Alt+0128). If you're using fonts older than 1998, or you don't like the design of the Euro character in a particular font, you can download a family of Euro fonts from the Adobe Web site: http://store.adobe.com/type/euroreg.html. Euro Sans has a regular weight that is the same as the official character adopted in Europe. Euro Mono is a condensed version of Euro Sans that is designed to work with monospaced fonts. Euro Serif is useful for settings of serif faces. All three fonts are free.

FIGURE 6.22 Euro Monospace, Euro Sans, and Euro Serif, from the Adobe Euro fonts.

Ligatures, Diphthongs, and the Dotless i

Ligatures are two or more intersecting characters fused into a single character. They are used to avoid collisions, most commonly between the finial of the lowercase f and the dot of the i or between the finial of the f and the ascender of the l. InDesign can use standard ligatures whether you're using OpenType, PostScript, or TrueType fonts. Check Spelling is smart enough to recognize them and not flag as misspelled any word that contains them. The use of ligatures may not be necessary with sans serif typefaces, where there's no danger of a character collision. First try setting the type without ligatures. If the characters collide, then turn on Ligatures. If they don't, well—if it ain't broke, don't fix it, especially since using ligatures may make these letter combinations appear to be more tightly set than the rest of your type. Ligatures can be turned on from the Control Panel menu or, when applied as part of a Paragraph Style, in the Basic Character Formats.

NOTE: InDesign CS5 ships with several OpenType fonts, including Adobe Garamond Pro, Chaparral Pro, Adobe Caslon Pro, Caflisch Pro, Minion Pro, and Myriad Pro.

FIGURE 6.23 Ligatures: necessary for serif typefaces, but typically unnecessary for sans serif.

Adobe Caslon Pro
No Ligatures

Adobe Caslon Pro
Ligatures

Futura
No Ligatures

OpenType fonts offer more ligatures such as ffi, ffl, fj, and ff combinations, and may contain discretionary ligatures such as ct, sp, and st. Discretionary ligatures are not for everyday use, but may be perfect for special occasions. The next time you're working on something fancy like a wedding invitation, discretionary ligatures might be just the extra seasoning you need.

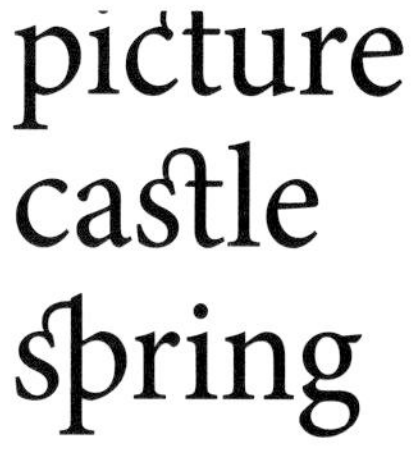

Diphthongs are ligatures that visually represent the pronunciation of a combined vowel. The most common examples are ae, AE, and oe, OE such as in Caesar, encyclopeadia, mediaeval, and oeuvre. Their usage is considered archaic

FIGURE 6.24 Minion Pro with discretionary ligatures.

œuvre
vitæ

FIGURE 6.25 Diphthong ligatures.

fickle

fickle

FIGURE 6.26 At display sizes, using a dotless i (top) in place of an fi ligature (bottom) makes it easier to equalize the spacing between the characters.

in modern English, especially American English. Both discretionary ligatures and diphthongs can be applied on a case-by-case basis through the Glyphs panel. Choose Discretionary Ligatures from the Show menu to isolate the available options.

Because ligatures can look odd in display type, you may be better off kerning to avoid character collisions, or replacing the i with a dotless i. On the Mac, the dotless i can be typed by pressing Shift+Option+B. In Windows, open Character Map, select Advanced View, and with Character Set set for Unicode, type 0131 (the Unicode ID number for the dotless i) in the Go to Unicode field. The dotless i will be highlighted in the character grid. Use the Copy button and InDesign's Paste command to insert the i into text. Both methods are faster than hunting and pecking in the Glyphs panel, which has no search tools.

Font Aid IV: A Typeface of Ampersands

An example of a character that has evolved from a ligature into a character in its own right is the ampersand (&), which is a stylized abbreviation of *et*, the Latin word for *and*. The term *ampersand* is a contraction of the phrase "and per se and." In the wake of the Haitian earthquake of January 2010, type designers from around the world contributed to Coming Together, a typeface created to benefit the earthquake victims. The typeface consists entirely of ampersands—representing the idea of people coming together to help one another. You can buy the typeface at www.ascenderfonts.com for $20.

FIGURE 6.27 Coming Together is an OpenType font of 400 ampersands created for Font Aid IV. All proceeds benefit victims of the Haitian earthquake.

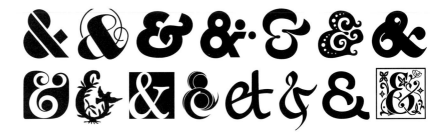

Ornaments

Sometimes referred to as *fleurons*, typographic ornaments were historically used to expand the typesetter's palette. Today they can lend a historic feel to a book cover, title page, chapter opener, or be used in repetitions to create a typographic wallpaper suitable for endpapers. They might also come in handy as bullets or end marks. Some were designed to be used in multiples to make decorative frames—although you'd find it a lot easier to achieve the same result in Adobe Illustrator. Some typefaces, like Chaparral Pro, contain playful ornaments.

FIGURE 6.28 A title treatment using Adobe Caslon Pro Ornaments (top) and Chaparral Pro Ornaments (bottom).

Swash Characters

Used sparingly, swash characters can add a flourish to your type. Typically, they are used at the beginning of words or sentences. Some italic styles of OpenType fonts have swashes—you can check by opening the Glyphs panel and looking for Swash in the Show menu. Some OpenType fonts may also have lowercase swash characters called *finals* or *terminal characters,* intended for use at the end of a word or line.

without Swash   *Ahoy There, Shipmates!*   *From Ibiza to the Norfolk Broads*   without Swash

Swash initial caps   *Ahoy There, Shipmates!*   *From Ibiza to the Norfolk Broads*   Swash and finials

FIGURE 6.29 Swash characters used with Adobe Caslon Pro Italic (left) and Raniscript (right).

Oldstyle Figures

The default figures in most typefaces are tabular lining figures, which were invented about 200 years ago. Lining figures have a fixed width so that they can be aligned in columns, and all have the same height (the cap height of the type). Because of this, they tend to stand out too much when combined with upper- and lowercase text.

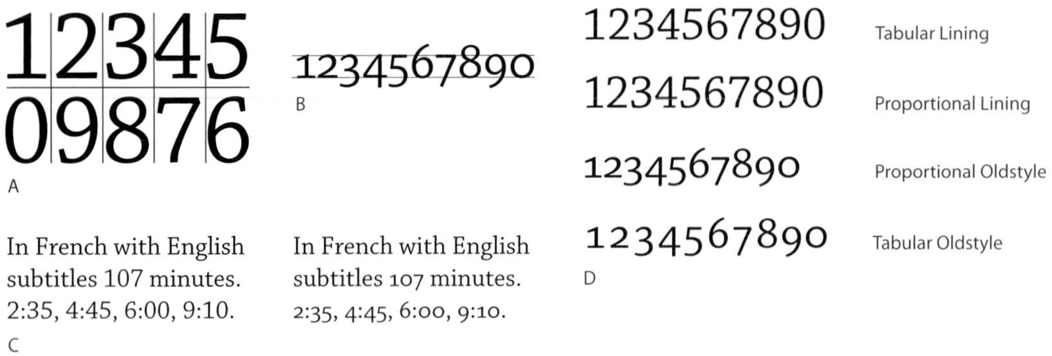

12345
09876

A

1234567890

B

1234567890 Tabular Lining

1234567890 Proportional Lining

1234567890 Proportional Oldstyle

1234567890 Tabular Oldstyle

D

In French with English
subtitles 107 minutes.
2:35, 4:45, 6:00, 9:10.

C

In French with English
subtitles 107 minutes.
2:35, 4:45, 6:00, 9:10.

FIGURE 6.30 Different figure
styles. Tabular figures all
occupy the same set width
(**A**); Oldstyle numbers have
ascenders and descenders (**B**).
A comparison of lining figures
and Proportional Oldstyle
figures in text (**C**). The four
different figure styles available
in OpenType Pro typefaces (**D**).

Proportional Oldstyle figures are as tall as the x-height of your type and are,
as their name suggests, proportionally spaced. They have a better type color in
body text than full-height lining figures. Figures 3, 4, 5, 7, and 9 have descenders, while 6 and 8 have ascenders.

OpenType fonts may also offer Proportional Lining figures (which are good
for working with text in all caps) and Tabular Oldstyle figures—the same letterforms as Proportional Oldstyle, but without the proportional spacing, so
therefore more appropriate for use in tables.

Contextual Alternates

Some OpenType script faces have alternate characters designed to connect
better in certain letter combinations and make your type look more like handwriting. Choose Contextual Alternates from the OpenType menu, and as you
type, the glyph to the left of your cursor may change according to the glyph
that follows it—if there is an alternate for that particular letter combination.
You can also choose the alternates on a case-by-case basis using the Glyphs
panel and choosing Alternates for Selection from the Show menu.

Titling Alternates

Some OpenType fonts have special "titling" characters intended for type set at
sizes of 72 point and above. The letters of titling alternates are more nuanced.
The thin parts of the strokes are relatively thinner, the serifs more refined,
and the letters are more condensed, giving them a more elegant look. The
large glyphs (A, B, C, etc.) on the chapter opening pages of this book all use
titling alternates.

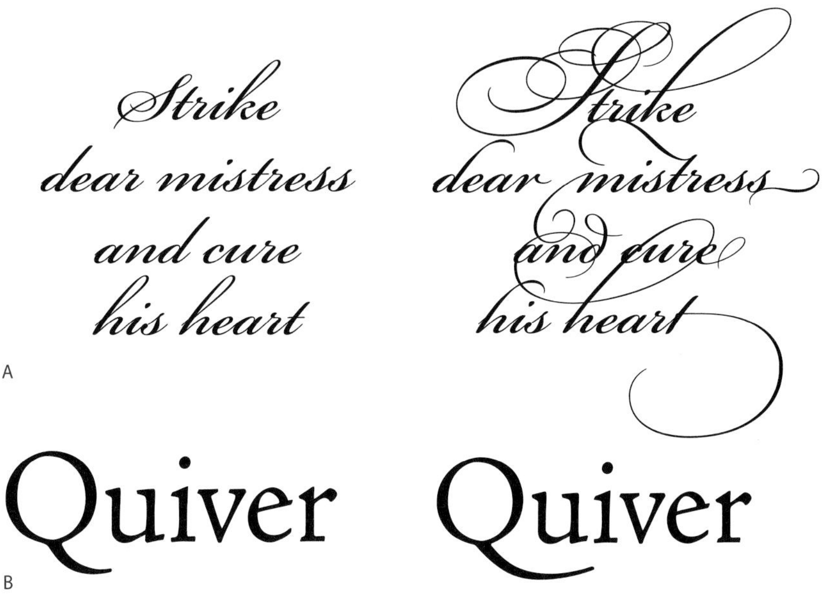

*Strike
dear mistress
and cure
his heart*

A

*Strike
dear mistress
and cure
his heart*

Quiver Quiver

B

FIGURE 6.31 Many OpenType Pro faces have a wide range of alternate characters that can be applied through the Glyphs panel. Here Bickham (A) and Adobe Jensen Pro (B) are shown before and after alternates have been applied.

TIP: You might expect the type preference Use Correct Optical Size to be related to optical sizes, but it actually applies to Multiple Master fonts.

Optical Sizes

Some OpenType fonts include four optical size variations: caption, regular, subhead, and display, so you can choose whichever is most appropriate for the size of your type. The title given the size variation (caption, for example) is your clue to its intended usage. As with titling alternates, the bigger the size, the more refined the characters.

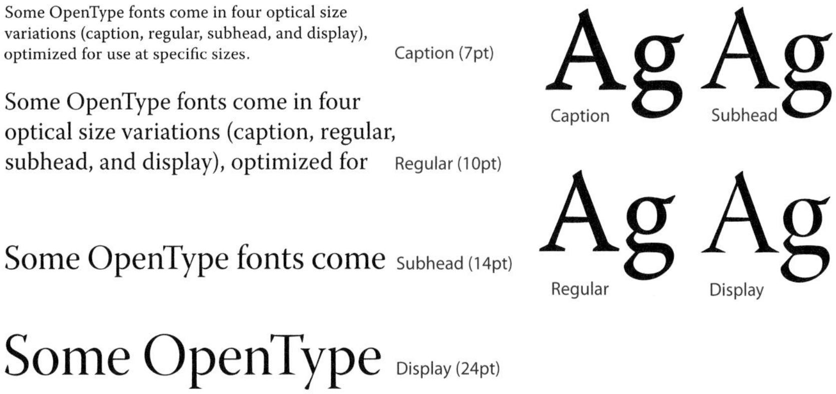

Some OpenType fonts come in four optical size variations (caption, regular, subhead, and display), optimized for use at specific sizes.   Caption (7pt)

Some OpenType fonts come in four optical size variations (caption, regular, subhead, and display), optimized for   Regular (10pt)

Some OpenType fonts come   Subhead (14pt)

Some OpenType   Display (24pt)

Ag Ag

Caption   Subhead

Ag Ag

Regular   Display

FIGURE 6.32 The different optical sizes of Warnock Pro.

CHAPTER 7

Alignment

USUALLY WHEN WE SPEAK OF alignment of type, we're referring to the horizontal position of text within a text frame. Each of the basic options—left, center, right, and justified—creates its own vibe, has its own strengths, and asks to be treated in particular ways to avoid common shortcomings. In this chapter, we'll look at the horizontal and vertical alignment of type within a text frame.

Horizontal Alignment

There are several terms for the different alignments in common usage. What InDesign refers to as Left alignment is also known as *ragged right, flush left,* or (confusingly) *left justified.* In InDesign terms, with Left Justify alignment all lines of the paragraph are the same length, except the last line. InDesign offers two other flavors of justified type, which have limited utility: Center Justify and Full Justify. The difference between them is the way the last line of the paragraph is handled. When I refer to *justified type,* I mean type with the last line of the paragraph left aligned.

Ragged can refer either to left-, center-, or right-aligned type. "Align towards spine" aligns text on a left-hand page so that it is right aligned. If the same text flows onto a right-hand page, it becomes left aligned. "Align away from spine" does the opposite: Text on a left-hand page is left aligned, while text on a right-hand page is right aligned.

Alignment Keyboard Shortcuts

Left	Cmd+Shift+L (Ctrl+Shift+L)
Center	Cmd+Shift+C (Ctrl+Shift+C)
Right	Cmd+Shift+R (Ctrl+Shift+R)
Justified	Cmd+Shift+J (Ctrl+Shift+J)
Justify All Lines	Cmd+Shift+F (Ctrl+Shift+F)

Because the length of every line will vary, an important distinction between the four main alignment types is what happens to the extra space on the line. With ragged alignments, the word spacing is consistent. Every word space is the same width as every other word space in the paragraph. The extra spacing is allotted to the right edge of the column (left alignment), allotted to the left edge (right alignment), or divided equally between the left and right edges (center alignment). With justified alignment, the size of the word spaces varies so that the lines can all be the same length. However, to maintain even type color when working with justified type, we strive to maintain the illusion that all our word spaces are the same.

Left Alignment

With left-aligned type, each line starts at the same place. The word spaces are consistent, giving the text block an even type color. The lines are of varying length, adding shape and interest — as well as white space — to what would otherwise be a rectangular block. The asymmetry of left-aligned text can appear informal because it resembles the uneven line lengths of handwriting.

When using left alignment, pay attention to the shape of the *rag* — the uneven side. The rag shape is determined by the column measure, the nature of the text (whether it contains predominantly long or short words), and whether hyphenation is turned on. Ideally, the rag should modulate subtly, without any sudden "holes" or awkward shapes. The line lengths should be clearly irregular (i.e., they shouldn't look like carelessly set justified type), but not so irregular that they create distracting shapes that slow reading. A bad rag occurs when some lines are too long and others too short, which can be distracting. To prevent this, you can shape the text manually by using forced line breaks or discretionary hyphens, or by preventing certain phrases, product names, and Web addresses from breaking over a line by applying No Break; see Chapter 9, "Breaking (and not Breaking) Lines, Paragraphs, Columns, and Pages." You can also, if necessary, apply a modest amount of tracking to cause a paragraph to rag differently.

Left vs. Justified Alignment

When it comes to the alignment of text meant for continuous reading, we are essentially concerned with the pros and cons of using left aligned versus justified type. There is no right or wrong here, and it largely comes down to a matter of personal preference. Whichever alignment you choose, however, there are certain steps and precautions to take to get the best results.

FIGURE 7.1 The four basic types of horizontal alignment: left, justified, center, and right.

Congress shall make no law respecting an establishment of religion, or prohibiting the free exercise thereof; or abridging the freedom of speech, or of the press; or the right of the people peaceably to assemble, and to petition the Government for a redress of grievances.

Left

Congress shall make no law respecting an establishment of religion, or prohibiting the free exercise thereof; or abridging the freedom of speech, or of the press; or the right of the people peaceably to assemble, and to petition the Government for a redress of grievances.

Left Justify

Congress shall make no law respecting an establishment of religion, or prohibiting the free exercise thereof; or abridging the freedom of speech, or of the press; or the right of the people peaceably to assemble, and to petition the Government for a redress of grievances.

Center

Congress shall make no law respecting an establishment of religion, or prohibiting the free exercise thereof; or abridging the freedom of speech, or of the press; or the right of the people peaceably to assemble, and to petition the Government for a redress of grievances.

Right

A paragraph style option called Balance Ragged Lines attempts to give you lines of roughly equal length. This is useful for heads and subheads and will reduce the amount of manual intervention necessary (in the form of forced line breaks, or nonbreaking spaces), but you're still going to need to check the type carefully for meaning. Balance Ragged Lines won't always break the line where you'd like it to. It's the designer's responsibility to make sure the lines break in a way that accentuates, rather than detracts from, the meaning of the text.

When applied to body text, Balance Ragged Lines can create more problems than it solves. Once multi-line paragraphs have Balance Ragged Lines applied to them, manually trying to make the lines of those paragraphs break how you want them to will be difficult. Balance Ragged Lines has no effect in justified text.

Asymmetrical Typography

In typography, asymmetry is associated with a particular design philosophy, the New Typography, first developed in Germany in the late 1920s and early 1930s and championed by Jan Tschichold and the Bauhaus. In his book *The New Typography*, Tschichold argued that the "old typography" practice of aligning type on a central axis was inflexible, inorganic, and unsuited to the requirements of modern typography "because of the manifold claims for our attention made by the extraordinary amount of print, which demands the greatest economy of expression." After the Second World War Tschichold lived in England, where he worked for Penguin Books and embraced the classical design principles of symmetry that he had earlier criticized. If there's a message here, to me it is this: There is no right or wrong alignment, only an alignment that best serves the needs of the text.

FIGURE 7.2 Hyphenation affects the rag of left-aligned text, as shown by the blue rectangles at the end of each line. The paragraph on the right is hyphenated; the one on the left is not, resulting in a harder rag (more variation in the line lengths).

Scrooge was better than his word. He did it all, and infinitely more; and to Tiny Tim, who did *not* die, he was a second father. He became as good a friend, as good a master, and as good a man, as the good old city knew, or any other good old city, town, or borough, in the good old world. Some people laughed to see the alteration in him, but he let them laugh, and little heeded them; for he was wise enough to know that nothing ever happened on this globe, for good, at which some people did not have their fill of laughter in the outset; and knowing that such as these would be blind anyway, he thought it quite as well that they should wrinkle up their eyes in grins, as have the malady in less attractive forms. His own heart laughed: and that was quite enough for him.

Scrooge was better than his word. He did it all, and infinitely more; and to Tiny Tim, who did *not* die, he was a second father. He became as good a friend, as good a master, and as good a man, as the good old city knew, or any other good old city, town, or borough, in the good old world. Some people laughed to see the alteration in him, but he let them laugh, and little heeded them; for he was wise enough to know that nothing ever happened on this globe, for good, at which some people did not have their fill of laughter in the outset; and knowing that such as these would be blind anyway, he thought it quite as well that they should wrinkle up their eyes in grins, as have the malady in less attractive forms. His own heart laughed: and that was quite enough for him.

Everybody's Got Something to Hide Except for Me and My Monkey

Unbalanced

Everybody's Got Something to Hide Except for Me and My Monkey

Balanced

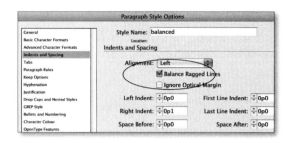

FIGURE 7.3 Applying Balance Ragged Lines to heads and subheads ensures lines of roughly equal length.

Justified Alignment (Justified with last line aligned left)

On every line of type, there is leftover space. With justified type, where the text is flushed left and right, that extra space is necessarily elastic—distributed between the word spaces and (potentially) between the letter spaces to give lines that are exactly the same length.

Justified type is symmetrical; the smooth edge on the right side of the columns creates a sense of balance. The uniformity of the right-hand margin also gives a more formal look to your page. Justified type is more economical than ragged type because it allows you to fit more words on the page. The difference may be insignificant in a short document, but in a magazine or book, it can mean a difference of several pages. All too frequently, justified type is set in

FIGURE 7.4 The same paragraph set as left aligned (left) and justified (right).

Hitler knows that he will have to break us in this Island or lose the war. If we can stand up to him, all Europe may be free and the life of the world may move forward into broad, sunlit uplands. But if we fail, then the whole world, including the United States, including all that we have known and cared for, will sink into the abyss of a new Dark Age made more sinister, and perhaps more protracted, by the lights of perverted science.

Let us therefore brace ourselves to our duties, and so bear ourselves that if the British Empire and its Commonwealth last for a thousand years, men will still say, 'This was their finest hour.'

Winston Churchill—June 18, 1940

Left Aligned

Hitler knows that he will have to break us in this Island or lose the war. If we can stand up to him, all Europe may be free and the life of the world may move forward into broad, sunlit uplands. But if we fail, then the whole world, including the United States, including all that we have known and cared for, will sink into the abyss of a new Dark Age made more sinister, and perhaps more protracted, by the lights of perverted science.

Let us therefore brace ourselves to our duties, and so bear ourselves that if the British Empire and its Commonwealth last for a thousand years, men will still say, 'This was their finest hour.'

Winston Churchill—June 18, 1940

Left Justified

FIGURE 7.5 Justification settings applied as part of a Paragraph Style (top) and locally through the Control Panel menu (bottom).

columns that are too narrow, resulting in what Robert Bringhurst refers to in *The Elements of Typographic Style* as "white acne or pig bristles: a rash of erratic and splotchy word spaces or an epidemic of hyphenation." However, if you have enough characters on every line (typically 40–60), and you use appropriate Justification and Hyphenation settings, there's no reason why you can't achieve even color with justified type.

How InDesign Justifies Type

InDesign's justification settings are best applied with a paragraph style, but can also be applied on a paragraph-by-paragraph basis by choosing Justification from the Control Panel menu.

Justification is achieved by varying the size of the word spaces on the line—or in the entire paragraph—in an attempt to get even word and letter spacing, or at least word and letter spacing that looks even. There are three important options that you can set to determine how InDesign justifies type: Word Spacing, Letter Spacing, and Glyph Scaling. Using InDesign's Justification options makes a dramatic difference in the appearance of your type.

If justification can't be achieved by adjusting word spacing alone, then InDesign adjusts the letter spacing according to the Minimum, Desired, and Maximum settings that you choose in the Justification Options dialog. After that, it moves on to the Glyph Scaling settings.

The world will little note, nor long remember what we say here, but it can never forget what they did here. It is for us the living, rather, to be dedicated here to the unfinished work which they who fought here have thus far so nobly advanced.

The world will little note, nor long remember what we say here, but it can never forget what they did here. It is for us the living, rather, to be dedicated here to the unfinished work which they who fought here have thus far so nobly advanced.

line 1
line 2

FIGURE 7.6 This figure shows my preferred settings for justified type. Allowing a small variation (± 2%) in Letter Spacing and Glyph Scaling (± 3%) dramatically improves type color. The paragraph on the left has default Justification settings applied; the paragraph on the right has my custom settings applied. Note the variation in the width of the word spaces, indicated by the blue shapes below.

Justification			
	Minimum	Desired	Maximum
Word Spacing:	85%	100%	115%
Letter Spacing:	-2%	0%	2%
Glyph Scaling:	97%	100%	103%

The more words there are on the line, the more word spaces there are to adjust, and the less noticeable those adjustments will be. You get more words either by making your type smaller or your column wider. It's a balancing act: If you make your column too wide relative to your type size, you'll be swapping one evil for another.

Word Spacing

No prizes for guessing that this refers to the space between words—the width of space you get when you press the spacebar.

Determining word spacing is more of an aesthetic consideration than an exact science. A good starting point is 100 percent, which is the width of the *space-band* specified by the font designer. However, you may want to reduce this to 90 percent or even less when working with any of the following:

- Condensed type

- Typefaces in light weights

- Typefaces that are tightly fit (if you have tight letter spacing, you'll want your word spacing to be correspondingly tight)

- Display type

Letter Spacing

This is the distance between letters and includes any kerning or tracking values that may be applied to the type. A character's width is determined not just by the character itself, but also by the space that the font designer adds around the character—known as the *side bearing*.

Because there are more letter spaces than word spaces on every line, changing the spacing between the letters by an imperceptible amount—plus or minus 2 percent—can dramatically improve the evenness of justified type.

Glyph Scaling

Glyph scaling is the process of adjusting the width of characters in order to achieve even justification—and a little glyph scaling goes a long way. Glyph scaling might sound like the kind of crime that the Design Police will bust you for in a heartbeat. In reality, though, moderate amounts of glyph scaling can—combined with your other Justification settings—improve type color significantly. Moderation is the key: Keep your Glyph Scaling settings to 97%,

TIP: Even if your body text is justified, other elements of your text will want to be ragged, both to avoid composition problems and to provide a contrast to the symmetry of your justified type. The following elements should not be justified: headlines and subheads, bylines, tables of contents, captions, pull quotes, footnotes, bibliographies, and indexes.

TIP: With both Word Spacing and Letter Spacing you need to find a balance between being strict and being reasonable. There's no point in specifying restrictive settings if your text-to-column width ratio makes it impossible for InDesign to honor these settings.

NOTE: It's important to bear in mind that InDesign's Justification and Hyphenation features work in conjunction with each other. Good word spacing will not be achieved by using the Adobe Paragraph Composer alone, but rather by combining it with the other justification features in InDesign's toolkit.

100%, and 103% for Minimum, Desired, and Maximum, respectively. No one will ever know that you varied the horizontal scale of your type. They will, however, appreciate the splendidly even word spacing.

Justified Alignment and Type Color

All alignment types influence type color, but none more so than justified alignment. The Justification settings determine the consistency of word and letter spacing by defining the ranges between which InDesign can flex word and character spaces. If these ranges are too tight your type will look pinched; too loose and your text blocks will be blotchy—full of gaping word spaces or too much space between the letters. Tight lines look darker, loose lines lighter. Neither is pretty, and both are difficult to read. Ideally, your text should have a middle gray value that doesn't call attention to itself.

The Adobe Paragraph Composer

TIP: When you are editing text composed with the Adobe Paragraph Composer, the type before and after the cursor moves. While you're editing the text, the paragraph is in progress, and InDesign is figuring out how to compose the paragraph, adjusting spacing and line breaks on the fly. This can be a little disconcerting if in a previous draft your client has signed off on specific line breaks. Line endings that change without apparent reason can make clients nervous, and they may require the whole text to be read again to make sure nothing is lost. If it's important to your workflow to maintain the line breaks as they are from one iteration of the document to the next, consider switching to the Single Line Composer.

A mainly behind-the-scenes InDesign feature that plays an important role in determining how the lines of paragraphs break is the Adobe Paragraph Composer. Before InDesign, page layout programs composed paragraphs line by line. Because there is a limited number of word spaces across which the extra space at the end of the line can be distributed, this often caused bad type color. Using the Adobe Paragraph Composer (the default choice of Composer), InDesign analyzes the word spaces across a whole paragraph, considers the possible line breaks, and optimizes earlier lines in the paragraph to prevent bad breaks later on. Looking at the whole paragraph is crucial because there are more places where space can be added or subtracted before this becomes noticeable. The result: fewer hyphens and better spacing. The Adobe Paragraph Composer works for both ragged and justified type, but it's with the latter that you really see its benefits.

As fabulous as the Adobe Paragraph Composer is, don't expect miracles. Good type color doesn't come easy, and you'll still have to fix some composition problems manually. This is where the Composition preference Show H&J Violations comes in handy. This preference allows you to easily identify problems so that you can fix them—by any means necessary. As a final reality check, keep in mind that even with the most carefully considered column widths, the most scientifically proven justification options, and the most judicious use of InDesign's Composition preferences, spacing problems still occur from time to time. So don't fire the proofreader.

Instead of a few chemical compounds of gold and silver, which at first were alone supposed to be photographic, we are now aware that copper, platinum, lead, nikel, and indeed, probably all the elements, are equally liably to change under the sun's influence. This fact may be of benefit to engravers, for if steel can be made to take photographic impressions, the more laborious

FIGURE 7.7 Choose Preferences > Composition and select H&J Violations to show spacing problems highlighted in yellow. The darker the yellow, the worse the problem.

We need to stop the World Bank and Inter- 1
national Monetary Fund (IMF) forcing poor 2
countries to open their markets to trade 3
with rich countries, which has proved so 4
disastrous over the past 20 years; the EU 5
must drop its demand that former Euro- 6
pean colonies open their markets and give 7
more rights to big companies; we need 8
to regulate companies — making them 9
accountable for their social and environ- 10
mental impact both here and abroad; and 11
we must ensure that countries are able to 12
regulate foreign investment in a way that 13
best suits their own needs. 14

Paragraph Composer

We need to stop the World Bank and International Monetary Fund (IMF) forcing poor
countries to open their markets to trade
with rich countries, which has proved so
disastrous over the past 20 years; the EU
must drop its demand that former European colonies open their markets and give
more rights to big companies; we need to
regulate companies — making them
accountable for their social and environ-
mental impact both here and abroad; and
we must ensure that countries are able to
regulate foreign investment in a way that
best suits their own needs.

Single Line Composer

FIGURE 7.8 The Adobe Paragraph Composer (left) versus the Single Line Composer (right). For the text composed with the Paragraph Composer, there are minor spacing problems on lines 8 and 9. For the text composed with the Single Line Composer, there is a major problem on line 9.

Centering Type

Center alignment assigns extra space on the line equally to the left and right of the type, giving equal weight to both ends of the line. It is widely used in magazine design for crossheads and in book design for title pages. It is also associated with birth announcements, wedding invitations, and … gravestones. Centering works best with a single line or a short paragraph; centering long paragraphs is usually a bad idea because every line has a different starting point, making the text less readable. When done right, centering can be formal and classical, and give an interesting shape to your text block; when chosen as a fall-back option, it makes layouts appear stodgy or generic. The equal white space on either side of every line makes the text feel static, as if it were being held in a vice-like grip. Beginning designers often gravitate toward center alignment because they are more comfortable with its solidity—each line is supported on either side by white space.

FIGURE 7.9 The same text centered (left), centered with Balance Ragged Lines turned on (center), and with the lines broken for sense using forced line breaks (Shift+Return).

Congress shall make no law respecting an establishment of religion, or prohibiting the free exercise thereof; or abridging the freedom of speech, or of the press; or the right of the people peaceably to assemble, and to petition the Government for a redress of grievances.

Congress shall make no law respecting an establishment of religion, or prohibiting the free exercise thereof; or abridging the freedom of speech, or of the press; or the right of the people peaceably to assemble, and to petition the Government for a redress of grievances.

Congress shall make no law respecting an establishment of religion, or prohibiting the free exercise thereof; or abridging the freedom of speech, or of the press; or the right of the people peaceably to assemble, and to petition the Government for a redress of grievances.

Centered

Balance Ragged Lines on

With Forced Line Breaks

Where some have found their paradise others just come to harm

Where some have found their paradise others just come to harm

Where some have found their paradise others just come to harm

FIGURE 7.10 Centered heads appear misaligned if the first line of text that follows does not fill the full measure (left). To compensate, the value of the extra space at the end of the line is added as a right indent to the head (right).

MOTION OF LIGHT
Rays of light are thrown off from luminous bodies in every direction, but always in straight lines, which cross each other at every point; but the particles of which each ray consists are so minute that the rays do

MOTION OF LIGHT
Rays of light are thrown off from luminous bodies in every direction, but always in straight lines, which cross each other at every point; but the particles of which each ray consists are so minute that the rays do

Combining center alignment with other types of alignment also has its drawbacks. The even white space on both sides of the line may create a symmetry that is at odds with the asymmetrical nature of the ragged-right text that follows. Centered display type over left-aligned body text will not appear optically centered if the first line of body text spans less than the full column measure. This is fixable, but even so, this difference in alignment diminishes the visual connection between the heading and the body text. Worse still would be to center an italic headline over roman type: The slant of the italic will make the headline appear off-center.

There's no reason why centered type can't look good, but it requires more than just clicking the Center Alignment button. The way the lines break may undermine the meaning of the text as well as create an ugly paragraph shape, so be prepared to wade in and add forced line breaks (Shift+Return) wherever necessary to carry the words that are to the right of the cursor down to the next line. Line breaks should enhance the meaning of the text as well as emphasize the central axis of the text—it should be obvious to your reader that the type is centered and not just badly justified.

Right-Aligned Type

Right-aligned, or flush-right, type is seldom used and is thus distinctive. It can be effective for short bursts of text like captions, pull quotes, or sometimes headlines. When used in a spread, it tends to work better when used on the left-hand page, when the text is "facing in" toward the spine, rather than the right-hand page facing out toward the outside margin, which can make your type look like it's trying to escape from the page.

If right-aligned text is overused, it can be offputting to the reader because the eye ends up focusing on the end rather than the beginning of the line. Also, the ragged edge makes it harder to find the start of the line. Applied thoughtfully, however, right alignment can be dynamic and a welcome change of pace.

Right-aligned text draws attention to itself. If you're going to use it, capitalize on this and emphasize, rather than play down, the unevenness of the rag. Just as with center alignment, this requires manually breaking the lines with forced line breaks (Shift+Return). Make sure to turn off hyphenation in right-aligned type: You don't want the smoothness of the flush right edge disturbed by hyphenation stubble.

Other Justification Options

As well as the usual justification options, there are also lesser-used options that may be appropriate in specific situations.

Align it right

This form of alignment
can be effective for
headlines and straplines
when the alignment is
towards the spine

Dignis ad quodignis pa expe net amet
adit quiaeror ad quo iundia dem illabor-
rum volorerum doluptasped elitatur
maiorum qui qui con eum dolorei cab-

delescipis aut landeli tistem elicid quo blatur aute volluptatur, ommolup tatectis que estia quiaesed quis ipsae ea di ut odipsant arumentius solorro que et posam verferciatin natiore nihicia esed quid quid ut des ut minusti demposant quiatestrum invendam explabo ratenist, te nis idelenit ut hillabo. Rum idem quia sanienimi, tem dolores accatem quiasit atempore il exce-pro ommolest, voluptiur, il illorro te omnihillia deritatate et re vel inti aut reperovid eum quunte vid moditae-ceped quibusd aectum rentur simpori

FIGURE 7.11 Right alignment juxtaposed with justified text columns.

FIGURE 7.12 On this facing pages spread, the picture captions are aligned toward the spine, while the page numbers are aligned away from the spine.

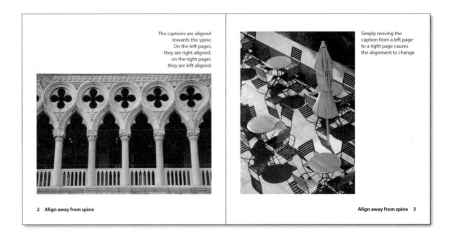

FIGURE 7.12 On this facing pages spread, the picture captions are aligned toward the spine, while the page numbers are aligned away from the spine.

Align Towards and Away from Spine

These options ensure that the alignment of your type mirrors itself when moved from a left-hand to a right-hand page or vice versa. For example, if you want picture captions that are right aligned on the left-hand pages and left aligned on the right-hand pages, choose Align Towards Spine. If you want page numbers that are aligned to the outside margins of facing pages, choose Align Away from Spine.

Down, down, down. Would
the fall never come to an end!
'I wonder how many miles
I've fallen by this time?'
she said aloud. 'I must
be getting some-
where near the
centre of the
earth.

FIGURE 7.13 Justify with last line aligned center.

Justify with Last Line Aligned Center

This is a once-in-a-blue-moon alignment option, occasionally useful for poetry and for creating interesting shapes with text blocks.

Full Justify

This alignment option will justify all the lines of a paragraph, even the last line. It is useful when you want display type to inhabit a fixed horizontal space. Set the alignment to Full Justify (Cmd+Shift+F or Ctrl+Shift+F) and then incrementally increase the point size (Cmd+Shift+> or Ctrl+Shift+>) to see how big the type can get before falling out of the text frame. When you go too far, press Cmd+Z (Ctrl+Z) to back up to your last step.

FIGURE 7.14 Use Full Justify to spread the type over the full column measure.

A CERTAIN LOOK IN THE EYE AND AN EASY SMILE
Justified

A CERTAIN LOOK IN THE EYE AND AN EASY SMILE
Full Justified

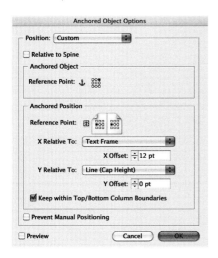

115 g unsalted butter
25 g all-purpose flour
60 ml water
1 teaspoon salt
1 egg yolk

Chill the butter and water to pre
the flour. Stir the flour, salt, and
butter — the resulting mixture sl

Pour in the chilled water a tables
addition.

Split the dough into two equal an
slightly, and wrap them in plastic
for at least 30 minutes to absorb

FIGURE 7.15 Side-by-side paragraphs, where the right-aligned text is an anchored text frame.

Combining Left and Right Alignment

Combining a right-aligned caption with a left-aligned column can be a visually effective use of white space. This involves creating a separate text frame for the right-aligned caption text and positioning it to the left of the main text frame. To maintain the visual relationship between the two types of text, it's necessary to anchor the caption text frame to a specific point in the text. Here's how:

1. Cut the caption text frame (Cmd+X/Ctrl+X).

2. Insert the Type cursor at the beginning of the paragraph that you want to anchor the caption to, and choose Paste (Cmd+V/Ctrl+V).

3. To adjust the position of the caption, with the caption frame selected right-click or choose Object > Anchored Object > Options. Make the Reference Point the upper-right corner, the X Relative to the Text Frame, with an X Offset that is the space you want between the caption frame and the main text frame. The Y should be Relative to the Line (Cap Height), with an Offset of 0. Optionally, check Prevent Manual positioning to prevent the relationship of the caption frame and main text frame from being disturbed.

Alison Steadman	Wendy
Jim Broadbent	Andy
Claire Skinner	Natalie
Jane Horrocks	Nicola
Stephen Rea	Patsy
Timothy Spall	Aubrey
David Thewlis	Nicola's Lover

FIGURE 7.16 "Movie credits" alignment: right-aligned next to left-aligned text on a central axis.

"Movie credits" alignment is best achieved by converting your text to a table with the right-aligned text in the left column and the left-aligned text in the right column. See Chapter 10, "Tabs, Tables, and Lists."

"Life is what happens while you're making other plans."

— John Lennon

Not Hanging

"Life is what happens while you're making other plans."

— John Lennon

Hanging

FIGURE 7.17 Top: A quotation in which the opening quote mark is not hanging. Bottom: The Indent To Here character is inserted after the opening quote mark.

Hanging Punctuation

Hanging punctuation is a form of optical alignment applied to maintain the clean left edge of the text. Hanging punctuation is used for bulleted and numbered lists (see Chapter 10), but it is also appropriate for display text—especially pull quotes and callouts that begin with a quote mark. Because the opening quote mark creates an optical hole on the left edge of the text, it's preferable to hang the punctuation using the Indent To Here character: Cmd+\ (Ctrl+\). This invisible character indents all subsequent lines in the paragraph to the insertion point.

Vertical Alignment

Type alignment usually refers to horizontal alignment of text. InDesign also has options for the vertical alignment of type. The default is for type to begin at the top of the frame, which is appropriate in most instances. There are times when Center or Bottom alignment of type within a text frame is necessary, however. With a text frame selected or your cursor inserted in the text, press Cmd+B (Ctrl+B).

FIGURE 7.18 The four types of vertical alignment within a text frame.

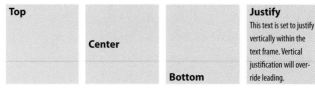

Top Alignment

The First Baseline Offset options (Object > Text Frame Options > Baseline Options or Cmd+B/Ctrl+B) determine the start position of the type in the text frame. Rarely is there reason to change from the default of Ascent, especially because using a baseline grid overrides these options, effectively giving the same result as choosing the Leading option. It is important to note, though, that there will be a small amount of space between the top of the text frame and the top of the first line of type. This means that aligning the top of a text column to the top of a picture requires special attention. The solution is to draw a guide to the cap height of the text and align the top of the picture to that. See Chapter 14, "Pages, Margins, Columns, and Grids."

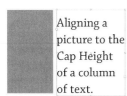

Aligning a picture to the Cap Height of a column of text.

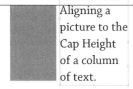

Aligning a picture to the Cap Height of a column of text.

FIGURE 7.19 Aligning pictures to the top of the text frame results in picture and text being visually misaligned (top). Instead, align the top of the image to that (bottom).

Typography | Typography

Vertically centered | Optical vertical centering with Baseline Shift

FIGURE 7.20 The text is vertically centered within the text frame, but visually appears far from it (left). The text is optically centered by applying a positive amount of baseline shift to the text (right).

Center Alignment

When centering vertically, the text may not appear to be optically centered, especially if there are few or no descenders. The solution is to shift the vertical position of the text with baseline shift.

Aligning Type in a Circle

When you create text inside a circle, it may be easier to work with the text frame and the circle shape as two separate elements. Here's how:

1. Size the text to your liking.

2. Select the text frame and choose Fit Frame To Content (Cmd+Alt+C/ Ctrl+Alt+C) to have the frame fit snugly around the type.

3. Select both the text frame and the circle, and align the two frames horizontally and vertically using the Align panel. If necessary, adjust for optical alignment.

4. Group the two items together with Cmd+G (Ctrl+G).

FIGURE 7.21 To create text inside a circle, it may be easier to work with the text frame and the circle shape as two separate elements.

Bottom Alignment

Bottom alignment is useful for picture captions to ensure that the baseline of the caption is aligned with the bottom of the picture in the adjacent column.

Justified Vertical Alignment

Justified vertical alignment can be used to force text to fill a vertical space or, with multiple columns, to make the text "bottom out" by adding extra space above the paragraphs and potentially to the leading of the shorter column.

This feature is highly convenient, and I use it when I think no one will notice or time is tight. But using vertical justification is something of a Faustian bargain. Yes, it makes your columns end on the same baseline, but it does so at a price. Vertical justification overrides leading, knocking your type off the baseline grid, if you are using one, and potentially making your type color uneven. That said, you do not surrender all control: The Paragraph Spacing Limit setting in

Text Frame Options lets you specify the maximum amount of space permissible between paragraphs. Once the Paragraph Spacing Limit has been reached, you must increase the leading. You can prevent this by specifying a massive amount in the Paragraph Spacing Limit (up to 8,640 points). That way, spacing will be added between paragraphs only (the lesser of the two evils), and the leading is unaffected.

How effective this is depends on how many paragraphs are in the column. If you have subheads and body text, for example, the extra space can usually be added unobtrusively above the subheads. But if the column contains a single paragraph, this approach isn't going to work. It's usually preferable to balance rather than vertically align uneven columns. Choose Object > Frame Options (Cmd+B/Ctrl+B), and select Balance Columns.

FIGURE 7.22 Bottom vertical alignment is useful for picture captions.

A picture caption vertically aligned to the bottom of the text frame.

FIGURE 7.23 Vertical justification results in inconsistent leading (right). Balancing columns (left) means that your text columns won't end on the same baseline as other text columns in the document.

Osto delis atumsandit autem il pratismolore dunt praesequat in ex ex enim zzrit dolore doluptat wis adit enis at, vel eliquat ulput lor sum ing ero commod molore molore velit ullum num zzriliscip esed mincillam ad eum irillan eu feugait ipit adio dolum alit adionsectem amet wis nim vulla faccum in ea aci et, quam velit volore te modolore tie dolore velenibh eniam in hent dolutatet

adigna faccummy nissequat aciliqu iscing eu feugait lor secte dolorercip endre tem vullam ipismol oreriurero estrud exeraese feum quipisi bla cor sequat. Olesequatie magna feu faci blam dolorem zzrit nosto euip ea adigna faccum velit autet lummod tem quametum quamcommod dolore molor sit, quat vent il et nonse commod tat iureet irit lortie dolorercin volobor.

Osto delis atumsandit autem il pratismolore dunt praesequat in ex ex enim zzrit dolore doluptat wis adit enis at, vel eliquat ulput lor sum ing ero commod molore molore velit ullum num zzriliscip esed mincillam ad eum irillan eu feugait ipit adio dolum alit adionsectem amet wis nim vulla faccum in ea aci et, quam velit volore te modolore tie dolore velenibh eniam in hent dolutatet adigna faccummy nissequat aciliqu iscing eu feugait lor

secte dolorercip endre tem vullam ipismol oreriurero estrud exeraese feum quipisi bla cor sequat. Olesequatie magna feu faci blam dolorem zzrit nosto euip ea adigna faccum velit autet lummod tem quametum quamcommod dolore molor sit, quat vent il et nonse commod tat iureet irit lortie dolorercin volobor.

Balanced Columns

Vertically justified

CHAPTER 8

Paragraph Indents and Spacing

TYPOGRAPHY, LIKE ALL COMMUNICATIONS MEDIA, relies on established conventions that are understood, often unconsciously, by its audience. The manipulation of horizontal or vertical space through indents or spacing creates important visual cues that distinguish one paragraph from another. Paragraphs represent units of thought, and a new paragraph signals the reader that a new idea is coming. While there are several ways to indicate a new paragraph, two methods are most prevalent: indenting the first line and adding spacing before the paragraph. In this chapter I'm primarily concerned with the hows and whys of these two time-honored conventions, but I also look at the use of other types of indents for differentiating specific types of paragraph.

First-Line Indents

The simple first-line indent plays a crucial role in the readability of documents, alerting the reader that one paragraph has ended and a new one is about to begin. First-line indents also provide a visual pause and necessary white space to what might otherwise look like a forbidding block of type.

You wouldn't think there would be too much to say about first-line indents. They're indents on the first line of a paragraph—'nuff said. Not if you're Jan Tschichold. The famous typographer wrote several articles about first-line indents and was unequivocal on the subject: "The beginnings of paragraphs must be indented. Paragraphs without indent ... are a bad habit and should be eliminated." And more: "Typesetting without indentation makes it difficult for the reader to comprehend what has been printed. And that is its most important disadvantage. While blunt beginnings seem to create a uniform and consistent impression when compared to normal typesetting, this impression is paid for with a serious loss of comprehension." (In *The Form of the Book: Essays on the Morality of Good Design*.)

How Big Should They Be?

There is no hard-and-fast rule, but 1 em is a good starting point. If you're using 10-point type, a 10-point first-line indent is suitable; anything less and the indent may be missed. Alternatively, you can use your leading increment: If your text is 10/12, then a 12-point first line indent is suitable. Some people prefer a slightly larger indent, especially when working with wide columns. Just make sure your first-line indent is smaller than the shortest last line of your paragraphs, to avoid creating ugly areas of trapped space between paragraphs.

How (and How Not) to Add First-Line Indents

First-line indents can be applied through the Control Panel, the Paragraph panel (Cmd+Option+T/Ctrl+Alt+T), or preferably, incorporated into a style sheet definition. Never create your first-line indents with tabs, or worse, by pressing the spacebar multiple times.

While first-line indents are generally well suited to reading matter, be it newspaper articles or literature, paragraph spacing may be more appropriate for reference material or instructional manuals. To some degree, it's a matter of preference, but here are some things to consider:

- Don't use first-line indents and paragraph spacing. It's an either/or proposition.

- Don't use first line-indents on centered or right-aligned type.

- If a paragraph follows a heading or subhead, the first-line indent is unnecessary.

- Dropping the first-line indent and adding a line of spacing before a paragraph is a simple way to indicate a separation without implying a hierarchical difference between two paragraphs.

"Not of late years. It is fifteen years since we—since I—came last from France."

"Indeed, sir? That was before my time here, sir. Before our people's time here, sir. The George was in other hands at that time, sir."

"I believe so."

"But I would hold a pretty wager, sir, that a House like Tellson and Company was flourishing, a matter of fifty, not to speak of fifteen years ago?"

"You might treble that, and say a hundred and fifty, yet not be far from the truth."

"Indeed, sir!"

FIGURE 8.1 A first-line indent of 1 em space (in this instance 10 points) is applied to the top excerpt. The bottom text uses a first-line indent of 3 ems. This is too large, creating awkward holes between the end of one paragraph and the beginning of the next.

   "Not of late years. It is fifteen years since we—since I—came last from France."

   "Indeed, sir? That was before my time here, sir. Before our people's time here, sir. The George was in other hands at that time, sir."

   "I believe so."

   "But I would hold a pretty wager, sir, that a House like Tellson and Company was flourishing, a matter of fifty, not to speak of fifteen years ago?"

   "You might treble that, and say a hundred and fifty, yet not be far from the truth."

   "Indeed, sir!"

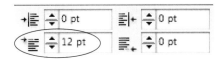

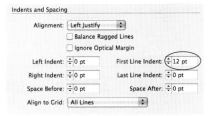

FIGURE 8.2 The first-line indent fields in the Control Panel Paragraph Formatting Controls (left) and in the indents and spacing options that are part of Paragraph Style Options (right).

'Ugh!' said the Lory, with a shiver.

'I beg your pardon!' said the Mouse, frowning, but very politely: 'Did you speak?'

'Not I!' said the Lory hastily.

'I thought you did,' said the Mouse. '–I proceed. "Edwin and Morcar, the earls of Mercia and Northumbria, declared for him: and even Stigand, the patriotic archbishop of Canterbury, found it advisable – "'

'Found what?' said the Duck.

'Found it,' the Mouse replied rather crossly: 'of course you know what "it" means.'

'I know what "it" means well enough, when I find a

First-Line Indents

To colour correct using an eyedropper tool:

1. (Optional) Place a colour sampler on a pixel in an area of the image that should be neutral gray. Choose a pixel in the shadows, midtone, or highlight, depending on the eyedropper tool that you plan to use. Use the Info palette to help you locate an appropriate pixel.

2. Choose Layer > New Adjustment Layer > Levels

3. Double-click the Set Black Point, the Set Gray Point, or the Set White Point Eyedropper tool. Use the Adobe Colour Picker to specify a neutral target colour.

If you're working in RGB, enter the same values for R, G, and B to specify a neutral colour. The neutral colour should be close as possible to the values of the colour sampler.

Paragraph Spacing

FIGURE 8.3 First-line indents versus paragraph spacing used to differentiate paragraphs.

Alternatives to the First-Line Indent

Not everyone loves a first-line indent. In Germany it's popular to have paragraphs begin flush left, without any indentation. The practice is also common in some newspapers, where space is especially tight. This can be problematic if the last lines of the paragraphs run the full column measure, which makes it difficult for the reader to discern one paragraph from another.

Running the paragraphs together and using a decorative mark between them maintains the flush look of the paragraph without compromising the meaning of the text. In medieval manuscripts, a pilcrow was used to differentiate paragraphs; in certain contexts, this can be an effective solution.

FIGURE 8.4 As an alternative to the first-line indent, a pilcrow (¶) is used to differentiate the paragraphs.

"Brave and generous friend, will you let me ask you one last question? I am very ignorant, and it troubles me—just a little." ¶ "Tell me what it is." ¶ "I have a cousin, an only relative and an orphan, like myself, whom I love very dearly. She is five years younger than I, and she lives in a farmer's house in the south country. Poverty parted us, and she knows nothing of my fate—for I cannot write—and if I could, how should I tell her! It is better as it is." ¶ "Yes, yes: better as it is." ¶ "What I have been thinking as we came along, and what I am still thinking now, as I look into your kind strong face which gives me so much support, is this:—If the Republic really does good to the poor, and they come to be less hungry, and in all ways to suffer less, she may live a long time: she may even live to be old." ¶ "What then, my gentle sister?"

Hanging Indents

There are two types of hanging indents: left-hanging (also known as *outdents*) and right-hanging (also called *last-line indents*). Left-hanging indents are commonly used in dictionaries and bibliographies, and sometimes on résumés. Right-hanging indents usually occur in price lists or restaurant menus.

Left-Hanging Indents

With left-hanging indents, all the lines of the paragraph are indented except for the first line, which sticks out beyond the left margin edge. These indents are achieved by first applying a left indent to the text block, and then applying a first-line indent of a negative value, typically the same amount as you entered for the left indent. For example, if you specify a left indent of 12 points, your first-line left indent will be –12 points.

To create a hanging indent, use the Control Panel or the Paragraph panel. You can also use the Tabs panel: Specify a left indent value greater than zero and drag the top marker to the left.

Right-Hanging Indents

Right-hanging, or last-line, indents can be used, in conjunction with right indents, to extend the last line of a paragraph beyond the edge of the text to accentuate its content.

Caribbean Pumpkin Curry Served over a quinoa corn
    cake with a red Calypso bean, smoked pepper sofrito, a spicy
    mango-coconut mojo, and crispy plantain slices $15.25

Wild Mushroom Roulade Marinated seitan, wild
    mushroom ragout, truffled mashed potatoes and celery root
    wrapped in yuba and baked in a crisp phyllo dough $16.50

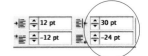

FIGURE 8.5 Using a last-line indent to make the last line extend beyond the right edge of the rest of the paragraph.

Left and Right Indents

Certain types of paragraph benefit from indentation on both their left and right edges. Indenting an entire block of text on the left, the right, or both is appropriate in the following situations:

- To indicate a quoted passage of text or an extract. Typically the type will be 1 point smaller than the body text, indented both left and right and with an even amount of paragraph space—usually a half-line space—added before and after the passage.

- In tables of contents or technical documents, where indenting signifies a lower level of the hierarchy.

- When working with verse. It's preferable to use left alignment, with the block indented. Center the block on the longest line and left indent all subsequent lines to the first line.

FIGURE 8.6 In this example, the verse is centered on the longest line, the position of the left edge is measured with Horizontal Cursor Position, and then all lines are left indented that amount. To do this, first center the line "Thyself thou gav'st … " (Cmd+Shift+C / Ctrl+Shift+C). Insert your Type cursor at the beginning of this line, and note the Horizontal Cursor Position on the Control Panel. Select all the lines, make them left aligned, and add a left indent that is the value of the Horizontal Cursor Position. (The last two lines are further indented by an em space.)

Farewell! thou art too dear for my possessing,
And like enough thou know'st thy estimate:
The charter of thy worth gives thee releasing;
My bonds in thee are all determinate.
For how do I hold thee but by thy granting?
And for that riches where is my deserving?
The cause of this fair gift in me is wanting,
And so my patent back again is swerving.
Thyself thou gav'st, thy own worth then not knowing,
Or me, to whom thou gav'st it, else mistaking;
So thy great gift, upon misprision growing,
Comes home again, on better judgment making.
   Thus have I had thee as a dream doth flatter—
   In sleep, a king; but waking, no such matter.

—William Shakespeare, *Sonnet 87*

Horizontal Cursor Position

health of those who were to live there. Conditions in such towns were frequently appalling. Frederick Engels, writing in 1844, described them thus:

> Every great city has one or more slums, where the working-class is crowded together. The streets are generally unpaved, rough, dirty, filled with vegetable or animal refuse, without sewers or gutters, but supplied with foul, stagnant pools instead. [1]

Moreover, the harsh, and all-too-frequently cruel, regime of the factories, if it did not daily inflict injuries upon the workers,

FIGURE 8.7 An excerpted passage 1 point smaller than the body text, with a 1-em left and right indent and a half-line space above and below.

A

A

Politics, n. A strife of interests masquerading as a contest of principles. The conduct of public affairs for private advantage.
Politician, n. An eel in the fundamental mud upon which the superstructure of organized society is reared. When we wriggles he mistakes the agitation of his tail for the trembling of the edifice. As compared with the statesman, he suffers the disadvantage of being alive.
— Ambrose Bierce, *The Devil's Dictionary*

B

FIGURE 8.8 Several applications of indents. Example **A** shows hanging indents used in an index. Example **B** shows dictionary entries where all lines are indented by 12 points and the first line has an indent of –12 pt. Example **C** shows indents used to indicate hierarchy in a table of contents. In Example **D** the text is aligned on a point—inserting a Tab character after a character's name flushes the dialogue line to that point.

Global Formatting with Styles

C

CASSIO	Thanks, you the valiant of this warlike isle, That so approve the Moor! O, let the heavens Give him defence against the elements, For I have lost us him on a dangerous sea.
MONTANO	Is he well shipp'd?
CASSIO	His bark is stoutly timber'd, his pilot Of very expert and approved allowance; Therefore my hopes, not surfeited to death, Stand in bold cure. A cry within: 'A sail, a sail, a sail!' Enter a fourth Gentleman.
CASSIO	What noise?

D

Summer Term
19 April–2 July
(Half Term 31 May–4 June)

Autumn Term
27 September–10 December
(Half term 25–29 October)

Opening Hours
9.30am–7.30pm
(Monday to Thursday)
9.30am–3.00pm
(Fridays and Half Term)

FIGURE 8.9 An "info box" on a 15 percent screen with text insets on all sides.

FIGURE 8.10 Quickly remove extra returns with a predefined GREP query.

Text Insets

Text insets are margins within your text frame. They give you the same result as applying left or right indents, but are more convenient to use if you are working with informational text in a colored or tinted rectangle.

Space Before and Space After

Time for another sweeping pronouncement: Never, ever, under any circumstances should you have more than one consecutive paragraph mark in your document. To put it another way, never create line spaces by pressing Return (Enter). There are no exceptions—at least none that I can think of. If text that you place in InDesign has extra returns (very likely), then zap 'em with Find/Change (Cmd+F/Ctrl+F). An easy way to do this is to use Multiple Return To Single Return, a predefined GREP Query.

Now, you might be thinking, what's the big deal? Why not type a harmless extra return between paragraphs—no one gets hurt. And it's true; the sun will still rise if you insist on maintaining this bad habit. But there are good reasons to avoid extra returns:

- Using returns for paragraph spacing allows no flexibility in the size of the space between paragraphs. Every time you create a new paragraph by pressing Return (Enter), the blank paragraph has the same formats (including the leading) as the paragraph before it.

- If your text flows into multiple columns or pages, a return at the top of the column or page creates unwanted vertical space.

 Instead of pressing Return (Enter) twice or—heaven forbid—more than twice, use Space Before or Space After from the Control Panel Paragraph Formatting controls or in Paragraph Style Options. I say *or* because using both, while occasionally necessary, is apt to get confusing. Most of the time, I use Space Before because that's what I've always used. Pick one and stick with it. As well as giving you complete flexibility in the size of the space between paragraphs, paragraph spacing is smart enough to disappear when not needed (such as at the top or bottom of a column or page).

Flowering begins along the parks southern boundary as early as February and at higher elevations in March and April. Regions over 4000 feet will show blooms much later, notably the higher Bernardino mountain region. The Joshua tree will flower in February or March but trees have been known to skip a season.

¶

Visitors who find it difficult telling the "Hairy Sand Verbena" from a "Forget Me Not" might seek further information in one of the parks visitor centers. Flowers are often recognized first by color group. They often carry descriptive names such as Canterbury Trumpet, Enlemann Hedgehog and

Extra Return between paragraph results in a blank line at the top of column 2

Flowering begins along the parks southern boundary as early as February and at higher elevations in March and April. Regions over 4000 feet will show blooms much later, notably the higher Bernardino mountain region. The Joshua tree will flower in February or March but trees have been known to skip a season.

Visitors who find it difficult telling the "Hairy Sand Verbena" from a "Forget Me Not" might seek further information in one of the parks visitor centers. Flowers are often recognized first by color group. They often carry descriptive names such as Canterbury Trumpet, Enlemann Hedgehog and Beavertail cactus.

Space Before ignored at the top of column two

FIGURE 8.11 Use Space Before rather than extra returns to separate paragraphs.

Book the First — Recalled to Life

A

I. The Period

B

It was the best of times, it was the worst of times, it was the age of wisdom, it was the age of foolishness, it was the epoch of belief, it was the epoch of incredulity, it was the season of Light, it was the season of Darkness, it was the spring of hope, it was the

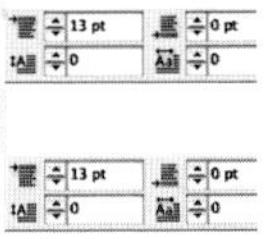

FIGURE 8.12 Space A is created by adding space before paragraph 2, "The Period." Space B is created by adding space before paragraph 3. The same result could have been achieved by adding space after paragraphs 1 and 2.

Proximity

Make sure any paragraph spacing accentuates rather than detracts from the connection between different pieces of text. Simply put, things that belong together should be in close proximity to each other. Organizing your material into clusters of information — subhead and paragraph, for example — will help establish the rhythm of your type. The reader will interpret the spaces between such clusters as representing a pause, the next cluster as being a new idea. To reinforce this relationship, your subheads should always be closer to the text that follows them than to the text that precedes them. This may seem obvious, but this rule is frequently broken.

To ensure that this relationship is never broken—by a column or page break, for example—set your Keep Options for the style definition of your subheads to Keep With Next 2 lines. (See Chapter 12, "Global Formatting with Styles.")

remains of the Blackfriars Rail Bridge, which once ran parallel, are the red columns in the river and the brightly colored cast-iron insignia of the company: London, Chatham and Dover Railway.

Tate Modern

Giles Gilbert Scott, 1947-63

Jacques Herzog and Pierre de Meuron, 1995-2000

The Tate Modern is now one of the most successful and popular art galleries in the world and London's most popular free tourist attraction. The building was originally Bankside Power Station, a monolithic steel construction

remains of the Blackfriars Rail Bridge, which once ran parallel, are the red columns in the river and the brightly colored cast-iron insignia of the company: London, Chatham and Dover Railway.

Tate Modern

Giles Gilbert Scott, 1947-63

Jacques Herzog and Pierre de Meuron, 1995-2000

The Tate Modern is now one of the most successful and popular art galleries in the world and London's most popular free tourist attraction. The building was originally Bankside Power Station, a monolithic steel construction

FIGURE 8.13 In the example on the left, the subhead floats between the paragraphs before and after, making it ambiguous which paragraph it refers to. On the right, the subhead clearly relates to the text that follows. The relationship between subhead and text is reinforced by the Keep With Next setting.

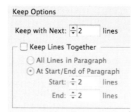

CHAPTER 9

Breaking (and Not Breaking) Words, Lines, Paragraphs, and Pages

AN IMPORTANT ASPECT of typography is controlling how words, lines, and paragraphs break —or are kept together—to enhance the meaning of the text and to facilitate easier reading. At the micro level, hyphenation determines how words are allowed to break—or are prevented from breaking—across a line. In addition, certain combinations of words, most commonly proper nouns, can be prevented from breaking over a line with a No Break attribute. On a more macro level, Keep Options serve a variety of related purposes. They can be used to prevent paragraphs from breaking over a column or page, to keep heads and subheads with a specified number of lines that follow them, and to make sure that certain classes of paragraph always start in a new column or on a new page.

Hyphenation

There's a lot of prejudice against the poor hyphen. Some designers feel that hyphens are ugly and to be avoided at all costs, as if a broken word is somehow inferior to a word with no hyphens. Used appropriately, however, hyphenation is a practical tool that helps you achieve even type color. By allowing words at the ends of lines to be broken into fragments, hyphenation keeps the amount of leftover space on a line to a minimum. As long as the breaks make sense, using hyphens is preferable to bad word spacing in justified type or uneven rags in left-aligned type. We're used to reading hyphenated text. We do it without thinking, rarely if ever pausing to consider the hyphen's service to the cause of readability.

Hyphenation rules vary from one style manual to another and from one language to another. Obviously we'd expect the Latvian dictionary in InDesign to break words differently than the English:USA dictionary; less expected, though, is that the English:UK dictionary hyphenates the same words differently than the English:USA dictionary. The UK dictionary breaks words by etymology, while the USA dictionary breaks them according to pronunciation. The moral of the story? Make sure you have the appropriate language dictionary selected.

Hyphenation can be labor intensive. Good hyphenation settings will address most issues, but InDesign can't read your mind. There will be times when you'll need to intervene to make sure words break how you want them to. Manually adjusting hyphenation should be included in the fine-tuning of your publication; text invariably gets edited throughout the production process, causing line

FIGURE 9.1 Choosing the language dictionary from the Control Panel (**A**) and in Paragraph Style Options (**B**). An example of how the USA and UK dictionaries hyphenate differently (**C**).

endings to change, so there's no point investing time in getting the hyphenation right until you know exactly what you're working with. Try to get the client to sign off on the text content before you start manually tweaking the hyphenation. And—an obvious point—always start at the beginning of the story and work forward.

Hyphenation Options

Setting Hyphenation options is an area where relatively few InDesign users dare to tread, yet these options have a profound impact on the appearance of your type. The Hyphenation dialog box is accessible via the Control Panel menu, the Paragraph panel, or as part of Paragraph Style Options.

Words with at Least

This refers to the minimum number of letters for hyphenated words. Changing this number from 5 to 6 or 7 will result in less hyphenation.

After First and Before Last

These rather confusingly named options refer, respectively, to the minimum number of characters at the beginning of a word and the minimum number of characters at the end of a word that can be broken by a hyphen. The rule of thumb is to leave at least two characters behind and take at least three forward.

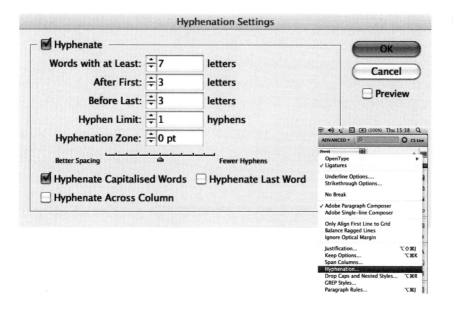

FIGURE 9.2 These restrictive hyphenation settings will result in fewer hyphens.

Like all rules of thumb, this has its exceptions. For example, when the first two letters are a prefix, it may be best to break the word at the prefix. Words like "realign" or "reappear" would look confusing if they were broken after "real" or "reap" because the word fragment looks like a whole word. A firm but flexible approach is therefore best when it comes to hyphenation settings. Two-letter fragments after the hyphen are always best avoided, but in rare cases even these may be the lesser of two evils. Ultimately it comes down to two things: how it looks, and whether it makes sense.

Hyphen Limit

This determines the maximum number of hyphens that can appear on consecutive lines. While you'd never want more than two consecutive hyphens, which gives a ladder effect on your column edge, it's debatable whether setting this option to 1 is the best method of preventing consecutive hyphens. If you're willing to work a bit harder, you can get a better result by setting this option to 0, allowing unlimited consecutive hyphens, then manually fixing any problems through a combination of tracking, rewriting, and adding discretionary hyphens.

Here are some options for fixing ladders, or cutting back on consecutive hyphens:

- Find a better break a few lines above and insert a discretionary hyphen.

- Find a line or lines where you can tighten the letter spacing with manual tracking.

- Take the tightest hyphenated line and set the last word to No Break. This will turn the word over to the next line.

- Rewrite, if you have the authority and it's appropriate.

FIGURE 9.3 Hyphen Limit set to 3 (left) and 1 (right).

Whereas disregard and contempt for human rights have resulted in barbarous acts which have outraged the conscience of mankind, and the advent of a world in which human beings shall enjoy freedom of speech and belief and freedom from fear and want has been proclaimed as the highest aspiration of the common people.

Whereas disregard and contempt for human rights have resulted in barbarous acts which have outraged the conscience of mankind, and the advent of a world in which human beings shall enjoy freedom of speech and belief and freedom from fear and want has been proclaimed as the highest aspiration of the common people.

Hyphenation Zone

Despite the alluring name, this is nothing more than an invisible boundary set from the right margin. A larger Hyphenation Zone allows more words to be carried down to the next line, thus resulting in fewer hyphens and a harder rag. A smaller Hyphenation Zone results in more hyphenated words and a softer rag. However, the utility of this option is severely limited by the fact that it applies to ragged text only and is limited to use with the Adobe Single-line Composer.

The Hyphenation Slider

There's always a trade-off between good spacing and hyphenation, especially when working with justified text. Nothing demonstrates this more clearly than the Hyphenation Slider. Better spacing or fewer hyphens: pick one, or leave the slider in the middle for a happy medium.

Hyphenate Capitalized Words

This does exactly what it says. Generally, you want to avoid breaking proper nouns, but if they occur frequently or there are a lot of them, or both, selecting this option yields better word spacing. If you do opt to break capitalized words, try to avoid breaking someone's name the first time it appears—after that, do whatever looks best in terms of type color. A name that is familiar to the English-speaking reader more easily lends itself to being broken than one that is not.

Suppose we wish to copy by the Daguerreotype, or Calotype process, any objects highly colored–blue, red and yellow, for instance predominat-ing– the last of course reflects the most light, the blue the least; but the rays from the blue surface will make the most intense impression, whilst the red radiations are working very slowly, and the yellow remains en-tirely inactive. This accounts for the difficulty experienced in copying

Hyphenation Zone set to 0.

Suppose we wish to copy by the Daguerreotype, or Calotype process, any objects highly colored–blue, red and yellow, for instance predominat-ing– the last of course reflects the most light, the blue the least; but the rays from the blue surface will make the most intense impression, whilst the red radiations are working very slowly, and the yellow remains entirely inactive. This accounts for the difficulty experienced in copying bright green

Hyphenation Zone set to 3 picas (36 pt).

FIGURE 9.4 The Hyphenation Zone is valid only with ragged text and when using the Single-line Composer.

chicken-houses? But it was no use, he could not remember: nothing remained of his childhood except a series of bright-lit tableaux occurring against no background and mostly unintelligible.

chicken-houses? But it was no use, he could not remember: nothing remained of his childhood except a series of bright-lit tableaux occurring against no background and mostly unintelligible.

FIGURE 9.5   Typically, it's best to avoid breaking the last word of a paragraph (top), but when that word is long, allowing a hyphen break can improve the spacing of the paragraph (bottom).

Vag Rounded

Adobe Jensen Pro

Goudy Old Style

Hiroshige

FIGURE 9.6   Some hyphen examples.

Hyphenate Last Word

This is just what the doctor ordered when it comes to preventing word breaks at the end of a paragraph. Deselect this option to prevent the last word of a paragraph being hyphenated. However, even this is not set in stone: If the last word in a paragraph is very long, then consider breaking it. Should you choose to set your Paragraph Style Options to not break the last word of a paragraph and you need to make an exception, inserting a discretionary hyphen won't work. Instead, you can manually override the paragraph style settings. With the paragraph selected, go to the Hyphenation dialog box and select Hyphenate Last Word.

Varieties of Hyphens

Typically 1/3 of an em, the hyphen in most fonts is nasty, brutish, and short, and it could easily be swapped with the hyphen from another font without anyone noticing. Certain fonts, however, have very distinctive—and beautiful—hyphens. To quote Robert Bringhurst, "In the republic of typography, the lowliest, most incidental mark is also a citizen" [Elements of Typographic Style, p. 77].

Discretionary Hyphens and Nonbreaking Hyphens

Discretionary hyphens, invoked with Cmd+Shift+Hyphen (Ctrl+Shift+Hyphen), are useful when a word at the end of a line is not in your hyphenation dictionary, or when you want to break the word at a place different than that chosen by InDesign's language dictionary. Discretionary hyphens have the good manners to disappear when not needed. If the text is edited so that the word is no longer at the end of the line, the discretionary hyphen is invisible. This makes them preferable to forcing line breaks with Shift+Return (Shift+Enter) when carrying a hyphenated word down to the next line. Forced line breaks can later come back to bite you if the text is edited, causing the line break to occur in the middle of a line rather than at the end.

A discretionary hyphen also serves another purpose: You can prevent a word from hyphenating by inserting a discretionary hyphen in front of it.

It was a bright cold day in April, and the clocks were striking thirteen. Winston Smith, his chin nuzzled into his breast in an effort to escape the vile wind, slipped quickly through the glass doors of Victory Mansions, though not quickly enough to prevent a swirl of

Bad hyphenation at the end of the first line

It was a bright cold day in April, and the clocks were striking hirteen. Winston Smith, his chin nuzzled into his breast in an effort to escape the vile wind, slipped quickly through the glass doors of Victory Mansions, though not quickly enough to

Problem made worse by adding a Return before "thirteen," causing the new paragraph to inherit the formats of paragraph 1.

It was a bright cold day in April, and the clocks were striking thirteen. Winston Smith, his chin nuzzled into his breast in an effort to escape the vile wind, slipped quickly through the glass doors of Victory Mansions, though not quickly enough to prevent a

The bad hyphenation is fixed by adding a forced line break before "thirteen," but this causes loose word spacing on line 1.

It was a bright cold day in April, and the clocks were striking thirteen. Winston Smith, his chin nuzzled into his breast in an effort to escape the vile wind, slipped quickly through the glass doors of Victory Mansions, though not quickly enough to prevent a swirl of gritty dust

Bad hyphenation fixed by adding Discretionary Hyphen before "thirteen."

FIGURE 9.7 Discretionary hyphens are preferable to forced line breaks when fixing bad breaks.

Nonbreaking hyphens—Cmd+Option+Hyphen (Ctrl+Alt+Hyphen)—are used to prevent a line from breaking at the hyphen, but they do not guard against the phrase from being broken elsewhere. They are used for phone numbers or web addresses.

Multilingual Documents

InDesign CS5 comes with 39 dictionaries, representing 27 languages plus many alternate dictionaries for English, Dutch, German, Norwegian, and Portuguese. The dictionary that is applied to your type determines how that type is hyphenated and spell-checked. If you are working on a multilingual document, as is common in countries like Canada or Switzerland, make sure you apply the correct language dictionary to the appropriate passages of text. Even if you have only an excerpt—a single paragraph in a second language for example—choose the appropriate language dictionary for that content so that the text is hyphenated correctly and so that it is spell-checked in the right language.

The quick brown fox jumped over the www.web-address.com

The quick brown fox jumped over the www. web-address.com

FIGURE 9.8 Nonbreaking hyphens prevent the URL from breaking at the hyphen but do not prevent it from breaking elsewhere.

Hyphenation and User Dictionaries

When a word—usually a technical term, proper noun, or expletive—is not found in your chosen language dictionary, you may wish to add it to your user dictionary. Insert your cursor in the word and right-click (or control-click on a Mac with a single button mouse) to select the Dictionary window under Spelling. Click Add to place the word in the chosen language's user dictionary.

If you wish to add a word and specify its hyphenation breaks, click Dictionary and then click Hyphenate to view the word's suggested hyphenation points. You can add your own hyphenation points by inserting tildes, ranking them as you go: One tilde indicates the best break, two tildes the second best, and so on. If you don't want the word to be hyphenated, add a tilde before its first character.

FIGURE 9.9 Adding a word to the User Dictionary and specifying its hyphenation break(s).

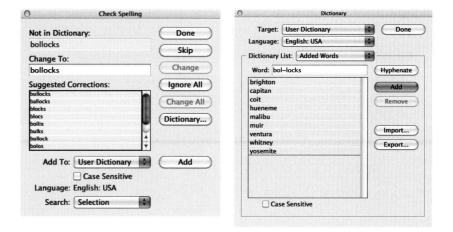

Sharing or Merging User Dictionaries

If you're part of a workgroup, make sure that each member of your team has the same user dictionary installed so that the same spelling and hyphenation rules are applied to a particular document regardless of who's working on it. While it's possible for multiple users to read and check against the same dictionary, only one person can add or edit words. For this reason, you'll need to assign one person responsibility for the custom dictionary.

Assuming that person is you, to share your custom dictionary with other members of your workgroup, choose Preferences > Dictionary and click the icon for New User Dictionary. Name the custom dictionary and save it in a folder on your file server where other members of your team can access it. (The file will have a .udc extension, identifying it as an InDesign dictionary.) Click OK and you'll now see two dictionaries listed, the default and the new one. When you run a spell check, InDesign will check the default dictionary first, then the custom dictionary. If neither contains the suspect word, it will be flagged as a possible misspelling.

Each member of your workgroup will now be able to load the custom dictionary by choosing Preferences > Dictionary, clicking the plus symbol to add a dictionary, and navigating to the server to select the custom dictionary file.

Alternatively, you can merge the user dictionary into the InDesign document. Choose InDesign > Preferences > Dictionary, and select Merge User Dictionary Into Document. On the plus side, this is one less thing to worry about. You can be sure that the text will hyphenate the same way if you're moving a document from one machine to another. On the other hand, you won't be able to use the same user dictionary for multiple documents.

TIP: The fastest way to add words to the custom dictionary is to create a text file that lists the words you wish to add, then select Edit > Spelling > Dictionary and click Import to load that file. Thereafter, you can enter words on a case-by-case basis by clicking the Add button.

Click to add new user dictionary

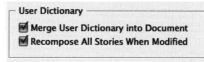

Save the user dictionary

FIGURE 9.10 Creating and sharing a user dictionary (left). Alternatively, you can merge the user dictionary into the document (right).

Hyphenation Dos and Don'ts

Do: Check your language dictionary. Hyphenation (and spelling) rules are based on the language dictionary specified for the text. You can choose which language to use from the Language menu on the Control Panel. Better yet, apply the language as part of a paragraph style definition. You can specify a default language in your Dictionary Preferences.

Do: Hang your hyphens. To use Optical Margin Alignment to hang the hyphens in the right margin, choose Type > Story and select the Optical Margin Alignment option. (See Chapter 7, "Alignment," for details.)

Do: Consult a dictionary for hyphenation breaks. When inserting discretionary hyphens, divide the word after a vowel to turn over the consonant to the next line. In present participles, turn over *-ing,* as in *walk-ing, driv-ing, design-ing.* When two consonants come together, put the hyphen between them. Try to divide the word so that the first part of the division suggests what is following: *conserva-tion,* not *con-servation; re-appear,* not *reap-pear; cam-ellia,* not *camel-lia.*

Don't: Use stupid hyphenation. Avoid breaks like *crap-ulous* or *the-rapist.*

Don't: Hyphenate display type and right- or center-aligned text. Be sure to deselect Hyphenation in the relevant Style Sheet definitions for headlines, subheads, and right- or center-aligned text blocks.

Don't: Hyphenate a word at the end of a paragraph. Remove the Hyphenate Last Word option in the Hyphenation dialog box to prevent this.

Don't: Hyphenate the last word. A single word at the bottom of a column or page should not break.

Don't: Double-hyphenate a word. This can happen if you have a long compound word that contains a hard hyphen occurring near the end of the line, but it requires a second hyphen. Select the type on either side of the hyphen and choose No Break to prevent the word from breaking.

Don't: Use more than two consecutive hyphens. Hyphens set in a column cause an ugly ladder effect down your right margin. Turn over one of the words by selecting it and choosing No Break, or by inserting a discretionary hyphen in front of the word.

H&J Violations

Setting your Hyphenation and Justification settings is important to do, but InDesign can't do the impossible. There are times when it won't be able to honor the settings you've chosen. Choose Preferences > Composition and check H&J Violations to highlight in three shades of yellow any lines that violate your H&J specs. The darker the yellow, the worse the problem. As with the Custom Tracking/Kerning Composition preference, this is distracting while you're designing pages, but very useful when fine-tuning a layout.

The No Break Attribute

The No Break attribute overlaps somewhat with the discretionary hyphen in terms of its utility. To prevent an individual word or a phrase from breaking, select it and choose No Break from the Control Panel menu. Whereas a non-breaking space will permit hyphenation, using No Break guarantees that the selected words will not be fragmented.

In addition to proper nouns and product names, the No Break attribute can also be used for the following:

- To prevent the word "I" from occurring at the end of a line.

- To prevent an em or en dash from occurring at the beginning of a line.

- To prevent short words like "A," "An," "The," and so on, from occurring at the end of a line when they are part of a title, such as A Winter's Tale.

- To keep together numerical expressions like "May 31" or "8 inches," or phrases like "Chapter 9."

- To prevent two or more consecutive lines from starting with the same word.

Every single surface of a modern For-mula One car, from the shape of the suspension links to that of the driver's
Nonbreaking space

Every single surface of a modern Formula One car, from the shape of the suspension links to that of the
No Break

FIGURE 9.11 Nonbreaking spaces permit hyphenation; No Break keeps the whole name or phrase on the same line.

Where No Break has the edge over nonbreaking spaces and discretionary hyphens is that it can be incorporated into a character style and, by extension, be applied automatically as a GREP style to proper nouns, product names, text strings, and so on, that you never want broken across a line.

Here's how:

1. Make a No Break character style: From the Character Styles panel menu choose New Character Style, name it "No Break," and in the Basic Character Formats select No Break.

TIP: If you need to see where the No Break attribute has been applied, you can temporarily change the color of the No Break character style.

TIP: Because No Break is tucked away under the Control Panel menu, you'll save yourself time by assigning it a keyboard shortcut.

2. Define the GREP style for the paragraph style where you want No Break applied. Right-click /control-click the style name in the Paragraph Styles panel and choose Edit. From the list on the left, choose GREP Style.

3. Click the New GREP Style button. From the Apply Style drop-down menu, select the No Break character style and click to the right of the To Text: field, then type the name or text string you want to prevent from breaking across a line. To apply No Break to multiple text strings, separate each one with a vertical pipe (|).

4. Select the No Break character styles you just created from the Character Style drop-down menu.

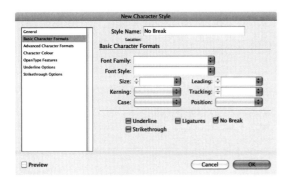
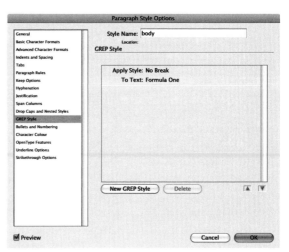

FIGURE 9.12 Applying a No Break character style as a GREP style.

Break Characters

There are several flavors of break character available on the Insert Break Character flyout menu under the Type menu. After the Paragraph Return, by far the most common is the forced line break (Shift-Return), which as already mentioned carries the text to the right of the cursor down to a new line without starting a new paragraph. This avoids taking on the unwanted indent and spacing attributes of the paragraph that it came from. The forced line break is also essential for contouring paragraphs when working with ragged text and for breaking lines for sense, especially in display text.

A discretionary line break is just like a forced line break, but has the good manners to disappear when the word occurs anywhere but at the end of the line, thus avoiding the possibility of the line breaking inappropriately.

The other breaks are self-explanatory and are inserted at the position of your cursor, introducing an invisible character into the text, which can be viewed when you have hidden characters shown: ⌄ ⌄ ● ⌄ ⌣ . When you insert one of these characters, text is forced to the next column in the current frame, to the next threaded frame, to the next page, or to the next odd or even page. Where you can predict the break—for example, if all chapter heads should start on a new right-hand page (recto)—then it's preferable to use Keep Options to incorporate this attribute as part of the paragraph style definition.

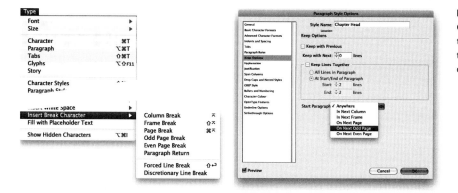

FIGURE 9.13 The Insert Break Characters menu (left) and the same options available through Keep Options as part of a paragraph style (right).

Keep Options

As well as controlling how the lines of a paragraph are kept together, Keep Options controls how a paragraph moves between text frames. Keep With Previous and Keep With Next ensure that heads and subheads don't become separated from the body text that follows them. Applying Keep With Previous to body text will carry a head at the bottom of a column or page over to the next column or page, but requires only one line of body text after the head. Alternatively, you can apply Keep With Next to the head itself and specify how many lines of the following paragraph must be kept with it.

With Keep Lines Together, you can make sure all the lines of a paragraph move together or that a specified number of lines move together at the beginning of the paragraph, the end of the paragraph, or both. This prevents widows and

Volorro el explissequi culparum ea dis dendici maximin ulparchil es as exerum volor magnistia dia nihicit qui berovit haruntest, omniata tiasped mi, quam, audi apitat doluptae. Ut quis dessita tiandionsed unte res exped molor anis.

Subheading

Sequam que volesciis alicabo reptate strunt

molupta turerum nihitatur, none dem idis as doluptu rereper oviduci tatiatur? Alis mod molupta cone voluptur aut reped que dolorepel explitate vitibusdam voluptate volo modi tectus atur, quam voloremquos autecus consect iatempe ritam, cus a provitDi occusci tem qui ulparion re consed mod exerspi enessit assuntur? Dundit, optati nectam si ut omniet quis dolupta

FIGURE 9.14 Keep with Previous applied to the body text after the subhead (top) and "Keep with Next 2 lines" applied to the subhead (bottom).

Volorro el explissequi culparum ea dis dendici maximin ulparchil es as exerum volor magnistia dia nihicit qui berovit haruntest, omniata tiasped mi, quam, audi apitat doluptae. Ut quis dessita tiandionsed unte res exped molor anis.

Subheading

Sequam que volesciis alicabo reptate strunt molupta turerum nihitatur, none dem idis as doluptu rereper oviduci tatiatur? Alis mod molupta cone voluptur aut reped que dolorepel explitate vitibusdam voluptate volo modi tectus atur, quam voloremquos autecus consect iatempe ritam,

Volorro el explissequi culparum ea dis dendici maximin ulparchil es as exerum volor magnistia dia nihicit qui berovit haruntest, omniata tiasped mi, quam, audi apitat doluptae. Ut quis dessita tiandionsed unte res exped molor anis.

Sequam que volesciis alicabo reptate strunt molupta turerum nihitatur, none dem idis as doluptu rereper oviduci

tatiatur? Alis mod molupta cone voluptur aut reped que dolorepel explitate vitibusdam voluptate volo modi tectus atur, quam voloremquos autecus consect iatempe ritam, cus a proviti occusci tem qui ulparion re consed mod exerspi enessit assuntur?

Dundit, optati nectam si ut omniet quis dolupta tiossit atenda nobit odi ium

FIGURE 9.15 The paragraph indicated in blue is shown with two lines kept together (top) and with all lines kept together (bottom).

Volorro el explissequi culparum ea dis dendici maximin ulparchil es as exerum volor magnistia dia nihicit qui berovit haruntest, omniata tiasped mi, quam, audi apitat doluptae. Ut quis dessita tiandionsed unte res exped molor anis.

Sequam que volesciis alicabo reptate strunt molupta turerum nihitatur, none dem idis as doluptu rereper oviduci tatiatur? Alis mod molupta cone voluptur aut reped que dolorepel explitate vitibusdam voluptate volo modi tectus atur, quam voloremquos autecus consect iatempe ritam, cus a proviti occusci tem qui ulparion re consed mod exerspi enessit assuntur?

orphans, as discussed in Chapter 5, "Letterspacing, Tracking, and Kerning." It is not a viable solution if you need your columns to end on the same baseline.

The Start Paragraph options ensure that certain headline levels always begin on a new page or in a new column or frame, and are especially useful for chapter or section heads.

Obviously, your paragraphs must break somewhere. Asking the impossible by setting too many Keep Options will result in Keep Violations, which like H&J Violations and Custom Tracking/Kerning can be highlighted by turning on the Composition preference (Preferences > Composition).

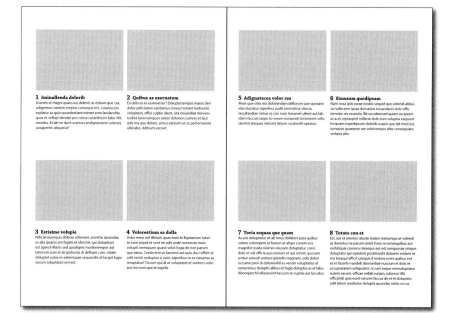

FIGURE 9.16 The Start Paragraph Next Frame attribute is useful when working with step-by-step guides to ensure that each numbered step automatically starts in a new frame.

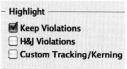

FIGURE 9.17 Select Keep Violations to highlight in yellow where InDesign can't honor the specified Keep Options.

CHAPTER 10

Tabs, Tables, and Lists

TABLES ARE EVERYWHERE: train and bus schedules, product comparisons, stock charts, sports league tables, and TV and radio listings to name but a few. Unlike narrative text, tables need to be read in two directions simultaneously, so it's important to keep the design simple. When creating tables, start out with a design that is homogenous, bland even, introducing rules, tints, and changes in emphasis only as necessary—and only if you can articulate *why* they are necessary. Lists are also ubiquitous: the top ten this, the 100 greatest that, 2-step programs, 50 ways to leave your lover, and so on. In this chapter I'll look at InDesign's robust and versatile table formatting features, then move on to the options for creating bullet and number lists, as well as a few useful things we can achieve with tabs.

Working with Tables

There's no denying it, tables are a drag. Faced with having to typeset lots of tabular information, filing a tax return starts to seem like an attractive prospect. Thankfully, InDesign's table options help ease the pain—but as well as using the tools at our disposal, it helps to arm ourselves with a commonsense, no-nonsense approach to the aesthetics of tables.

Unfortunately, clients sometimes treat tables the way we might treat a junk room: just cram as much stuff in there as possible, then force the door shut. Remember: Even though it's a table, it still needs to be read. Normal rules of legibility still apply.

In terms of typeface choice, table text is typically one or two points smaller than body text. My point about legibility notwithstanding, condensed faces may be preferable because they are more economical with space. Sans serif faces with relatively high x-heights and open counters (Helvetica, Univers, Myriad) are more readable at small sizes than serif faces. Make sure your typeface has lining numerals (that is, numerals without ascenders and descenders) rather than proportional old style numerals. If it's an OpenType font with a choice of numeral style, select Lining Numerals as the default figure style. Unlike in body text, in tables you want all the figures to have the same set width so that they line up with each other.

The mantra "Keep it simple" is perhaps never more important than when working with tables. The way the table is constructed should establish the hierarchy of information, rather than different fonts, weights, and point sizes. InDesign provides borders, column and row strokes, and tinted cells. These should all be used sparingly. Too many rules and tinted blocks and you'll overemphasize the cellular structure of the table, causing your data to look trapped within the cells. Rather than a full border around the table, consider using top and bottom rules only to create a more "open" table with room to breathe.

In terms of alignment within tables, it pays to be flexible. Centering column heads over numbers is preferable if the number of numerals in each column varies. If there are the same, or close to the same, number of numerals in each column, left alignment may be preferable. Be prepared to adjust for optical alignment where necessary.

Vertical alignment can be important for column heads. Where these run to more than one line, bottom alignment is cleaner and makes it easier for the eye to scan along the column. Justified alignment and first-line indents have no place in tables; the table cells are too narrow. If table cell entries run to more than one paragraph, break them into separate cells. When working with currency columns, the currency symbol should be positioned according to the widest numerical entry in the column. For all other entries in that column, the currency symbol should be horizontally aligned to this point using figure spaces.

For long tables that run across several pages, repeat the header row on each page; a footer row is only necessary at the end of the complete table.

Brighton–London Victoria
Mondays–Fridays

Outward	Time	Time	Time	Time	Time	Time	Time
Brighton	07:04	07:06	07:06	07:15	07:15	07:19	07:30
Preston Park	07:18	07:18	07:36				
Burgess Hill	07:28	07:28	07:45				
Hassocks	07:20	07:20	07:39	07:39			
Haywards Heath	07:44	07:44	07:48				
Balcombe	07:59						
Three Bridges	08:05						
Gatwick Airport	07:30	07:47	07:47	08:02	08:02		
East Croydon	07:46	07:57	07:57	07:56	08:23		
Clapham Junction	08:02	08:06	08:06	08:05	08:39		
London Victoria	08:09	08:16	08:16	08:20	08:20	08:12	08:35
Duration	01:05	01:10	01:10	01:05	01:05	00:53	01:05

				Home			Away						
Team	P	W	D	L	F	A	W	D	L	F	A	GD	PTS
1 Man Utd	31	14	1	1	37	5	9	3	3	27	10	49	73
2 Chelsea	31	10	5	0	31	10	10	3	3	24	13	32	68
3 Arsenal	31	12	4	0	33	10	7	6	2	26	14	35	67
4 Liverpool	31	9	6	1	38	12	7	5	3	17	12	31	59

FIGURE 10.1 Two examples of tables where the cell shading reinforces the primary reading direction: vertical in the case of the train timetable, horizontal in the case of the league table.

Creating a Table

Tables are contained in a text frame. If you insert a table into an existing story, it will move with the flow of the text. Treat the table as a discrete paragraph. Then, should you choose to reduce the table width, you can horizontally align the table within the frame using the Text Alignment option in the Paragraph formats of the Control Panel. You use the Type Tool to edit tables, and formatting table text is the same as formatting any other. You can also drag and drop or place graphics (Cmd+D/Ctrl+D) into table cells. It helps to think of each table cell as being its own text frame.

FIGURE 10.2 The anatomy of a table.

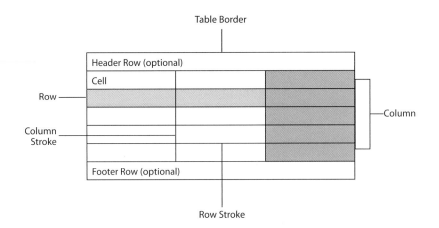

There are three approaches to creating a table: from scratch, converting existing text to a table, and importing a table from Microsoft Word or Microsoft Excel.

From Scratch

1. Draw a text frame with the Type Tool, or insert your type pointer into an existing text frame.

2. Choose Table > Insert Table.

3. Specify the numbers of rows and columns.

4. Click OK.

   Optional: If the table will span more than one column or frame, specify the number of (repeating) header or footer rows. If you create a table without a header or footer, you can convert the first row to a header or the last to a footer by choosing Table > Convert Rows. If you have a Table Style prepared, you can apply it here. For more on Table and Cell Styles see Chapter 12, "Global Formatting with Styles."

FIGURE 10.3 Creating a table from scratch.

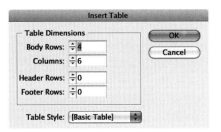

Converting Text to a Table

If you plan to convert text to a table, it pays to set up the text with tabs separating the columns and paragraph returns separating the rows. Select your text and choose Table > Convert Text To Table. It may not look pretty at first, but by adjusting the column widths, merging cells where necessary, and applying appropriate paragraph styles to the text, you'll be well on your way. You can also make this conversion in reverse by inserting your Type Tool in a table and choosing Table > Convert Table To Text.

FIGURE 10.4 Converting tab-delimited text to a table.

Brighton–London Victoria »	»	»	»	»	»	»	¶
Mondays–Fridays »	»	»	»	»	»	¶	
Outward » Time »	Time »	Time »	Time »	Time »	Time »	Time¶	
Brighton » 07:04 »	07:06 »	07:06 »	07:15 »	07:15 »	07:19 »	07:30¶	
Preston·Park »	07:18 »	07:18 »	07:36 »	»	»	¶	
Burgess Hill »	07:28 »	07:28 »	07:45 »	»	»	¶	
Hassocks » 07:20 »	07:20 »	07:39 »	07:39 »	»	¶		
Haywards·Heath »	07:44 »	07:44 »	07:48 »	»	»	¶	
Balcombe»07:59 »	»	»	»	»	¶		
Three·Bridges »	08:05 »	»	»	»	»	¶	
Gatwick·Airport »	07:30 »	07:47 »	07:47 »	08:02 »	08:02 »	¶	
East·Croydon »	07:46 »	07:57 »	07:57 »	07:56 »	08:23 »	¶	
Clapham·Junction »	08:02 »	08:06 »	08:06 »	08:05 »	08:39 »	¶	
London·Victoria »	08:09 »	08:16 »	08:16 »	08:20 »	08:20 »	08:12 »	08:35¶
Duration » 01:05 »	01:10 »	01:10 »	01:05 »	01:05 »	00:53 »	01:05#	

Brighton–London·Victoria#	#	#	#	#	#	#	#
Mondays–Fridays#	#	#	#	#	#	#	#
Outward#	Time#	Time#	Time#	Time#	Time#	Time#	Time#
Brighton#	07:04#	07:06#	07:06#	07:15#	07:15#	07:19#	07:30#
Preston·Park#	07:18#	07:18#	07:36#	#	#	#	#
Burgess·Hill#	07:28#	07:28#	07:45#	#	#	#	#

Importing a Table

There's no point in reinventing the wheel: You can place an Excel spreadsheet or a Word table in InDesign. Choose File > Place (Cmd+D/Ctrl+D) and select Show Import Options. If you're placing a Word or RTF document, you can choose to remove the style and formatting from text and tables, either converting the tables to unformatted tables or to unformatted tabbed text. If the table you're importing exists in the context of a longer document, it's better to choose Preserve Styles And Formatting and then strip out the formatting from the table once the story is placed. To remove the formatting from an imported table, do the following:

1. Select the Table by inserting the Type cursor in any of the table cells, and choose all cells with Cmd+Option+A (Ctrl+Alt+A).

NOTE: If you aren't using the Type cursor when you place a table, the table will be independent of the text flow. To insert the table into the text flow, cut the table, select the Type Tool, click inside the story, and paste.

2. Go to the Paragraph Styles panel and click the Clear Overrides button at the bottom of the panel to remove any local character and paragraph formatting.

3. Go to the Cell Styles panel (Window > Type & Tables > Table) and do the same. This will zap any cell formatting (row or column stroke weight, cell colors), so that you can proceed with a completely unformatted table.

When placing an Excel file, you can specify a cell range and apply a table style to the incoming table.

FIGURE 10.5 Importing an Excel table (saved with the .xls file extension).

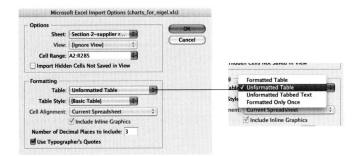

Table Selection Methods

NOTE: Selecting a cell and the text within a cell are two distinct things. To select a cell, drag from the top left of the cell. Alternatively, because it's all too easy to inadvertently resize rows and columns when trying to select individual table cells, put your Type cursor in the cell and choose Table > Select > Cell or press Cmd+/ (Ctrl+/).

Selecting a whole table allows you to change the formatting of all the table's cells. To do so, move your pointer to the upper-left corner of the table—it becomes a southeast-pointing arrow—and click. Alternatively, with your Type cursor inside the table, choose Table > Select > Table (Cmd+Option+A/Ctrl+Alt+A).

To select a column, move the pointer to the top edge of the table; your pointer becomes an arrow shape. Click to select the entire column. Alternatively, press Cmd+Option+3 (Ctrl+Alt+3). To select a row, move your pointer to the left edge of the table and click to select the row. Alternatively, press Cmd+3 (Ctrl+3). You can also click inside a table and choose Table > Select > Column or Row. To specifically select Header, Body, or Footer rows, click inside the table and choose Table > Select > Header Rows, Body Rows, or Footer Rows.

To select a cell, insert the Type cursor in the cell and press Esc or Cmd+/ (Ctrl+/).

To select the text within a cell, use the normal text selection methods.

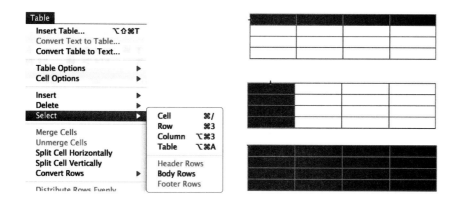

FIGURE 10.6 Selecting a row, a column, and a whole table.

Linking to Spreadsheet Files

When you place a graphic in InDesign, a link is created to the original graphic. You manage links through the Links panel, either initiating a round-trip edit of the graphic in its native application (Adobe Photoshop, Adobe Illustrator, and so on) or updating the link if the original file has been edited. This is not the default behavior with text and spreadsheet files: Once you place them in InDesign, they become independent of the original file unless you select Create Links, which is found under Preferences > File Handling.

Creating a link to an Excel spreadsheet means that every time the original Excel spreadsheet is changed, you can update the table in the InDesign document. There are, however, two big caveats to this.

First, updating the file in Excel will cause you to lose formatting applied to the table in InDesign. Bummer. For this reason, you're probably better off copying and pasting the new data from Excel to InDesign (see "Table Selection Methods"). If your tables are particularly data-heavy and prone to frequent updating, however, it may be useful to create links to your spreadsheets—just so long as it's going to take less time to reapply the formatting with table styles than it would take to copy and paste in the new data.

Second, turning on the Create Links preference causes text files to be linked from that point forth, which is unlikely to be a good idea. So, once you have placed the spreadsheet that you want linked, make sure to return immediately to your File Handling preferences to turn it off again.

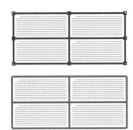

FIGURE 10.7 Use the proxy preview in the Control Panel to determine which sides of the cell border are being affected. Selected rules appear in blue; deselected lines in gray.

Adding Borders, Strokes, and Fills to a Table

When you insert a table based upon the Basic table style, by default it will have a border and a row, and column strokes will be turned on. Your first job is to turn off these options and add back only those that you need. Here's how:

1. Select the table by clicking in its upper-left corner. This will change the top control panel into Table mode—a one-stop styling center.

2. Select the Preview check box to the right of Strokes in the Control Panel. Selected lines appear in blue; deselected lines in gray. Click the gray horizontal and vertical lines within the preview to add rules not already selected. Enter 0 in the Stroke value box to the left. To deselect all lines, triple-click the proxy preview.

3. Return your cursor to the table, and open the Table Setup dialog box (Cmd+Option+Shift+B/Ctrl+Alt+Shift+B). Set up your own stroke and fill properties for the whole table. You can always go back and change individual rows or columns through the Control Panel using the proxy preview or through Table > Table Options or Cell Options.

Row strokes or fills can enhance the readability of complicated tables with wide measures by helping the eye to track along the table rows. Depending on the nature of the data, you may want to experiment with Alternating Patterns. You can apply your fills or strokes to every other row, every second row, every third row, or, using the First and Next menus, come up with a Custom Row pattern. The same is true with columns.

Row or column shading should reinforce the primary reading direction. According to the data in the table, is the reader more likely to read down the column or across the row?

| Team | P | W | D | L | F | A | W | D | L | F | A | GD | PTS |
		Home					Away						
1 Man Utd	31	14	1	1	37	5	9	3	3	27	10	49	73
2 Chelsea	31	10	5	0	31	10	10	3	3	24	13	32	68
3 Arsenal	31	12	4	0	33	10	7	6	2	26	14	35	67
4 Liverpool	31	9	6	1	38	12	7	5	3	17	12	31	59

FIGURE 10.8 Applying alternating fill colors to a table makes it easier to compare statistics.

Inserting and Deleting Rows and Columns

You can insert rows and columns using the menu options, or on the fly by holding down Option (Alt) as you drag a row or column border. You can also create a new row by pressing Tab when the insertion point is in the last cell of the table. Make sure frame edges are shown (select View > Extras) so you can see the individual table cells.

To delete all or specific parts of your table, choose Table > Delete > Row, Column, or Table.

To delete cell contents without deleting the cells themselves, choose the Type cursor, drag over the cells containing the text you want to delete, and press Delete or Backspace.

Resizing Rows and Columns

To resize individual rows and columns, drag the row or column border to change the row height or column width. To keep the table at the same size, hold Shift while you drag. This method affects only two rows (or two columns) at once—as one field grows larger, the adjacent field grows smaller. To resize all the rows and columns proportionally, hold down Shift while dragging the bottom table edge or the right table edge respectively.

To resize the whole table, position the pointer over the lower-right corner of the table so that the pointer becomes a diagonal arrow, and then drag to increase or decrease the table size. To maintain the table's height and width proportions, hold down Shift. Note, however, that this doesn't work if the table spans more than one frame.

If you want the selected rows or columns to have a uniform height or width, choose Table > Distribute Rows Evenly or Distribute Columns Evenly.

In certain cases, a design may require a single cell be split into two distinct cells. For example, if you want to make one cell wider without making all the cells in that column wider, you first need to split the cell horizontally. Place your cursor in the cell to be split, and choose Table > Split Cell Horizontally.

One resizing caveat: InDesign doesn't show rows that fall outside the text frame (although it does show columns that do). Turn on Show Frame Edges (Alt+Cmd+H/Ctrl+H) when resizing tables. Then resize the text frame once you have resized the table to ensure that the whole table is visible.

TIP: When adding columns, if you hold down the Option/Alt key and drag the column divider more than one and one-half times the width of the column being dragged, new columns with the same width as the original column are added.

TIP: Choosing Exactly from the Control Panel or Table panel sets a fixed row height. Fixed row heights don't grow when you add text, and a small red dot will appear in the lower-right corner of the cell if it is overset. With an overset cell you have two options: Make the content smaller or the table cell bigger.

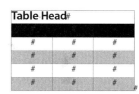

FIGURE 10.9 Inserting and deleting rows.

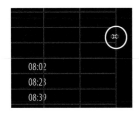

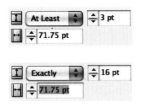

FIGURE 10.10 Resizing columns (top) and rows (bottom).

FIGURE 10.11 Specifying row height and column width using the Control Panel.

FIGURE 10.12 The Keep Options hold specified rows together and set the location where the keep will start.

Specifying Row Height

Row heights can grow with the content of the cell or be an absolute value. The default height of a row is determined by the leading of your text. The At Least option found under Table > Cell Options > Rows And Columns specifies a minimum row height that will grow as you add text or increase the point size of the text within the cells. "Exactly" sets the row height to a fixed value even if the row is empty. If your text or graphic exceeds this height, a red dot in the lower-right corner indicates that the content is overset. To avoid having to hunt for the overset, set the individual cell insets to 0 and choose the Clip Contents To Cell option before placing the graphic.

Breaking Tables Across Frames

If the table is taller than the text frame in which it resides, to continue the table you can thread the frame with another frame in the same way you would thread a regular text frame.

Specifying Keep Options (Cell Options > Rows And Columns) determines where a row should start. The default is "Anywhere" (that is, after the previous row), but this can be changed to In Next Text Column, In Next Frame, On Next Page, On Next Odd Page, or On Next Even Page. You can also request that a selected range of rows be kept together in the same text frame by selecting Keep With Next.

If you want a header or footer row to repeat information in the new frame, choose Table > Headers And Footers.

If you didn't set up a header or footer row initially, you can easily convert an existing row to a header or footer row by selecting the row and choosing Table > Convert Rows > To Header or To Footer.

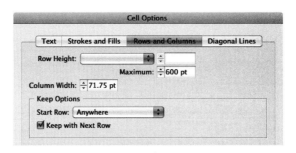

Working with Table Cells

Cells are the building blocks of a table, and each cell in your table has the same properties as an individual text frame.

Using Cell Options, you can determine the Cell Inset Spacing and the Vertical Alignment. On a cell-by-cell basis, you can also change Row Strokes, Column Strokes, First Baseline Options, and Diagonal Lines. Table text can be formatted in exactly the same way as text in a text frame, and paragraph and character styles are equally beneficial (see Chapter 13). The only restriction on table formatting is that text can be rotated in increments of 90°, 180°, or 270° only. (If you really must have text rotated at any other angle, format the text in its own frame and then cut and paste the text frame into a cell as an inline frame.)

NOTE: Table cells do not have a gutter setting to specify the distance between them. To calculate the space between columns, add the right inset of column one to the left inset of column two.

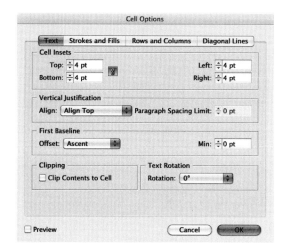

FIGURE 10.13 The Cell Options dialog box.

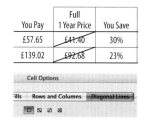

FIGURE 10.14 Applying diagonal lines to cells.

Cutting/Copying and Pasting Data

Should you wish to cut or copy and paste data from one table to another with the same number of rows and columns, select the first table (Cmd+Option+A/Ctrl+Alt+A) and choose Copy or Cut, then go to the destination table, insert your cursor in the first cell, and press Esc. It's important here that you select the cell by pressing Esc rather than selecting the data within the cell (which would place a table within a table). When you choose Paste (Cmd+V/Ctrl+V), the incoming data will replace the existing data in the table. This saves time if you're working with tabular information that needs frequent updating. It also works if you are copying and pasting data from an Excel spreadsheet into an InDesign table.

Merging and Splitting Cells

You can click the icons on the Control Panel to merge (⊠) and unmerge (⊟) cells, or you can choose these options from the Table menu, where you can also split cells horizontally or vertically.

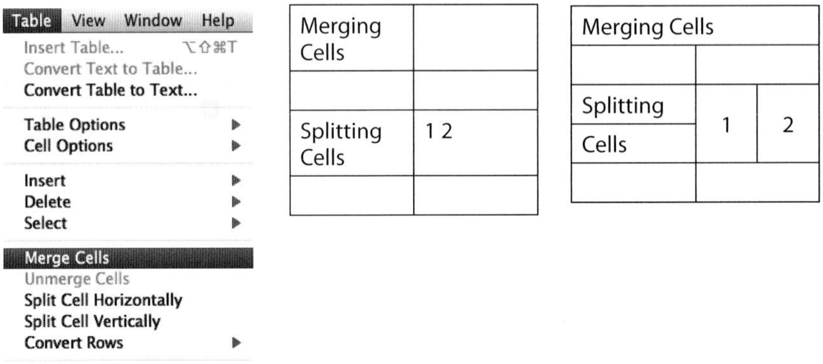

FIGURE 10.15 In addition to merging (and unmerging) cells, you can also split cells horizontally (right) and vertically (left).

Graphics in Table Cells

Placing graphics in tables is useful for creating specification sheets or product comparison tables, or just for jazzing up what might otherwise be a deathly boring chunk of data. Because table cells are essentially text frames, pictures in those table cells are effectively inline or anchored objects and thus move with the table. To get a graphic into a table cell, it may sometimes be easier to start out with an independent graphic. Rather than place the graphic directly into a table cell, which is apt to cause confusion if the graphic is substantially larger than the cell and only a small portion of it is visible, first place the graphic close to the table, but not in it. Size the graphic to the dimensions of the table cell you wish to place it in, then cut the resized graphic and paste it into the target cell, which makes it into an anchored object. If the graphic is bigger than the

FIGURE 10.16 In this example, the graphics have an inset of 0, making them flush with the edges of the table cell.

Album	Year	Label	Producer
 Hunky Dory	1971	RCA	Ken Scott / David Bowie
 Low	1977	RCA	David Bowie / Tony Visconti

cell, choose Table > Cell Options > Text and select the Clip Contents To Cell check box. Choose Table > Cell Options > Text (Cmd+Opt+B/Ctrl+Alt+B) and set the Cell Insets value to 0. The graphic will fill the cell vertically, but not horizontally; you will need to adjust the column width accordingly. To crop, triple-click with the Selection tool and drag the image around within its frame.

Tables and Text Wrap

You can wrap text around an image in a table by making the image into an anchored object. However, it can be difficult to adjust the text wrap exactly as you'd like, especially when trying to wrap the first line of the type around the anchored object. For this reason, it's easier to create the text wrap in a text frame outside the table, making sure that the frame is the same width as the table cell you want it to occupy. Group the image and text together, and then cut and paste the grouped object in place.

FIGURE 10.17 This text wrap was constructed outside of the table and then pasted into the table as a grouped object.

Historical Populations		
Census	Population	%±
1900	658,111	—
1910	925,708	40.7%
1920	1,182,911	27.8%
1930	1,578,009	33.4%
1940	1,734,308	9.9%
1950	2,681,322	54.6%
1960	3,638,939	35.7%
1970	4,628,199	27.2%
1980	5,179,784	11.9%
1990	6,023,577	16.3%
2000	6,783,760	12.6%

FIGURE 10.18 To create a rounded-corner table, cut or copy and paste a table into a rounded-corner rectangle.

Rounded-Corner Tables

Personally, I have a phobia of rounded rectangles, but rounded-corner tables are often requested. Here's how to make one:

1. Create your table without a table border.

2. Cut the table (Cmd+X/Ctrl+X).

3. Create a rounded-corner rectangle (Object > Corner Options), then insert the Type cursor into this and choose Paste Into (Cmd+Option+V/ Ctrl+Alt+V). The table becomes an inline object and can be repositioned using the Selection tool.

Joining and Splitting Tables

Although there is no command for joining tables, you can do this manually. First, make sure the table you're copying to has enough empty rows and columns to accommodate the data. Then copy or cut the contents to be carried over. Select the first empty row in the destination table and paste the contents in. Be sure to select the row(s) and not the single cell, as this would cause the new content to be placed as an inline graphic.

FIGURE 10.19 To join tables, copy and paste Table 2 into the empty rows of Table 1.

Team	P	W	D	L	F
1 Man Utd	31	14	1	1	37
2 Chelsea	31	10	5	0	31
3 Arsenal	31	12	4	0	33
4 Liverpool	31	9	6	1	38

Team	P	W	D	L	F
5 Everton	31	9	3	3	28
6 Portsmouth	31	6	7	2	22
7 Aston Villa	31	8	3	5	25
8 Blackburn	31	7	5	4	21

Table 1   Table 2

Team	P	W	D	L	F
1 Man Utd	31	14	1	1	37
2 Chelsea	31	10	5	0	31
3 Arsenal	31	12	4	0	33
4 Liverpool	31	9	6	1	38
5 Everton	31	9	3	3	28
6 Portsmouth	31	6	7	2	22
7 Aston Villa	31	8	3	5	25
8 Blackburn	31	7	5	4	21

FIGURE 10.20 Sometimes it can be easier to edit tables in the Story Editor. You click the triangle to the left of the table symbol to hide or disclose the table's contents.

To split a table, select the rows you want to split off and cut them to the Clipboard (Cmd+X/Ctrl+X). Insert the Type cursor wherever you want the new table to be and paste (Cmd+V/Ctrl+V).

Tables and the Story Editor

You can view any overset table text in the Story Editor. Right-click the overset marker at the frame edge and choose Edit In Story Editor to see the contents of the table. Clicking the triangle to the left of the Table icon in the Story Editor will alternately hide and disclose the contents of a table. The Story Editor can also be useful for selecting copy before or after a table, particularly if you want two tables in a row with no paragraph return between them.

Unexpected Uses for a Table

Beyond their obvious utility, tables can also be helpful in the following situations.

If you want to put a screened background behind a specific paragraph, a table is an elegant solution. Select the text in the paragraph—but not the final hidden carriage-return character—and choose Table > Convert Text To Table to make a one-cell table. You can then stroke and fill the table as you wish and—because it's a table—it will grow as you add type and move as part of the text flow. You control the paragraph spacing between the table and the paragraphs above and below using Table Options > Table Setup.

Et assintur re experere evelis res natinci minisciis magnimus ut volo es moditi asperit, nossequi sundae ducius ea dellendes dolum que sequam, ut es audi con rest.

Convert the paragraph into a single cell table and then apply a fill color to that cell. Use Cell Options to control the inset spacing of the text.

Dus maio mi, ne et voloris nones etur aceaqui aturia volore si nullace pudipsum fuga. Cum rem conecta pero offictempos ut aspit dolut aut maionse catur?

TOUR INFO

Duration: 2 Weeks

Cost per person: $5000 (based upon double occupancy)

Departure Dates: March 10, June 15, September 24.

FIGURE 10.21 Tables used to create shaded paragraphs, info boxes (a one-column, two-row table), and movie credits where a double baseline is arranged against a single baseline.

Bulleted and Numbered lists

Bulleted and numbered lists are formatted with automated hanging indents with either a bullet character or a number as the first (hanging) character. A character style can be applied automatically to the bullet or number to change its color, size, or baseline position. This formatting can be included in a paragraph style definition.

To apply either a bulleted or a numbered list to selected text, Option-click (Alt-click) the Bullets And Numbering icon (▤) on the Paragraph Formats level of the Control Panel, and then choose the list type, the bullet or numbering style, and the alignment. As always, select Preview to see how your changes affect the selection. Select a character style to be automatically applied to the bullet or number; if you don't have one already made, choose New Character Style and make one on the fly. Once you're satisfied with the bulleted or numbered list, click OK, then capture the formatting in a paragraph style by choosing New Paragraph Style from the Paragraph Styles panel menu. (For more on paragraph and character styles see Chapter 12.)

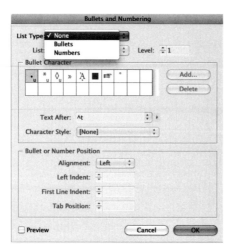

FIGURE 10.22 The Bullets And Numbering dialog box, where you specify the numbering or bullet style as well as the list's alignment and amount of indent.

Bulleted Lists

Solomon Grundy...

- Born on a Monday
- Christened on Tuesday
- Married on Wednesday
- Took ill on Thursday
- Grew worse on Friday
- Died on Saturday
- Buried on Sunday

That was the end of Solomon Grundy.

FIGURE 10.23 A bulleted list with a half-line space before the first and after the last bullet item.

Here are some things to consider when making bulleted lists:

- Sometimes, especially if your bullet character is a different font, the bullet may not vertically align perfectly. If necessary, adjust the baseline shift for the character style that is applied to the bullet. If the items begin with a cap, center the bullet vertically within the cap height. If the items begin with lowercase characters, center the bullets within the x-height.

- An em space is usually a sufficient amount of indent.

- Keep the punctuation to a minimum while adhering to the house style. Unless the bullet point is a full sentence, don't end it with a period.

- Add space before the first and after the last item in the list. A full line space is too much, so use a half-line space before and after. Once you have made a bullet paragraph style, make two variants based on it: bullet_first that has a half-line space before, and bullet_last that has a half-line space after. A caveat here is that if you're working with a baseline grid that is a full leading increment, the grid will override the paragraph spacing, effectively giving a whole line space before or after. For this reason, make sure that the bullet_first and bullet_last paragraphs are not aligned to the grid.

- Even if your body text is justified, bulleted lists work better left aligned.

- Indenting the text after the bullet means you lose the strong flush-left alignment of your text. For this reason, some people prefer outdenting the bullet to strengthen the left axis of the text. This requires indenting the body text by the same amount that you indent the bullet.

When working with long item lists, it can be a much more efficient and aesthetic use of space to split the list within a single column of text. To do this, select the text and choose the Split widget from the Control panel; alternatively, you can incorporate the instruction to split across a specified number of columns as part of the paragraph style definition. Note that split columns cause havoc with your Keep Options, especially if some of the paragraphs run to multiple lines.

Numbered Lists

The same considerations apply to numbered lists. Applying autonumbering is pretty self-explanatory: Instead of a bulleted list, choose a numbered list and then select the style of numbering, the character style you want applied to the number, and the alignment, and you're done. There are, however, a couple of aspects of working with numbered lists that can cause frustration: right- or decimal-aligning numbers in lists that have single- and double-digit numbers, and managing the numbering of lists across unthreaded text frames.

Right-aligning numbers: Set the Alignment drop-down menu to Right to align the numbers to the rightmost character or decimal point. Because InDesign doesn't allow text to hang outside the frame, this won't work unless you also increase the left indent, decrease the first-line indent, or both, to move the text to the left and create enough space for the numbers to fit to the left of the text.

If you plan to export the InDesign story to an RTF file, you'll need to convert the automatic numbers (or bullets) to text, otherwise they'll be stripped out of the converted document. Select the list and choose Type > Bulleted And Numbered Lists > Convert Numbering To Text. You will now be able to select

Lorem ipsum dolor sit amet, consectetur adipiscing elit.

- maecenas lacus libero, sagittis ac sollicitudin id, tempor nec arcu
- aliquam convallis feugiat quam vel sodales
- vestibulum hendrerit pulvinar leo id sollicitudin

Integer adipiscing, risus vitae vehicula dapibus.

FIGURE 10.24 Outdenting the bullet character maintains the flush-left alignment of the text.

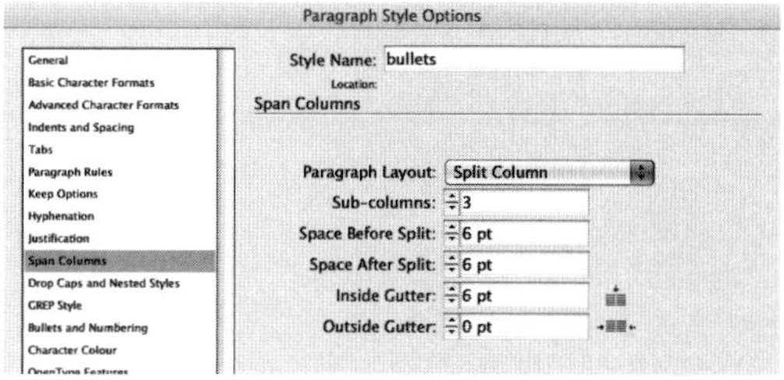

FIGURE 10.25 Splitting bulleted list items into three columns using Split columns.

Professional cameras and video/audio equipment are strictly prohibited. Live video/audio recordings made without the permission of the artiste/promoter are prohibited.

Not allowed through the campsite gates

- Glass
- Illegal substances
- Portable Laser Equipment and Pens

- Unauthorised Professional Film or Video Equipment
- Audio Recorders
- Spray Cans

- Fireworks
- Flares
- Animals (other than registered guide or hearing dogs)

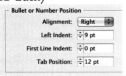

the numbers or bullets, and they will survive intact when you export the story; the numbers will no longer be "live," however.

Numbering across frames: You can have numbered lists continue across unthreaded frames from frame to frame, from page to page, or even across documents if those documents are collected as a Book. The most obvious use of this is a figure caption.

In order to do this, you'll need to make a list style. Numbered lists have the [Default] list style applied to them, which doesn't allow numbering across unthreaded text frames.

FIGURE 10.26 Right-aligning the numbers in a list that combines one- and two-digit numbers.

Create a new list style and apply that style to the paragraphs you want to sequentially number. In the Bullets And Numbering dialog box, choose New from the List drop-down menu, name the style, and select Continue Numbers Across Stories.

Apply this list style to paragraphs you want to autonumber across frames. Even better, incorporate the list style into a paragraph style. Set it up correctly once, use it an infinite number of times thereafter. See Chapter 12 for more on using paragraph styles.

FIGURE 10.27 Choosing a list style to ensure numbering across unthreaded stories.

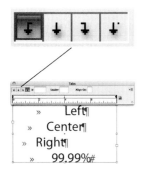

FIGURE 10.28 The different types of tab character.

Tabs

Tabs are used for positioning text at specified positions on a line. Tabs are automatically incorporated into bulleted or numbered lists, but they can also be added manually to create reply forms, to align numbers on a decimal point, or to separate columns of information into a table-like layout. Tabs come in four flavors: left, center, right, and decimal.

Setting Tabs

1. Insert your Type cursor where you want to add horizontal space, and press the Tab key.

2. Choose Type > Tabs or press Cmd+Shift+T (Ctrl+Shift+T). With your Type cursor in the text frame, click the magnet symbol at the lower right of the Tab Ruler to snap the Tab Ruler above the text frame.

3. On the Tab Ruler, choose the type of tab you want and click a location on the ruler to position the tab.

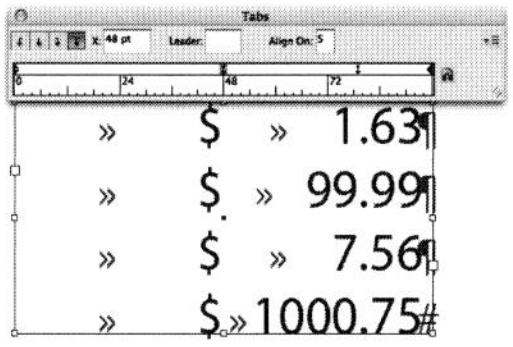

FIGURE 10.29 Typically, decimal tabs align on a decimal point, but they can align on any character.

Creating Decimal Tabs

A decimal tab aligns characters on a decimal or another character you specify. Place the tabs in your text. Select a decimal tab on the Tab Ruler, then, in the Align On box, type the character you want to align on—typically a decimal point, but you can use anything, such as a dollar sign or pound sign when working with price lists.

Using Tab Leaders

Tab leaders are used on menus, price lists, and tables of contents. Their purpose is to guide the eye from one piece of text to the next. There are other solutions, arguably preferable, but so long as the distance between the text and the number isn't too wide, leaders can be effective.

For open leaders, add a space after the period in the Leader Character field. For more control over the appearance of the leader characters, apply a character style to the leader dots.

Leader characters don't necessarily need to be dots. Using the underscore as the leader character is a way to create a simple line that's useful in reply forms.

FIGURE 10.30 Four instances of using a tab leader: On the left, the underscore character is used; on the right, a full stop (period). In the lower example of the address form, a character style with an underline is used instead of a leader character, allowing more control over the weight of the rule. In the lower example of the menu, the leader character is a full stop followed by a space.

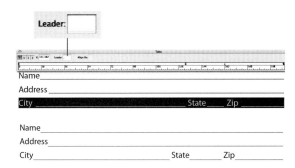

Wild Mushroom Roulade Marinated seitan, wild mushroom ragout, truffled mashed potatoes and celery root wrapped in yuba and baked in a crisp phyllo dough. Served with grilled pears and a porter porcini mushroom sauce $16.50

Portobello Potato Salad Breaded portobello mushrooms, pan sautèed and served over a warm gold and purple potato salad with cucumbers, tomatoes, Mandarin oranges, French lentils, mint, and winter greens $13.95

NOTE: You can set repeating tabs based on the distance between the tab and the left indent or the previous tab stop by choosing Repeat Tab in the Tabs panel menu. You can also delete any existing tabs by choosing Clear All.

Tabs in Tables

When you're working in a table, pressing Tab moves your cursor to the next cell. If you want to insert a tab in a cell, choose Type > Insert Special Character > Other > Tab. (On the Mac, you can also press Option+Tab.) That's a long way to go every time you want a tab in a table; if this is something you find yourself doing a lot, then it's worth making your own keyboard shortcut (Edit > Keyboard Shortcuts), or, once you've inserted one tab, copy and paste it for the subsequent instances.

Right-Indent Tab

A right-aligned tab (Shift-Tab) allows you to align all subsequent text to the right edge of the text frame. You can also use a Right-Indent Tab with a tab leader: Set a tab stop anywhere in the paragraph and apply a leader character to it. Place your cursor at the end of the paragraph and press Shift-Tab, and the leader character will appear.

FIGURE 10.31 The Right-Indent Tab (Shift-Tab) flushes the text to the right edge of the frame.

31 | Magazine Title   October 2010

Part of the reason for the ugliness of
adults, in a child's eyes, is that the
child is usually looking upwards, and
few faces are at their best when seen
from below.   — George Orwell

CHAPTER 11

Drop Caps

THE USE OF DECORATIVE FIRST LETTERS as a design element has evolved from a long tradition of illustrated first letters stretching back to before the invention of the printing press. Before printing, books were dictated to scribes, and each book was regarded as a unique treasure. The scribes incorporated individual flourishes to distinguish their work from others. It was with the decorative first letter that a scribe could really cut loose and show his stuff. Each major section usually began with an illuminated letter made with metallic, mineral, or vegetable pigments that were bound by glue or gum to the paper or parchment.

The purpose of the initial letter, or *versal*, was to call attention to the beginning of the book. By the 14th century, versals had evolved from enlarged heavy letters into elaborate illustrated works of art, most often used to decorate religious texts. An illuminated versal might flow down the whole side of a page, or extend up and around the top of the page. Sometimes a versal included illustrations and took over the entire page. In 1455, when Gutenberg printed his 42-line Bible—the first book to be printed in the western world with movable type—he acknowledged the importance of this tradition by leaving space in the printed text for a scribe to add a decorative first letter. As printing evolved, so did the forms of initial caps used by designers. The current variations include hung caps, several forms of dropped caps, and raised or stick-up caps. InDesign uses the term *drop cap* for all initial cap styling.

FIGURE 11.1 Two pages from the Gutenberg Bible (1455), the left showing an illuminated first character painted by a scribe, the right showing smaller initial characters in red to indicate new sections.

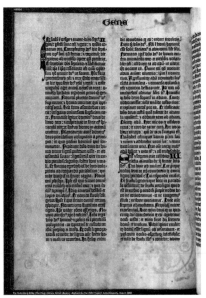

FIGURE 11.2 Some drop caps in contemporary magazines.

A THERE WAS NO POSSIBILITY of taking a walk that day. We had been wandering, indeed, in the leafless shrubbery an hour in the morning; but since dinner (Mrs. Reed, when there was no company, dined early) the cold winter wind had brought with it clouds so sombre, and a rain so penetrating, that further out-door exercise was now out

B THERE WAS NO POSSIBILITY of taking a walk that day. We had been wandering, indeed, in the leafless shrubbery an hour in the morning; but since dinner (Mrs. Reed, when there was no company, dined early) the cold winter wind had brought with it clouds so sombre, and a rain so penetrating, that further out-door exercise

C THERE WAS NO POSSIBILITY of taking a walk that day. We had been wandering, indeed, in the leafless shrubbery an hour in the morning; but since dinner (Mrs. Reed, when there was no company, dined early) the cold winter wind had brought with it clouds so sombre, and a rain so

D THERE WAS NO possibility of taking a walk that day. We had been wandering, indeed, in the leafless shrubbery an hour in the morning; but since dinner (Mrs. Reed, when there was no company, dined early) the cold winter wind had brought with it clouds so sombre, and a rain so penetrating, that further out-door exercise

E THERE WAS NO POSSIBILITY of taking a walk that day. We had been wandering, indeed, in the leafless shrubbery an hour in the morning; but since dinner (Mrs. Reed, when there was no company, dined early) the cold winter wind had brought with it clouds so sombre, and a rain so

F THERE WAS NO POSSIBILITY of taking a walk that day. We had been wandering, indeed, in the leafless shrubbery an hour in the morning; but since dinner (Mrs. Reed, when there was no company, dined early) the cold winter wind had brought with it clouds so sombre, and a rain so penetrating, that further out-door exercise

FIGURE 11.3 Drop and initial cap examples: (**A**) This three-line drop cap is followed by small caps applied to the first four words. (**B**) The size of the drop cap is increased to create a drop cap/stick-up cap hybrid. (**C**) This is a simple stick-up cap. (**D**) Here, a stick-up cap is combined with a large first-line indent. (**E**) The drop cap is cut and pasted into a separate text frame that is anchored to the main text frame, floating in the outside margin, and "molded" around the shape of the text frame. (**F**) The drop cap is cut and pasted into its own text frame, which is anchored in the main text frame. A text wrap is applied to the drop cap text frame.

Creating a Simple Drop Cap

Contemporary magazine and book publishing continues this centuries-old tradition by beginning chapters and articles with large initial letters. The treatment can be incorporated into a paragraph style or applied locally through the Control Panel.

FIGURE 11.4 Using the Control Panel to apply a simple drop cap. Note that Optical Margin Alignment is turned on in the Story panel, allowing the crossbar of the T to stick out into the left margin.

T he Nellie, a cruising yawl, swung to her anchor without a flutter of the sails, and was at rest. The flood had made, the wind was nearly calm, and being bound down the river, the only thing for it was to come to and wait for the turn of the tide.

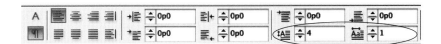

To create a drop cap, insert your Type cursor into the paragraph and type the number of lines for the drop cap in the Control Panel, then specify the number of drop cap characters you want—usually one, but this isn't always the case.

For more options, choose Drop Caps And Nested Styles from the Control Panel menu. In this dialog you can align the left edge of the drop cap to the left edge of the text frame, as well as scale drop caps with descenders to avoid collisions between the descending part of the drop letter and the line that follows it.

Certain letters will not look optically aligned because the left sidebearing (the space incorporated into the letter's design) causes the letter to appear slightly indented. This can be addressed by selecting Align Left Edge in the Drop Caps And Nested Styles dialog.

If you plan to apply the same formatting to more than one paragraph in your document, it saves time (and ensures consistency) to incorporate the drop cap attributes into the style definition. The Drop Cap paragraph style is commonly based on your body text style with any first-line indent removed.

Choose New Paragraph Style from the Paragraph Styles panel. To edit an existing style, Ctrl/right-click on the style and choose Edit.

Name the new style; "first par" and "body first" are common naming conventions. If you have a "body" style, you may want to base your "body first" style on this. Choose "body" from the Based On: drop-down menu.

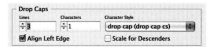

It was the best of times, it was the times, it was the age of wisdom, it w of foolishness, it was the epoch of b the epoch of incredulity, it was the sea: it was the season of Darkness, it was th

It was the best of times, it was the w it was the age of wisdom, it was the : ishness, it was the epoch of belief, it of incredulity, it was the season of Ligh season of Darkness, it was the spring c

Align Left Edge

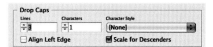

Jellorrum quia secea qui con cones conemolor amusdae con renimus s ventiberum consequi di nimi, te ve a qui dolut essi dion repellantio ipiend mostios andaesenimos et voluptatia dit

Jellorrum quia secea qui con cones : conemolor amusdae con renimus s ventiberum consequi di nimi, te ve a qui dolut essi dion repellantio ipiend mostios andaesenimos et voluptatia dit

Scale for Descenders

FIGURE 11.5 Making optical adjustments according to the character shape and style of the drop cap.

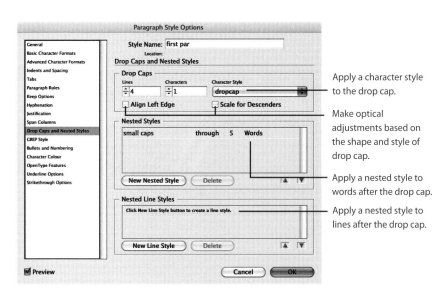

FIGURE 11.6 Incorporating a drop cap into a paragraph style definition.

Choose Drop Caps And Nested Styles from the list in the left column. Specify the number of lines to sink the first character and the number of characters that you want to include.

You can use the Character Style drop-down menu to apply an existing character style to the drop cap, or you can choose New Character Style to make and apply a character style.

Drop Cap Aesthetics

There are no hard-and-fast rules concerning how big a drop cap should be, but common sense should prevail. Size matters, although in this context bigger isn't always better. The purpose of the drop cap is to signal to the reader where to begin. To do so, the drop cap doesn't need to scream at the reader and shouldn't overwhelm any headline that precedes it. The drop cap comes below the headline in terms of page hierarchy; usually, though not always, it will be smaller than the headline. Also, don't repeat the letter that you use as the drop cap at the beginning of the text.

In addition to the initial drop cap for the first paragraph of a chapter or article, it's common practice to use smaller drop caps as section markers (set up as a style based on the parent drop cap style). This is visually effective to break up the monotony of columns of type, and it's necessary if the text doesn't have illustrations, subheads, or other graphic elements. That said, if you sprinkle drop caps too liberally throughout a document, they cease to be elegant and functional graphic devices and start to become repetitive and annoying. Don't use more than two drop caps per page. Paragraphs that get drop-cap treatment should not be close to each other on a page, and preferably the drop caps should be different letters.

FIGURE 11.7 Kerning a drop cap. The example on the left shows the result of applying a three-line drop cap in Adobe Garamond Pro. The serif of the W collides with the "h." Insert the type cursor between the two letters and press Option+Right Arrow (Alt+Right Arrow) to kern the space between the W and the "h" (right).

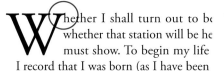

Whether I shall turn out to be whether that station will be held must show. To begin my life I record that I was born (as I have been

Whether I shall turn out to whether that station will be must show. To begin my life I record that I was born (as I have bee

Kerning Drop Caps

A problem with automatically generated drop caps is that the big first character often collides with the body text that follows. You may need to kern to avoid such problems. Note that when you kern between the drop cap and the first character of the text, kerning is applied to all the lines adjacent to the drop cap.

With a decorative letter, selecting Align Left may not be sufficient to optically align the drop cap. In addition, you'll want to kern the drop cap to the left margin. To do this you'll first need to add a space before the drop cap. Note that adding a space will mean you have to drop two characters instead of one—if you see yourself likely to do this more than once, make a paragraph style with this specification. You can then insert your cursor between the space and the

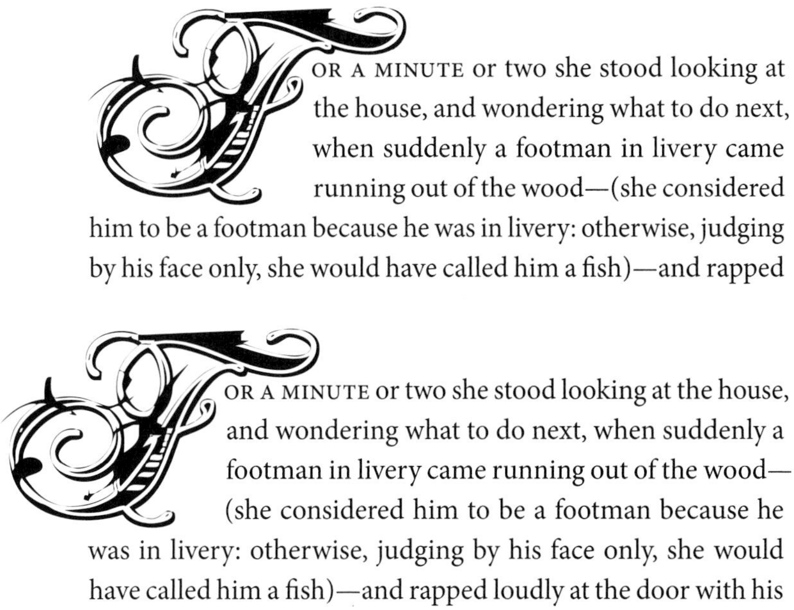

OR A MINUTE or two she stood looking at the house, and wondering what to do next, when suddenly a footman in livery came running out of the wood—(she considered him to be a footman because he was in livery: otherwise, judging by his face only, she would have called him a fish)—and rapped

OR A MINUTE or two she stood looking at the house, and wondering what to do next, when suddenly a footman in livery came running out of the wood—(she considered him to be a footman because he was in livery: otherwise, judging by his face only, she would have called him a fish)—and rapped loudly at the door with his

FIGURE 11.8 When working with highly decorative drop caps, the Align Left Edge and Scale For Descenders options may not be sufficient for the optical spacing of the opening letter, as you can see in the top example. In the bottom example, a thin space (Cmd+Shift+Option+M/Ctrl+Shift+Alt+M) was added before the dropped letter, and this space was then kerned back, which moved the F into the left margin.

drop cap and kern by pressing Option+Left Arrow (Alt+Left Arrow) until the character is optically aligned with the left margin edge. Instead of using a regular space, however, you can add a thin space by pressing Cmd+Shift+Option+M (Ctrl+Shift+Alt+M)—if you do that, you won't have to kern as much.

Creating a Picture Drop Cap

Converting a drop cap to outlines —by selecting Type > Create Outlines or pressing Cmd+Shift+O (Ctrl+Shift+O)—allows you to place an image into the letter shape. It's a compelling idea, but unless the drop cap is very large and in an extra-bold typeface, there's unlikely to be enough space within the letter shape for the image to be visible. There's also the danger of visually disassociating the drop cap so that the reader scans the first line without the first letter.

Creating a Contoured Drop Cap

Putting your drop cap character in its own text frame allows you to contour the text to the shape of the drop cap. Apply a text wrap to the drop cap text frame, then use the Direct Selection tool to sculpt the text wrap outline to conform to the shape of the letter. Make sure that the space around the drop cap is optically the same on the right side as it is beneath the drop cap.

FIGURE 11.9 Using the first letter as a picture frame: an almost irresistible idea that seldom works well. The "window" onto the picture is rarely big enough for the picture to be clearly visible.

RIGHTON IS CONSIDERED to be one of the UK's premier night-life hotspots and is also associated with many popular music artists. There are also live music venues including the Concorde 2, Brighton Centre and the Brighton Dome, where ABBA received a substantial boost to their career when they won

FIGURE 11.10 A contoured drop cap. The W is in its own text frame, and a text wrap is applied and then adjusted to correspond to the letter shape.

Whether I shall turn out to be the hero of my own life, or whether that station will be held by anybody else, these pages must show. To begin my life with the beginning of my life, I record that I was born (as I have been informed and believe)

Adding Small Caps

An often-used device to create a visual bridge between drop cap and body text is to put the words following the drop cap in small caps. This creates a transition from the large decorative character into the upper- and lowercase text so that the drop cap does not look like an isolated graphic. Just how many characters are put into small caps is a matter for discretion—it may be just the first word, the first phrase, a specified number of words, or the first line. Whatever you choose, be consistent throughout the publication.

It's possible to use a nested style to specify character-level formatting for one or more ranges of text within a paragraph. For a drop cap character with a different color or font (or both) than the rest of the paragraph, define a character style with these attributes, then nest that character style within the paragraph style. Thereafter, you can apply all the formatting with a single click.

FIGURE 11.11 Small caps applied to five words to ease the transition from the big first character to the upper- and lowercase body text. To apply the small caps to a whole line, create a nested line style.

IT WAS THE BEST OF times, it was the worst of times, it was the age of wisdom, it was the age of foolishness, it was the epoch of belief, it was the epoch of incredulity, it was the season of Light, it was the season of Darkness, it was the spring of hope, it was the winter of despair, we had everything before us, we had nothing before us, we were all going direct to Heaven, we were all going direct the other way—in

*C*ALL ME ISHMAEL. SOME YEARS AGO — NEVER MIND HOW long precisely—having little or no money in my purse, and nothing particular to interest me on shore, I thought I would sail about a little and see the watery part of the world. It is a way I have of driving off the spleen and regulating the

FIGURE 11.12 Combining nested styles with Drop Caps to transform raw text. With a single click, in addition to the paragraph and character attributes, a Character Style is applied to the drop cap and a Line Style applied the first line of the paragraph.

Creating Nested Small Caps

1. Create a small caps character style. If you are using an OpenType font, choose OpenType All Small Caps from the Case drop-down menu to keep the case of your small cap range consistent without having to rekey any initial caps as lowercase letters.

2. To "nest" the small caps character style in the paragraph style, Ctrl-click or right-click the paragraph style in the Paragraph Styles panel and choose Edit to open the Paragraph Style Options panel, then choose Drop Caps And Nested Styles from the lefthand column.

3. Click New Nested Style and specify the number of words to apply the nested style to. If you haven't already styled the type, you can create a new character style by clicking [None] in the window and selecting New Character Style from the drop-down menu. Note that the drop-down menu option appears only after you have selected the various options in the window.

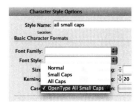

FIGURE 11.13 If available, choose OpenType All Small Caps when creating a small caps character style.

To automate the application of small caps to the entire line, create a new line style.

Other Uses of Drop Caps

Drop caps can have uses beyond the obvious. Here are a few examples of other ways in which drop caps can be applied.

FIGURE 11.14 Drop caps used for question and answer section (**A**), step-by-step instructional text (**B**) and for page numbers (**C**) in a table of contents.

Q **What's the difference between Optical and Metrics kerning?**

Metrics kerning uses a font's built-in kerning information. Its effectiveness depends on how many kerning pairs are in the font. Optical kerning ignores the built-in kerning pairs and adjusts the space between the characters based upon the character shapes.

Q **How do I prevent certain text frames from being affected by a text wrap?**

Select the text frame then Choose Object > Text Frame Options (Cmd+B/ Ctrl+B), then check Ignore Text Wrap.

A

1 Insert your Type tool into the paragraph you want to affect.

2 In the Control Palette Paragraph Formats type a number for Drop Cap Number of Lines.

3 Type the number of drop cap characters you want (usually 1) in the Drop Cap One or More Characters field.

B

27 Hilary, Cate and friends dazzle at the Oscars and BAFTAs

37 Style file: Get in line for the designer's pattern of choice

C

45 We've shopped around to find you all the biggest trends

60 How to outshine everyone in the season's best occasionwea

Difficult Drop Caps

Drop caps are just one way of kicking off a paragraph; they're not always the best solution. If you have the occasional opening paragraph that needs customizing, no big deal—so long as it's an exception. If you find yourself fussing over every chapter or article opening, then use another type of opening device—an initial cap, perhaps—or simply remove the first line indent and add a paragraph space before the section or chapter opening text.

Before you decide on a particular opening device, familiarize yourself with the material. Here are some instances when drop and initial caps don't work well:

- When the first character of the paragraph is a number.

- When an opening paragraph begins with a quotation mark. You will need to drop both the opening quotation mark and the initial cap. The opening quote mark will probably look disproportionately large. You'll want to reduce its size, adjust its vertical position by applying a baseline shift, and kern the space between it and the drop cap that follows it. Exact amounts will vary according to the nature of the font, so there's subjectivity involved here. You should also hang the opening quote mark.

- When opening paragraphs can't accommodate the drop cap's depth. Trying to sink a cap three lines into a one-line paragraph can create some visual confusion, although InDesign does an excellent job of coping with that by allowing the next paragraph to come up. However, if you find that you are repeatedly using a three-line drop cap on paragraphs that are only two lines deep, then you might consider using a raised cap instead.

Curiouser and curiouser!' cried Alice (she was so much surprised, that for the moment she quite forgot how to speak good English); 'now I'm opening out like the largest telescope that ever was! Good-bye, feet!' (for when she looked down at her feet, they seemed to be almost out of sight, they were getting so far off). 'Oh, my poor little feet, I wonder who will put on your

Curiouser and curiouser!' cried Alice (she was so much surprised, that for the moment she quite forgot how to speak good English); 'now I'm opening out like the largest telescope that ever was! Good-bye, feet!' (for when she looked down at her feet, they seemed to be almost out of sight, they were getting so far off). 'Oh, my poor little feet, I wonder who will put on your

FIGURE 11.15 Because this paragraph begins with a quotation, the quote mark is dropped instead of the initial cap (top). To drop the initial cap as well, as shown in the bottom example, select 2 for the number of dropped characters. Reduce the size of the punctuation and adjust its vertical position by applying a baseline shift. Finally, kern the space between the punctuation and the C.

■ When your articles or chapters begin with poetry, song lyrics, or other quoted material. To apply the drop cap here would add an extra (and unnecessary) level of decoration, possibly confusing the reader. You could use the drop cap after such a passage, but it is no longer signaling the beginning of the chapter, article, or section, and so is extraneous and can tend to look fussy as a result.

FIGURE 11.16 InDesign copes elegantly with short opening paragraphs, bringing the second paragraph up next to the drop cap and maintaining its first-line indent. If you find yourself making many such "exceptions," you probably need an opening device other than a drop cap.

W INSTON was dreaming of his mother.

He must, he thought, have been ten or eleven years old when his mother had disappeared. She was a tall, statuesque, rather silent woman with slow movements and magnificent fair hair. His father he remembered more vaguely as

CHAPTER 12

Global Formatting with Styles

STYLES HAVE BEEN AROUND since the dawn of desktop publishing, continually evolving in their ease of use and range of capabilities. A bedrock feature of any page layout program, styles enable better design and more efficient workflow. No matter how good your conceptual grasp of typography, it won't amount to much unless you can apply type formatting consistently and efficiently using styles.

Defining Our Terms

Paragraph and character styles are collections of attributes that can be applied to text with a single click. Paragraph styles can incorporate both character *and* paragraph formats—font, font size, alignment, paragraph spacing, color, you name it. Character styles can incorporate character formats only. As the name suggests, paragraph styles are applied to whole paragraphs; character styles are applied to a *selected range of text* within a paragraph.

Object styles are applied to frames—text frames or picture frames—and can include such attributes as fill color, stroke color and weight, text frame options, picture fitting options, and many more.

Table and cell styles are applied to tables. Table styles cover the attributes of the overall table, such as whether it has a border or uses row or column strokes. Cell styles refer to the attributes of the individual cells—like text insets—that make up a table.

Where things get more complicated, more interesting, and exponentially more powerful is when you nest character styles within paragraph styles, which in turn can be incorporated into object styles. Add into the mix GREP styles (which automatically apply character styles to predefined ranges of text within paragraph styles) and sequential styles (which let you apply styles to a cascade of paragraphs), and the possibilities are mind boggling.

Collectively, I will refer to the paragraph, character, and object styles in a document as a style sheet.

Why Use Styles?

The difference between using styles and not using styles is the difference between you controlling InDesign and InDesign controlling you. Here are some reasons to use styles:

- Styles ensure consistency in formatting throughout your document, making for a better-designed piece.

- Styles enable you to instantly change the formatting of your entire document, no matter how large or complex, by changing your style definitions.

- And the best reason of all: Styles save you hours and hours of drudgery.

Despite these irrefutable facts, many designers either underutilize styles or avoid them altogether. I'm frequently amazed by the number of designers—many of whom should know better—who don't use styles or who use them in a half-assed way. What's up with you people? Do you like the grind of repetitive work? Are you masochists? Or perhaps you're paid by the hour.

I've had designers tell me "I don't like to use styles because I like to experiment with different designs" or "I don't want my pages to all look the same." These are exactly the reasons you *should* use styles. Far from stifling creativity, styles enhance it by making experimentation quick and easy. And just because your style names may be the same or similar from one document to the next, that doesn't mean the style definitions can't be completely different.

[Basic Paragraph]

The best advice I can give about [Basic Paragraph] is to ignore it—if you have different definitions for [Basic Paragraph] in your documents, when you copy text from one document to another you can get some nasty surprises. By default the [Basic Paragraph] style is applied to text you type. You can't rename or delete this style, but you can edit it and choose [Edit Basic Paragraph] to bring up the Paragraph Style Options panel where you can change the properties of the style. Alternatively, you can designate a different style to be the default: Simply choose that style when you have no text or text frame selected.

Creating Styles

Time spent creating style sheets is an investment that will repay you many times over throughout the lifespan of a publication. You can set up your styles at the beginning of the design process or add and edit your styles as your document evolves. If you're like me, a style sheet is never finished but is always refined and improved.

Creating the Style "Blind"

Using the Paragraph Style Options panel, you can create as many styles as you need without having a single character on your page. With experience, you can visualize what a style will look like without needing to see it realized on your page, which makes setting up a style sheet much faster.

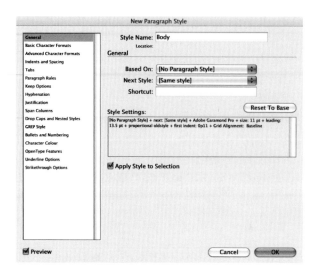

FIGURE 12.1 The New Paragraph Style menu incorporates all the character and paragraph formats available on the Control Panel.

Basing Styles on Other Styles

Hierarchy is a big concept in typography. Hierarchy gives a document structure and aids effective communication. The Based On option is important for establishing hierarchy in your styles. Typically, though not exclusively, hierarchy is established through size. Take a simple example: Your headings and subheadings will probably use the same font: Head1 will be bigger than Head2, which in turn will be bigger than Head3. By basing one style on another, you create more than just a visual link between the styles; when you edit the base or "parent" style, the attributes that it shares with its "offspring" styles also change. This lets you effect changes across a range of styles with just a single edit to the parent style. For example, if you want to switch the font of your heads from Helvetica to Univers, change Head1 (the parent style) and all the styles that are based on it will change too (except for attributes like the font size, which are unique to the individual styles).

Using the Based On option to create related styles and establish hierarchy

1. Adjust the Character and Paragraph settings on the Control Panel to format the paragraph the way you want it to look.

2. With your cursor in the newly styled paragraph, open the Paragraph Styles panel and choose New Paragraph Style from the menu. The Style Settings window will reflect your choices.

3. Name the style and (optionally) specify a shortcut keystroke. If you want to add additional formatting, click the attributes list on the left and specify the options you want to add to your style. With Preview selected, you can see your formatting changes added to the selected paragraph. To apply your new style to the text you are basing the style on, select Apply Style To Selection.

4. Click OK.

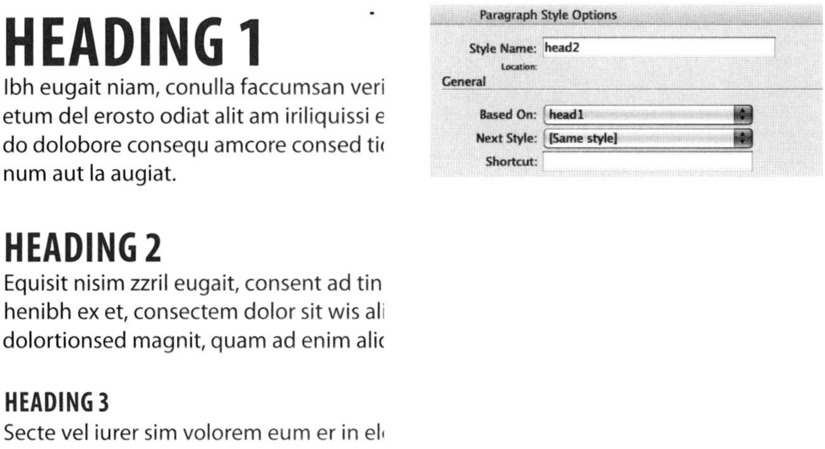

HEADING 1

Ibh eugait niam, conulla faccumsan veri etum del erosto odiat alit am iriliquissi e do dolobore consequ amcore consed tic num aut la augiat.

HEADING 2

Equisit nisim zzril eugait, consent ad tin henibh ex et, consectem dolor sit wis ali dolortionsed magnit, quam ad enim alic

HEADING 3

Secte vel iurer sim volorem eum er in eli

Paragraph Style Options

Style Name: head2

Location:

General

Based On: head1

Next Style: [Same style]

Shortcut:

FIGURE 12.2 Basing styles on a parent style (in this case, Head3 on Head2, Head2 on Head1) means you can edit the parent style to set off a domino effect that causes all the styles based upon it to change.

Applying Styles

When you select text or click an insertion point, the style that was applied to that text is highlighted in the Paragraph Styles panel, the Character Styles panel, or both. If you select a range of text covering multiple styles, no style is highlighted (the word *Mixed* appears at the top of the appropriate panel).

To apply a paragraph style, place your Type Tool cursor anywhere inside the paragraph—there's no need to select the whole paragraph—then click the style name in the Paragraph Styles panel. To apply a paragraph style to more than one contiguous paragraph, drag your cursor through those paragraphs. Again, you don't need to select the whole paragraph; you just need to make contact with at least part of each of the paragraphs.

Applying a paragraph style doesn't remove any existing character formatting or character styles applied to that paragraph—unless you clear any overrides (see the next section). When you apply a style, if the text has additional formatting that is not part of the style definition, a plus sign (+) appears next to the current paragraph style in the Paragraph Styles panel.

Assign a keyboard shortcut to your styles and you'll be able to apply them even faster. To add a shortcut, open the Paragraph Styles panel, turn on Num Lock, and then hold down a combination of Shift, Option/Alt, and Cmd/Ctrl and add a keypad number. Two caveats: letters and non-keypad numbers will not work; your keyboard must have a Num Lock key and a numeric keyboard. Unfortunately, you can't use function keys as shortcuts for style names.

For text-heavy documents it may be quicker to apply styles in the Story Editor (with or without shortcuts) simply because you can scroll through long passages of text faster than in Layout view.

FIGURE 12.3 It can sometimes be quicker to apply styles in the Story Editor, without the distraction of graphics and column breaks.

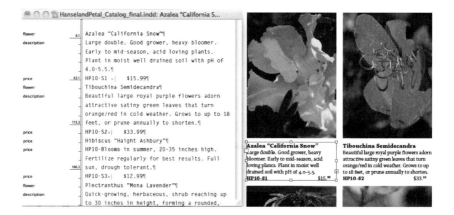

Clearing Overrides

When you add formatting to text that already has a paragraph or character style applied, you are overriding the style definition. To put it another way: You've defined a paragraph style, applied it to a piece of text, and then contradicted your style definition by adding additional formatting. You can tell which text has overrides applied because when it's selected a plus sign (+) appears next to the style name. Hover the cursor over the style name in the Paragraph Styles panel and a tool tip pops up with details of the local formatting.

Maybe this local formatting is what you want, maybe not. Maybe you've inherited the document from someone else—someone who hasn't used styles as effectively as you would have liked—and you want to clear the overrides.

There are several ways to approach this:

- To clear all local formatting, but retain any character styles applied to the paragraph, Option/Alt-click the style name in the Paragraph Styles panel. Alternatively, click the Clear Overrides button in the Control Panel.

- To remove only the local character formatting (retaining any local paragraph formatting), Cmd/Ctrl-click the Overrides button (the Paragraph icon) at the bottom of the Paragraph Styles panel.

- To remove only the local paragraph formatting (retaining the character formatting), Cmd+Shift+click (Ctrl+Shift+click) the Clear Overrides button.

- To clear all local formatting *and* character styles: Option+Shift+click (Alt+Shift+click) the style name in the Paragraph Styles panel.

We hold these truths to be self-evident, that all men are created equal, that they are endowed by their Creator with certain unalienable Rights, that among these are Life, Liberty and the pursuit of Happiness.

Base Paragraph

We hold these truths to be self-evident, that all men are created equal, that they are endowed by their Creator with certain unalienable *Rights,* that among these are **Life, Liberty** and the pursuit of **Happiness**.

Override

FIGURE 12.4 On the left, the base paragraph; on the right, local overrides are circled. The blue emphasis is applied as a character style and is thus not considered an override.

Quick Apply

When you have many styles, you might need to scroll through long lists and manage three different panels to get to the style you're after. To dramatically speed up your workflow, use Quick Apply to find a style by typing the first few characters of its name. Here's how:

1. Select the text or frame to which you want to apply the style and press Cmd+Return (Ctrl+Enter) to bring up the Quick Apply panel.

2. Start typing the name of the style, and you'll be taken to the closest match.

3. Use the Up Arrow and Down Arrow keys on the keyboard to move through the list.

4. Press Return/Enter to apply the style.

Quick Apply will remember the style you just used, so if you want to use a style that you just applied, press Return/Enter to apply it.

To clear overrides while using Quick Apply, employ the same keyboard shortcut listed under Clearing Overrides. For example, to apply a style using Quick Apply *and* clear local formatting at the same time, press Cmd+Return (Ctrl+Enter) and then press Option/Alt as you click the style name.

Editing Styles

The beauty of styles is that you can change their definitions at any time. Changing a style definition means that all the text formatted with that style changes to match the new style definition. This has been a staple feature of all page layout programs since the Stone Age.

Styles allow you unprecedented flexibility in experimenting with the appearance of your document. A few simple clicks and you can totally transform the appearance of your pages. It's a beautiful thing.

The safest way to edit a style is to Ctrl-click (right-click) the style name in the appropriate Styles panel and choose Edit from the menu. That way, there's no danger of inadvertently applying the style where you don't want it.

Once you're in the Styles Options dialog box, make as many or as few changes as you want, click OK, and Bob's your uncle. If you're feeling cautious, duplicate the style first (just drag the style name onto the Create New Style icon at the bottom of the panel).

Redefining Styles

Instead of editing the style, you can modify a paragraph with local overrides, decide that's how you'd like the style to look, and then redefine the style based on the modified paragraph: Just select the paragraph, open Paragraph Styles, Right/Alt-click the style name, and choose Redefine Style from the menu.

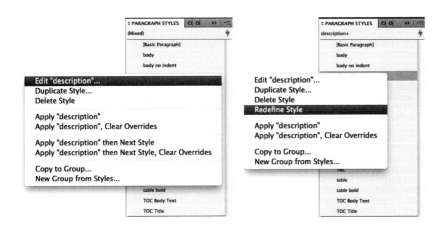

FIGURE 12.6 Ctrl-click (right-click) the style name to edit the style or, if the text is selected with the Type Tool cursor, to redefine the style so that it incorporates the overrides.

Loading Styles from Another Document

You will be at your most efficient in InDesign when you spend the time to create a robust yet flexible set of styles (a style sheet), then reuse and repurpose it many times. Every publication, be it the *National Enquirer* or the *New York Times*, follows a similar structure: heads of different levels of hierarchy, subheads, captions, callouts or pull quotes, and several closely related variants of body text. When you initially set up paragraph styles, it is more important to establish the relationship between these styles—that is, which styles are based on (and thus inherit their properties from) other styles—than what the styles actually look like. Once the relationships have been established, a change to a "parent" style can ripple through to all other styles that are based on it. With such a style sheet, you can effect a dramatic transformation in the appearance of the document in just a handful of moves.

Once you have established styles in one document, you can reuse and repurpose those styles (or a subset of them) in any other document. The same is also true of master pages and the color swatches that influence certain styles. Choose Load Paragraph Styles (or Load All Text Styles if you also want to load character styles), navigate to the document containing the styles you wish to import, and then click Open. You can import specific styles and determine how to deal with any style-name conflicts: Where the style name is the same in both documents, you can choose to use the incoming style definition or to rename the incoming style, which will have "copy" appended to its style name. (You can later rename the style if you wish.)

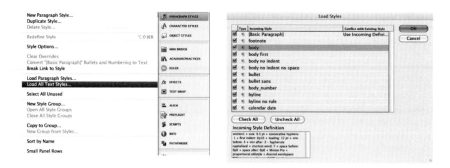

FIGURE 12.7 Choosing Load All Text Styles from the Paragraph Styles or Character Styles panel menu allows you to import styles from another document.

Organizing Styles

A well-organized style sheet is a boon to productivity. Here are some tips and personal preferences.

NOTE: Style names are case sensitive; for example, Body Text and body text are two distinct styles. Be precise when naming your styles, or you may end up with two versions of a style and no idea which is the real one.

Naming: Keep in mind that you'll likely need to come back to a document months or even years down the road, so you'll want a style-naming strategy that is transparent. Alternatively, you may need to hand over your InDesign document to someone else to finish. So that you don't have to spend time explaining why you named your styles after your favorite Radiohead songs, keep them logical and follow established conventions: body, head, subhead, caption, and so on.

Sorting: When you choose Sort by Name from the Paragraph, Character, or Objects Styles panel menus, InDesign lists your styles in alphanumeric order. For this reason, you might consider putting a two-digit identifier in front of your most commonly used styles to force them to the top of the panel. Putting a unique two-character identifier at the beginning of your most frequently used styles—such as 01_head for a first level head—also makes it easier to access them using Quick Apply by typing those two characters to access the style.

Style Groups: These folders on the Styles panels allow you to group related styles together. This visually reinforces the relationship between those styles, but also allows you to more easily manage long lists of styles by hiding and disclosing the contents of the style groups as necessary. To create a style group, click the Style Group icon at the bottom of the style panel, name the group, and then drag styles into the folder. Alternatively, you can Shift-click to select the styles you want to group together (Cmd-click/Ctrl-click to make a noncontiguous selection), then choose New Group From Styles from the panel menu to place your selection in a new folder.

Small Panel Rows: This view option is accessed through the flyout menu and is useful if you have many styles (and good eyesight) and want to list more of them on the Styles panel.

Select All Unused: Throughout the lifecycle of a project you'll likely end up with several unwanted styles in your various styles panels. Leaving these around is apt to create confusion—either for you or for anyone else who may work on the document. You can get rid of them on a case-by-case basis, but the quickest way to zap them all at once is to choose Select All Unused from the menu in any of the Styles panels and then click the Delete icon at the bottom of the panel.

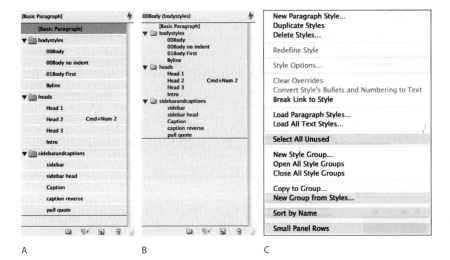

A   B   C

FIGURE 12.8 Organizing styles. Paragraph styles organized into style groups (**A**); the same Styles view as Small Panel Rows (**B**); some useful housekeeping options highlighted on the Paragraph Styles panel menu (**C**).

Creating Default Styles

If you create paragraph styles, character styles, or object styles (as well as color swatches) with no document open, those styles are available in every new document. There's a case to be made for creating a set of default styles so you're ready to go every time you create a new document. Just because the names are the same doesn't mean the styles have to look the same. Most documents have headlines, subheads, body text, captions, and so on. What you make them look like is entirely up to you. What's important is the hierarchy of the styles.

Make sure no InDesign document is open when you create your default styles or load them from an existing InDesign document. That way they'll show up in every InDesign document you create thereafter.

Combining Typefaces

Setting up paragraph styles involves choosing and combining typefaces—a skill that, like cooking, ultimately relies heavily upon intuition and experience. There are no definitive "right" ways to combine typefaces, but here are some factors to consider that will give you more confidence when making your choices.

Versatility

Choosing a typeface is a bit like choosing a pair of shoes. If you're planning to go to the beach, a pair of flip-flops may be all you need. But if you're going to the beach, then rock climbing, then out for dinner, you'll need footwear that's more versatile—likewise with a typeface.

A versatile typeface will have a range of weights — light, regular, semibold, bold, and so on — that allows you to indicate hierarchy of information. When a London newspaper, *The Guardian*, went through a major redesign in the fall of 2005, it switched to using a single font family — Guardian Egyptian — that has 96 different weights and widths. Obviously, the demands of a daily newspaper and its associated supplements are more than is typical, but you get the idea.

The Benefits of OpenType

A PostScript Type 1 typeface has a character set of 256; an OpenType type-face has potentially thousands of characters. If your design calls for small caps, fractions, old style numbers, or contextual alternates, then choose an OpenType font (preferably a Pro version) with an extended character set. Another huge advantage of OpenType fonts is that they are cross-platform.

Historical Connotations

Depending on the nature of your text, you might use history to inform your choice of typeface. For example, a book on modernist architecture could suggest Futura, while a book of 18th-century Italian poetry may be more appropriate in Bodoni. Perhaps more important than choosing a historically appropriate typeface is not choosing a wrong one: For example, it might be jarring to use a typeface that was designed after the period that the subject matter addresses.

Same Type Designer

When looking for a complement to a given typeface, you could do worse than look at other typefaces by the same type designer—the rationale being that the two faces will have a related sensibility. Some fonts are designed to be used together, their pairings suggested by their names: for example, Stone Serif and Stone Sans (Sumner Stone). Other possible combinations:

- Optima and Palatino (Hermann Zapf)

- Gill Sans and Perpetua (Eric Gill)

- Gotham and Mercury (Jonathan Hoefler and Tobias Frere-Jones).

Lorem ipsum dolor
Sit amet, consectetur adipiscing elit. Quisque id massa quam, in tempor nisi. Nunc fermentum varius ipsum nec rutrum. Sapien ut orci ultrices consectetur quis vitae nisl.

Quisque lobortis
Posuere elit, eu cursus nisl ullamcorper vitae. Quisque vehicula metus nec quam ultricies tempus. Sed eu turpis odio.

Optima/Palatino

Lorem ipsum dolor
Sit amet, consectetur adipiscing elit. Quisque id massa quam, in tempor nisi. Nunc fermentum varius ipsum nec rutrum. Sapien ut orci ultrices consectetur quis vitae nisl.

Quisque lobortis
Posuere elit, eu cursus nisl ullamcorper vitae. Quisque vehicula metus nec quam ultricies tempus. Sed eu turpis odio. Quisque vulputate diam vitae purus luctus sit amet rhoncus nisi iaculis.

Gill Sans/Perpetua

Lorem ipsum dolor
Sit amet, consectetur adipiscing elit. Quisque id massa quam, in tempor nisi. Nunc fermentum varius ipsum nec rutrum. Sapien ut orci ultrices consectetur quis vitae nisl.

Quisque lobortis
Posuere elit, eu cursus nisl ullamcorper vitae. Quisque vehicula metus nec quam ultricies tempus. Sed eu turpis odio. Quisque vulputate diam vitae purus luctus sit amet rhoncus

Gotham/Mercury

FIGURE 12.9 Combining typefaces by the same type designer.

Contrast

Contrast is one of the most effective ways of establishing hierarchy, and choosing different fonts is one way of adding contrast. Other parameters to mix and match are size, weight, structure, color, and form; for example, caps contrasted with lowercase, roman contrasted with italic.

If you want contrast, then go for it. Don't use typefaces that are too similar: Your readers won't pick up on the change, or the difference will be so subtle as to be disconcerting. Worse, it might look like a mistake. Similarly, when combining weights within the same typeface family, stay weights apart—light with semibold, regular with bold, and so on.

FIGURE 12.10 Some approaches to combining typefaces based on contrast.

Helter Skelter — Bold / Light

Helter Skelter — Condensed / Extended

Helter Skelter — Hand-drawn / Machine-made

Helter *Skelter* — Roman / Italic

Helter Skelter — Big / Small

Helter Skelter — Positive / Negative

Helter Skelter — Sans Serif / Serif

Helter *Skelter* — Minimalist / Decorative

It may sound like an overly simplistic formula, but you won't go far wrong if you use serif faces for your body text and sans serif for your headings and subheads. Sans serifs tend to be bolder and blockier, and thus better at grabbing the reader's attention. Also, the absence of serifs makes it possible to track sans serif headlines tighter, adding to their solidity. To make a subhead distinct from body text, it is enough to choose a contrasting typeface; subheads don't necessarily need to be bigger.

A Typical Style Sheet

Print and web designers often refer to lists of styles as a *style sheet*. What follows is a basic style sheet that would be appropriate for a magazine, newsletter, or newspaper.

Matching X-Heights

If you plan to use contrasting typefaces on the same line—for example, in a run-in head—make sure they have the same x-height, or adjust their relative sizes accordingly to ensure there are no jarring transitions from one font to the next.

POVERTY

No adjustments

Ucit lant audae volupta turernatem dolo officabore lautem audae velluptis inullaut ulparum, est inverae que sita

No adjustments

POVERTY

Cap heights matched

Ucit lant audae volupta turernatem dolo officabore lautem audae velluptis inullaut ulparum, est inverae que sita

X-heights matched

FIGURE 12.11 Matching x-heights and cap heights.

Head1

Heads will likely be in a bold or black weight. Depending on the typeface, they may be negatively tracked and tightly leaded, which contributes to a dark type color. The purpose of the Head1 headline is to make the reader want more. Typically, such headlines do this by posing a question or telling part—the best part—of the story.

Head2

A secondary-level head or subhead will often be in the same typeface as Head1, and be based on that style with a reduction in size to indicate a lower level on the hierarchy. Space is added before (and possibly after) to separate this form of head from the surrounding text. This format helps the reader navigate the body text and breaks the text block up into chunks to provide visual relief.

Head3

A third level of heading could be a run-in head, one in which the heading is part of the same paragraph as the body text that follows. The run-in head would need to be a character style, which could be nested in the paragraph style definition. The parent style for such a head may reflect the main head style or appear closer to body text.

Body

As the most widely used style in the document, this is the paragraph style to create first. You can often use it to quickly format a document by applying Body style to all the text in a story, and then going back and applying the other styles as appropriate. The Body style will likely (though not necessarily) be a serif face in regular or book weight at a size of 8 to 11 points, with first-line indents to indicate the beginning of a new paragraph.

Body No Indent

This is based on Body, with first-line indent set to 0. It is often used following a Head3.

Body First

A version of Body No Indent, adding a drop cap or initial cap treatment to bring special emphasis to the start of stories or to major sections within a story.

Byline

The author's credit is typically based on Body and is differentiated by bold weight and by paragraph spacing above, below, or both.

Caption

Captions are typically set smaller than the body text and possibly in a different typeface. With so many competing demands on people's time, captions may be what people read first. A caption should provide enough information for the browsing reader to decide whether to dive into the main article. Designers are not usually responsible for writing captions, but if this is in your remit, be aware that more than just stating the obvious, a caption should clearly establish the relationship between the image and the text.

Intro

To create an entry point for the reader, magazine designers will often set an article's opening paragraph (or its first lines) in larger type, possibly in bold type, possibly in a contrasting font. An intro paragraph may even be set over a wider measure than the body text. Sometimes the byline will be incorporated as well.

The Mother of All Styles: The Book Feature

You can supercharge your style management by using InDesign's Book feature to apply one set of styles to a group of documents. Choose File > New >
Book to open the Book panel. Add documents to the book by clicking the Add
button or by dragging files into the panel. Use the Up Arrow and Down Arrow
keys to change to the order of the documents. Once the book is set up, you
can synchronize the styles and color swatches in your "booked" documents all
at once or one at a time. The Book feature also provides a fast way to add the
styles from one document to a bunch of others.

Specify a Style Source or "master" document by clicking in the leftmost
column of the Book panel, then synchronize the documents in the book.
Styles and swatches are copied from the Style Source to all the documents in
the book, replacing any that have identical names. Styles and swatches in the
documents that aren't in the style source are unchanged.

You can synchronize the book while its documents are closed. InDesign opens
the closed documents, makes any changes, and then saves and closes the
documents. Documents that are open when you synchronize are changed,
but not saved.

To synchronize selected documents, Cmd-click the document icons (or Shift-
click for a continuous selection). If no documents are selected, the whole
book will be synchronized.

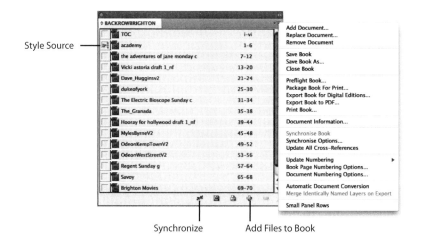

Style Source

Synchronize   Add Files to Book

FIGURE 12.12 The Book
panel and its menu.

Picture Credit

The picture credit can be as small as 5 or 6 points, and it's often rotated 90 degrees to sit in the gutter or at the bottom of a page outside the body text. Sans serif is often the type style of choice for credits, to aid legibility at a smaller size.

Pull Quote

A pull quote is an excerpt "pulled" from the text and used as a graphic element. Pull quotes are intended to catch and hold the reader's interest. They should be thought provoking and succinct. Pull quotes also add visual interest to a layout, especially when you have few photographs or illustrations to work with.

The pull quote is display text. It should offer a strong visual contrast to your body text and be positioned to catch the eye of a potential reader who's skimming or flipping pages.

The pull quote should be positioned on or before the page where the excerpted text appears. Long sentences should be edited into tight, provocative pull-quote versions. They can be set off with rules, reversed, set in a contrasting color, or combined with decorative quotations marks.

Sidebar

A sidebar is an article that, as the name suggests, typically runs by the side of the main article, though it can mean any supplementary article. It is graphically separate from the main text but contextually linked to it. Begin by basing Sidebar on the Body style and adjust the look to set it apart.

Sidebar Head

The heading of a sidebar article, often based on Head1.

Character Styles

Character styles are designed to apply formats to specific ranges of text within paragraphs. These styles can be relative to the paragraph style they are applied within, or they can be explicit. For example, if you want a character style that is an italic version of the paragraph style you're working with, you can create a single-option style. Here's how:

1. Open the Character Styles panel and select New Character Style from the menu.

2. Name the new style and click Basic Character Formats to open the Character Style Options dialog box.

3. Select Italic for Font Style, but leave the other attribute fields blank.

When you apply this character style to text within a paragraph styled in Garamond 10 pt, it will become Garamond Italic 10 pt; if you apply another paragraph style or change the style definition—to say, Caslon 11 pt—then the character style will be Caslon Italic 11 pt. If, however, you want your emphasis to always be Centaur Italic 10 pt, then make sure you include all these attributes in the Character Style Options. Unlike paragraph styles, character styles replace any local formatting—and because you can't apply two character styles to the same text, as soon as you apply a new character style, the old one is removed.

A caveat when working with relative character styles: Because of different naming conventions from one typeface to another, you can sometimes end up with missing fonts. For example, let's say you make an italic character style and then change the paragraph style definition to Helvetica. Depending on the version you've selected, Helvetica uses either "Oblique" or a number-coded font style instead of italic. When you apply the character style, pink highlighting will indicate that there is no such font as Helvetica Italic.

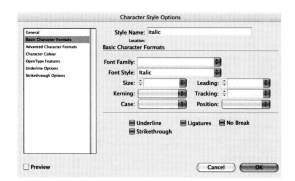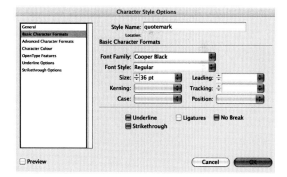

FIGURE 12.13 On the left, creating a single-attribute character style that will inherit all its attributes, with the exception of Font Style; on the right, a style that is more explicit.

Importing Styles from a Microsoft Word Document

If you select Show Import Options in the Place dialog box when you import a Word .doc, .docx, or RTF file, you get to choose whether to preserve or remove the styles and formatting in the Word document. The best choice really depends on how good the formatting in the Word file is. On one hand, if the Word operator has done a good job, there's no reason to duplicate their efforts. On the other, if there is so much dodgy formatting that stripping it out is causing you to have murderous thoughts, then opt to remove the lot at time of import and start with a blank slate. A slightly less drastic approach would be to remove styles and formatting but preserve local overrides—that way you can convert these to character styles as shown in the "Preserving Character Styling in an Imported Microsoft Word Document" sidebar.

As a best-case scenario, you can select Customize Style Import in Microsoft Word Import Options and choose Style Mapping to map incoming Word styles to styles defined in the InDesign document. If the Word styling has been implemented logically, it's merely a question of going through the list of styles and deciding what gets mapped to what. When you click OK to place the document, it immediately takes on the appropriate formatting and you get to leave work early. Even better, if the names of the Word styles are identical to the InDesign styles, then the InDesign styles take precedence and you don't even need to worry about mapping styles.

FIGURE 12.14 When you map Word styles to InDesign styles the placed text is automatically formatted.

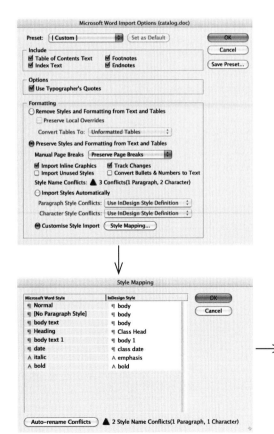

your professional skill set by mastering this exciting program.

Prerequisite: Macintosh experience.

DIANE BURNS a pioneer in electronic publishing, founded TechArt International, one of the first Macintosh-based design firms in the country. Today it is one of the leading firms for print and Web design specializing in East Asian languages. She has presented publishing seminars for Stanford University, MacWorld Expo, and Seybold Seminars, and is the author of several articles and books, including *The QuarkXPress Handbook*.
6 meetings
June 13-27: Mon., 6:30-9:30 pm; also
June 11: Sat., 10 am-4:30 pm
June 12 and June 19: Sun., 10 am-4:30 pm
June 14: Tues., 6:30-9:30 pm
San Francisco: Room 219, South of Market Center,
95 Third St.
$795 (EDP 015354)

Photoshop

Photoshop is essential to any graphic designer's toolbox. This course introduces the fundamental concepts of Photoshop: using layers, painting tools, blending modes, tonal correction, and retouching and sharpening images. You also learn the fundamentals of scanning, image resolution, and appropriate file formats. Emphasis is given to real-world production and collaging techniques. This course is for anyone planning a career in the graphic arts.

Prerequisite: Macintosh experience.

ALICIA BUELOW is a San Francisco-based digital artist specializing in Photoshop illustration. She created packaging images for Adobe Illustrator and Adobe PageMaker. Her clients include *National Geographic*.

history of widely use
and the purposes for
intended. In-class ex
type design, visual a

ALASTAIR JOHNST
of typography and d
100 books, winning
Award of Excellence
latest book on type,
by Oak Knoll and th
Poltroon Press, Berk
10 meetings
June 6 to Aug. 8: M
San Francisco: Roo
95 Third St.
$440 (EDP 025221)

Illustrator

Adobe Illustrator is
creating vector grap
designer's toolbox.
this course enables
drawing tools to cre
to use the pen tool,
color palettes, and c
amazing typograph
and Web designers.

Prerequisite: Macinto

HUGH D'ANDRADE
designer and illustra
book jacket design.
Publications and Bil
6 meetings
June 8-29: Wed., 6:3
June 18 and June 2
June 26: Sun., 10 ar

Preserving Character Styling in an Imported Microsoft Word Document

Microsoft Word documents invariably contain much egregious formatting that you'll want to zap immediately before you can start designing your layout. The problem is, along with all the crap, there may be some useful information—typically text with emphasis—that you need to preserve. So before you apply styles and clear overrides, you may need to convert local formatting to character styles.

For example, let's say you need to preserve the italicizing of an imported document:

1. Go to Find/Change and enter **Italic** in the Find Format field.

2. In the Change Format field, click the magnifying glass to the right and select your italic-only character style (if you don't have one, open the Character Style pop-up menu to create a new one).

3. Click Change All.

Now all the italic text is isolated as a character style. You can press Cmd+A (Ctrl+A) and right-click to select the Clear All Overrides option. This wipes out all the unnecessary formatting but keeps the italics, which are now in a character style and immune to Clear Overrides. What's more, you can now control the appearance of your emphasis text—say, for example, you wanted to use boldface instead of italic—by editing its character style definition. It's the difference between making one change and having to make many.

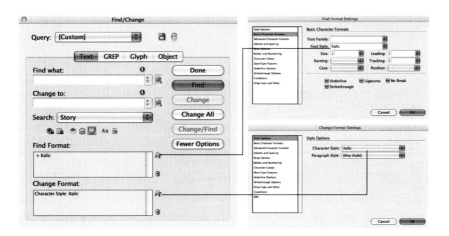

FIGURE 12.15 Changing local formats (overrides) to character styles using Find/Change.

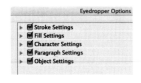

FIGURE 12.16 You can copy settings (including styles) to selected text using the Eyedropper. Double-click the tool to specify which settings to include. Click the empty tool in the paragraph you wish to copy the styles from, then click the other paragraphs with the full tool to transfer the selected settings.

NOTE: The amount of offset added to paragraph rules does not alter the paragraph spacing of the paragraph.

Using the Eyedropper to Apply Styles

To quickly apply a style to multiple paragraphs, use the Eyedropper to sample the character and paragraph styles from one piece of text and apply them elsewhere. Choose the Eyedropper Tool and click the paragraph containing the style you want to sample, then with the Eyedropper loaded, click the other paragraphs that you want to apply the style to (click and drag to select a range of text if you are transferring a character style). The Eyedropper remains loaded with the style so that you can apply it multiple times. Double-click the Eyedropper to specify which settings to include.

Paragraph Rules

If you've ever drawn a rule above a line of text only to have the text reflow and leave the rule in the dust, you'll find paragraph rules (Cmd+Option+J/Ctrl+Alt+J) an invaluable feature. With paragraph rules, you can add a rule above the text, below the text, or both, and that rule will move with the paragraph when the text is edited—no more chasing after the text to reposition those lines.

Choose Rule Above in the Paragraph Rules menu to set the rule to start at the baseline and extend up. Using a positive offset shifts the line up relative to the baseline; a negative offset shifts the line down relative to the baseline.

Choose Rule Below to set the rule to start at the baseline and extend down. Using a positive offset shifts the line down relative to the baseline; a negative offset shifts the line up relative to the baseline.

The techniques shown in Figure 12.17 involve shifting the rules relative to the baseline of the type, sometimes so much so that the terms above and below become meaningless.

Sequential Styles

Because it is common for one particular style to always be followed by another style, you can use the Next Style Paragraph Style option to define a sequence of styles that can be applied with a single click. In any document where the text styling follows a consistent pattern—a large proportion of documents—this can save hours of donkey work as well as ensure consistency. A simple example of a style sequence might be a subhead style that is always followed by a body no indent style. For more of a wow factor, sequential styles can be applied to listings-style text—like a directory listing at the back of a magazine—to make fast work of what might otherwise seem a daunting task.

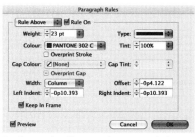

A column rule offset over the type, with the text color set to [Paper] and the text frame Transparency Style Options set to Multiply creates letter-shaped "windows" onto the text image beneath.

COLUMN WIDTH RULE

A Rule Above set to span the full column width. The text is given a small (2pt) left indent to allow some space on the left side of the rule.

TEXT WIDTH RULE

As above but with the width set to Text and the left indent of the Rule set to -2 pt.

RULE ABOVE AND BELOW

A 1-point Rule Below set to column width sitting on top of a 12-point Rule Above.

RULE ABOVE AND BELOW

A 6-point Rule Below indent left and right sitting on top of a 1-point Rule Above.

LOZENGE RULE

An 11-point Rule Below with a Dotted Style on top of 10-point solid rule. The Rule Below has a negative left and right indent. This effect tends to work better when the subhead type is set in ALL CAPS, making it easier to optically center the letters within the rule.

Imagine, for example, an event listing where the date style is followed by the title style, which in turn is followed by the description style. Define *date*'s Next Style as *title*, and define *title*'s Next Style as *description*. Select the full sequence of text. In the Paragraph Styles panel, Ctrl-click (right-click) on *date* (the parent style), and then choose Apply (Style Name) Then Next Style from the pop-up menu to style three paragraphs in one. Note that you have to choose at least two paragraphs to bring up the Apply (Style Name) Then Next Style option. If the text sequence repeats, you can define the next style for *description* (the last style in the sequence) as *date* (that is, the first style in the sequence). Using this approach, you can theoretically format pages of text with a single click. I say "theoretically" because for this looping approach to work, your text has to adhere rigidly to the style sequence—one paragraph out of place, or one piece of information that runs to more than a single paragraph, and the whole thing comes tumbling down like a house of cards. If there are some blocks of information that run to multiple paragraphs, you can replace the paragraph marks with line breaks (Shift+Return) so that the lines break visually but are technically the same paragraph. However, if you have to spend a lot of time massaging your text in this way before applying your spiffy automation techniques, you might question just how automated those techniques really are.

Next Style also determines the style the next paragraph takes on when you press Return (Enter) for the next line. This is useful if you are writing your text in InDesign, but otherwise underwhelming.

FIGURE 12.18 One click does it all: Applying a style sequence to the text on the left results in the formatted text on the right.

18 West
Mutations features hip house and soulful beats from Mutiny, Raymondo Rodriguez and Kris Bones. AKA Bar, West Central Street, WC1 (020-7836 0110) 6pm–4am, £7, free before 9pm
ART
Acquired Rhythm Taste sees John Shepeard (Juno) select vintage electronic dance.
The Warwick, Essex Road, N1 (020-7688 2882) 8pm–1am, free.
Bang Face
Neo-rave explosion of acid, jungle, old school rave, drum'n'basss, nu skool, break core and techno with Andrew Weatherall, Remarc, DMX Krew and the Hard Crew.
Electrowerkz, Torrens Street, EC1 (020-7837 6419) 9pm–5am, £10.

18 West
Mutations features hip house and soulful beats from Mutiny, Raymondo Rodriguez and Kris Bones.
AKA Bar, West Central Street, WC1 (020-7836 0110) 6pm–4am, £7, free before 9pm

ART
Acquired Rhythm Taste sees John Shepeard (Juno) select vintage electronic dance.
The Warwick, Essex Road, N1 (020-7688 2882) 8pm–1am, free.

Bang Face
Neo-rave explosion of acid, jungle, old school rave, drum'n'basss, nu skool, break core and techno with Andrew Weatherall, Remarc, DMX Krew and the Hard Crew.
Electrowerkz, Torrens Street, EC1 (020-7837 6419) 9pm–5am, £10.

Nested Styles

Nested styles allow you to embed a character style—or multiple character styles—in a paragraph style definition, so that you can apply multiple formats with a single click or keyboard shortcut, potentially eliminating hours of repetitive drudgery and freeing you up to be more creative. The best nested styles are those that are simple to set up and that you use frequently.

To create a nested style, you must first create the character styles you will be adding to a paragraph style definition. Then follow these steps:

1. Ctrl-click (right-click) on the paragraph style you want to edit.

2. Select Drop Caps And Nested Styles from the list on the left side of the Paragraph Style Options dialog box.

3. Click New Nested Style and choose from your list of available character styles.

4. Specify how to "turn off" the character style. Depending on the nature of the nested style, either choose a specified number of words or characters, or a condition from the pop-up menu that appears when you click the last item following your specified style. You can also type a specific character such as a colon (:) into this field. Without a delimiter, the character style never gets turned off and will affect the whole paragraph. Choosing Through includes the character that ends the nested style, while choosing Up To formats only those characters that precede the designated character.

TIP: Use a keyboard shortcut to insert the End Nested Style Here character. Create your own custom keyboard shortcut to quickly place this character in your text. I use Ctrl+Cmd+Option+X (on a Mac).

If you have more than one nested style listed for a paragraph style, you can use the Up button or Down button to change the order of the styles in the list, determining the order in which the formatting is applied. The formatting defined by the second style begins where the formatting of the first style concludes.

This is all well and good, but what if there's nothing consistent about your paragraphs that you can use to turn off the nested style? You can insert an End Nested Style Here character into the text itself. This invisible character turns off character styling at that specific point.

Here are some practical applications of nested styles.

TIP: It's possible to accommodate just about any kind of variation by entering multiple characters in the delimiter field of a nested style. If you enter all the possible characters that could end a sentence—.?!—InDesign will use the first one it encounters to turn off the nested style.

FIGURE 12.19 Four simple and practical examples of nested styles showing the settings used to create them.

This is a run-in head: elessendio el exero consenisit iliquat velesed tatie velessenibh erilisit niscin et nulputpat diat illa feuipisl utpat ex etue

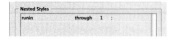

Run-in Head

37 FILM Don't Judge The Damned United by David Pearce's novel, says Richard Kelly

40 TV Gives Peace another chance with C4's Red Riding Trilogy

45 TABLE TALK Everything you needed to know about skyscrapers

Contents Page

one **two** three **four** five **six** seven **eight** nine **ten**

Alternating styles using the [Repeat] option, useful for giving emphasis when a bulleted list would take too much space.

1 EVERYTHING IN ITS RIGHT PLACE Enit prate feugueril ute faciliquat auguercipsum dunt dolor il ex ea auguera esequate dolum velesectet luptat. *4.11.*

2 KID A Nulla feu facilit aliquam, venis nullut lor summy nulla atumsan ulla con ulputat ipisim vero dolore feuipsu! *4.44.*

3 THE NATIONAL ANTHEM Scilit lobore esendre raesent inciniam, core magna feugiam conullaore doluptat luptat, cor senim quis nisim illa facilit? *5.51.*

Listing or Track List

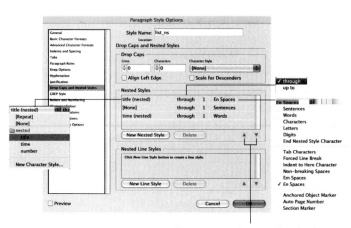

Uses arrows to change order of styles.

Product or Track Listing

In this example, nested styles are combined with a numbered list. For the majority of the paragraph, no nested style (that is, None) is applied through 1 Sentence. The end of the sentence is recognized by a period, question mark, or exclamation mark. Note that a "word" can be a series of numbers that are not separated by spaces; for example, 4.44 or 5.51.

Run-in Heads

Run-ins are usually third-level subheads that have the heading on the same line as the body text that follows. The heading is distinguished from the body text with a contrasting font. The key with run-in heads—and for all nested styles—is some identifiably consistent element. This might mean separating the subhead from the body text with a colon or an en space.

Contents Page

A common style of a contents page calls out the page number in a different color or weight of font. Additional run-in elements can include identifying tags for the department in which the article appears. In the example shown, the departments are called out in a second color. Because some heads are one word and others two, an End Nested Style character (Type > Insert Special Character Other > End Nested Style Here) is inserted after to "turn off" the character style. Because the End Nested Style Here character has no keyboard shortcut, it is time-saving to create one.

Repeating Styles

To repeat a sequence of nested styles, effectively creating a loop of styles within the same paragraph, add a Nested Style at the end of the sequence. Choose [Repeat] from the Nested Style pop-up menu and specify the number of styles to repeat.

Nested Line Styles

You can use a nested line style to apply a character style to a given number of lines in a paragraph. The most obvious application of a line style is for specifying small caps or similar treatment as part of a paragraph opening device. Another usage is when you want to emphasize a line-by-line contrast within the paragraph, perhaps with an alternating highlight.

TIP: When you create a style sheet you may not be the only person who uses it. Or you may find yourself returning to style sheets that you created weeks, months, even years before. So that you and the other members of your team don't get confused by nested styles, adopt a naming convention that is transparent. For example, append "_ns" after the style names.

FIGURE 12.20 Two examples of a nested line style: applying small caps to the first line of a paragraph (top) and to alternating lines using the Repeat function (bottom).

Aᴛ ᴀʟɪᴄᴛɪᴏ ʀʀᴜᴍǫᴜɪ ᴀᴜᴛᴀᴛᴜʀ? Gᴇɴᴛ ʀᴇʀɪʙᴜs ᴀ dolligni bla venim ab idelicias id que perit, quas et volorem nus evelic temporit, occusae plicim venis duntio. Hil ipsum, ut et, sediorpor adi ut asin nimin cuptisti voluptatem faces enda con cuscimp

At alictio rrumqui autatur? Gent reribus a dolligni bla venim ab idelicias id que perit, quas et volorem nus evelic temporit, occusae plicim venis duntio. Hil ipsum, ut et, sediorpor adi ut asin nimin cuptisti voluptatem faces enda con cuscimp orent, sus dolore arcitia qui

GREP Styles

Gʀᴇᴘ allows you to search for patterns in your text. You can implement Gʀᴇᴘ by using Find/Change (Edit > Find/Change or Cmd+F/Ctrl+F), where you can change the found patterns to anything you choose, or (more simply) through Gʀᴇᴘ styles. A more automated approach is to add a Gʀᴇᴘ style to a paragraph style definition. This automatically applies a character style to consistent patterns within the text.

NOTE: For more on GREP, see Michael Murphy's "InDesign CS4: Learning GREP" in the Lynda.com online training library and Peter Kahrel's "GREP in InDesign CS3," O'Reilly Media.

To create a Gʀᴇᴘ style, you specify a Gʀᴇᴘ expression—that is, the text you're looking for—and choose a character style to apply to it. All paragraph text that matches the Gʀᴇᴘ expression is formatted with the character style. An obvious application is when you want a product name or the name of your publication to be formatted with specific character styling—bold, italic, a certain color, whatever. Once the Gʀᴇᴘ style is created, it will affect all instances of the text string that are formatted with that paragraph style (and its derivative styles), and any time you type that combination of words it will automatically take on the right formatting.

To apply a Gʀᴇᴘ style to multiple text patterns, separate each with a vertical pipe (|). For example, to apply a character style to the words *red* and *blue,* type **red|blue** in the To Text: field. Make sure the Preview option is selected so that you can evaluate whether the Gʀᴇᴘ style is working—especially when building more complex expressions.

6.00am Breakfast **10.00**
Saturday Kitchen **11.30**
Football focus **12.10**
The Politics Show
13.00 FILM The GREP
Adventure

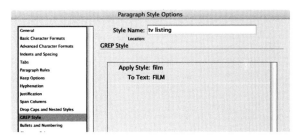

FIGURE 12.21 A simple GREP style applied to a TV listing to call out the word *FILM* in color. A nested style wouldn't work here because the position of *FILM* will vary from paragraph to paragraph.

Object Styles

Object styles take the concept of paragraph and character styles and apply it to text and graphics frames as well as to lines and pen paths. Within one object style you can save such attributes as fill color, stroke weight, stroke color, the number of columns in the frame, drop shadow, and so on. You can also capture Frame Fitting Options, which make object styles tremendously useful and save time when incorporating images into your layout.

Formatting Callout Boxes

As part of an object style definition, you can specify a paragraph style to be applied to the content of a text frame, allowing you to apply item and text attributes with a single click. This makes object styles very convenient for applying formats to small text with single-line stories, like captions or photo credits.

Taking automation to the next level, when you select the Apply Next Style option you trigger a style sequence as we did in sequential styles. This can be especially useful in a number of instances.

For example, let's say you're designing a journal where all the articles follow the same format: head, strapline, byline, body first, body. Start by setting up the Next Style specifications for each of these paragraph styles:

1. Open the Object Styles panel and choose New Object Style from the menu.

2. Name the new style and click Paragraph Styles in the Basic Attributes list of the Object Styles panel.

3. Choose the *head* style from the menu and select the Apply Next Style option.

NOTE: InDesign CS5 allows you to generate live or static captions derived from an image's metadata and (as specified in Object > Captions > Caption Setup) choose which paragraph style gets applied to the caption. Unfortunately, you cannot specify an object style to be applied to the caption text frame.

You can now apply the object style to the text frame and jumpstart the formatting of the publication.

Repeating elements like sidebar boxes and pull quotes can be made into Library items or Snippets so that they can be easily reused and repurposed. An alternative approach is to set up an object style to apply frame formats as well as a sequence of styles to the content of the frames.

Did you know?
The oldest living tree in the world is a California Bristlecone Pine named Methuselah. It is about 4600 years old.

Did you know?

The oldest living tree in the world is a California Bristlecone Pine named Methuselah. It is about 4600 years old.

Using Object Styles with Anchored Objects

If you've ever positioned a graphic, a caption, or a pull quote next to its associated piece of text, only to have to reposition it when the text is edited, then you'll appreciate anchored objects. Inline graphics have been around for years: If you want a graphic inserted into the text flow, you cut it to the clipboard, place your pointer in the text frame where you want the graphic to go (usually on a separate line), then paste it. Thereafter it moves with the text, remaining anchored to its position in the text flow. You may have to futz around with its position relative to the text, and certain unpredictable things may happen, but for the most part, it's an approach that works—until, that is, you want to position a graphic relative to a portion of text, but *outside* the text frame. Cue anchored objects ...

Anchored objects can be positioned outside a text frame and will maintain their positions relative to that text frame no matter what. You can even have them positioned relative to the spine, so that anchored objects are always outside the text frame they are anchored to—in the left margin for left pages, the right margin for right pages.

An anchored object can be a text frame, a picture frame, or any combination of grouped objects.

To create an anchored object, insert your cursor at the beginning of the paragraph and then choose Object > Anchored Objects > Insert to get a blank frame that is anchored to the text. If you already have the object frame created, you can cut it (Cmd+X/Ctrl+X), insert your type cursor into the main story, and paste the frame as an inline graphic. In either case, to determine the placement of the anchored frame relative to the main text frame, Ctrl-click (right-click) the object, choose Object > Anchored Objects > Options, and change the anchored object's Position from Inline or Above to Custom.

Positioning the anchored object exactly where you want it can be a bit fiddly, which is why you'll want to capture its setting as an object style. Select the object, open the Object Styles panel, and choose New Object Style from the menu. Name the new style and save. Thereafter, you can apply the object style to other graphics frames you want to anchor to the text frame. The frames won't snap into place immediately—but as soon as you cut and paste them into the text frame, they will be positioned correctly relative to the text frame.

Just like paragraph and character styles, you can base one object style on another, creating a parent-and-child relationship so that when you change the base, or parent, style, the child style changes as well.

6   **The evolution of hate** Am quissecte tie dit alit lam, vent accum velit ad tionseniam, vel digna feugiatet incipsum quis nummy nostrud esequi bla. Re euissit la faccumsandre feui tate commy niam zzriure min henim quipsum irit, con hendree tummod.

12   **Arctic Monkey magic** conseniam vel euipsusto dolor se ver in ecte dunt utpat. Iriustie mincidunt autat. Lummy nibh eugiamet lobore tie dolore min velenim vullum vel euguer inibh elestrud eugue endiam.

14   **Life after Castro** Ut aliquisis aliquisi tie velendi psuscipsusto od mincili quationsed. Endipsum quam, con henim iurem vercipit accum alit in henit, consequiscip erosto odolumsan esecte consequisi eugiam velenim dolessim quissi et wismodo eugiam.

18   **Style** nulla faciduissi el ullamet venim verillandre commolor senim. aliquis nos eros nonsectet venisl in vercip etum vel ut elit nim quamet prat, corem ip ercip erilisit, sum nisit lorper in vel exero commy nisit do odolore vulputa

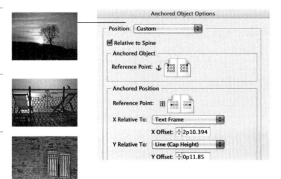

FIGURE 12.23 The Object Style Options panel is a dynamic control center, bundling many styling options in one location. It can save a lot of time once you have a set direction with your design. You control which settings the object style affects by including or excluding a category in the style definition. In the example shown, an object style is applied to the images anchored to the right of the text frame to ensure consistent positioning with a single click.

Each document begins its life with [Basic Text Frame] and [Basic Graphics Frame] object styles. By default, these styles are applied to any text or graphics frames you create. You can edit these basic styles, but you can't delete them. If you want to change the defaults for a text or graphics frame, choose Default Text Frame Style or Default Graphics Frame Style from the Object Styles menu, and then designate a new default from your available object styles.

FIGURE 12.24 Specifying a default object style.

Table and Cell Styles

Table and cell styles continue the automated, do-it-once-reuse-again-and-again approach. While a boon to any sort of table-heavy document, they are not a total solution. Table styles include such attributes as table borders and row and column strokes. Cell styles include formatting such as cell insets, paragraph styles, and strokes and fills. What neither do is set the relative width of the columns, nor do they know what cells you want to merge (how could they?). Therefore, once a table style is applied you'll still need to adjust column widths and merge appropriate cells.

Here's the tricky thing about these styles: A table style is built like a Russian nesting doll. Inside a table style you can include cell styles, and inside cell styles you can include paragraph styles. For example, when you create a table style, you specify which cell styles are applied to which parts of the table: header and footer rows, left and right columns, and body rows. If you don't specify the cell style for a particular element, InDesign assigns a default Same As Body Rows style behind the scenes.

Cell styles don't necessarily include all the formatting attributes of a selected cell. When you create a cell style, you can determine which attributes are included. That way, applying the cell style changes the desired attributes only, such as the fill color, and ignores all other cell attributes.

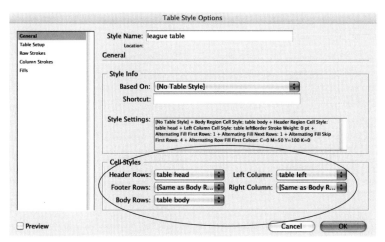

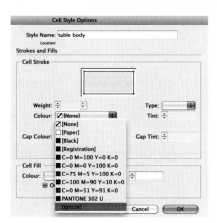

FIGURE 12.25 Table Style Options (top) include row and column strokes, alternating fills, and the table border. The table style includes what cell styles are applied to specific parts of the table (circled). Cell Style Options (center) include cell insets, as well as any row or column strokes or fills applied to specific ranges of cells. Cell styles also reference what paragraph styles are applied to the contents of cells (circled).

CHAPTER 13

Working with Text Wraps

TEXT WRAPS OFFER a great design opportunity by giving you an effective way of adding visual interest to a page. With text wraps, a boring picture can become an intriguing shape or a boxy layout can be made unique and exciting. However, like most tricks, text wraps should be used sparingly and with care. Done well, a text wrap improves both the text and the image; done poorly, your layout will look gimmicky and amateurish. Once you start looking out for bad text wraps, you realize they're everywhere. It's shockingly easy to make a bad text wrap. What frequently gets overlooked is that when you place a graphic inside a block (or blocks) of type, the column measure is narrowed. All the careful planning of type size to column width ratio goes out the window. This chapter looks at how to make a good text wrap—and how to avoid the common pitfalls that cause bad ones.

Applying Text Wraps

While it doesn't require rocket science to make a good text wrap, it does require common sense—and often some tweaking. Here are a few simple precautions:

- Avoid text wraps in a single column where the text wraps around all four corners (or the entire shape) of the bounding box or graphic. Such text wraps disrupt the horizontal flow of the text, and readers may be confused about whether to jump over the graphic or continue reading back and forth in the column.

- Use text wraps with justified type. Because left-aligned type has an uneven or ragged edge, it doesn't emphasize the shape of the graphic the way justified type does. That said, it's harder to achieve good type color with justified type, so make sure the columns are not too narrow.

- Avoid having the left edge of lines in a paragraph start at different horizontal locations (apart from a first-line indent). When you do this, the reader's eye has to search for the start of the line and may lose the rhythm of the text, ending up on the wrong line.

- It's essential to visually balance the space around the graphic. This is about more than just selecting equal values for all the text offsets. The vertical space around the wrapped object depends on where it sits relative to the baselines of the type around it.

- When working with text wraps on rectangular images, align the top of the picture frame to the cap height or x-height of the text in parallel columns. Whichever you choose, be consistent. Align the bottom of the picture frame with a text baseline.

- Check all lines affected by the wrap. If you have composition problems you can try slightly adjusting the position or scale of the graphic. If this doesn't work, use a combination of tracking, hyphenation, and (if appropriate) rewriting.

- When using more than one text wrap in your document, keep the offset amount consistent.

- Don't attempt the impossible. If the shape of your wrap object is too irregular, the result will be too many different line lengths, too much hyphenation, and great gaping holes in the text. If you're working with multiple columns, consider placing the image on the edge of one of those columns, rather than between columns.

The Text Wrap Panel

Text wraps are applied through the Text Wrap panel. Options A–E let you choose what kind of text wrap you want, while options F–H allow you to finesse the text wrap.

A. No Text Wrap

B. Wrap Around Bounding Box creates a rectangular wrap around the bounding box of the wrap object.

C. Wrap Around Object Shape creates a text wrap around the contours of the wrap object.

D. Jump Object keeps text from appearing to the right or left of the wrap object.

E. Jump To Next Column forces all text below the wrap object to the next column or text frame.

F. Top Offset and Bottom Offset determine the distance between wrap object and text. Positive values move the wrap away from the edges of the frame. Negative values position the wrap boundary inside the edges of the frame or object. This relationship is reversed if you invert the text wrap by selecting the Invert option.

G. Wrap To determines which side(s) of the object the text will wrap.

H. Contour Options set how the edges of the object are found when Wrap Option C is applied to the picture frame.

TIP: When adding a text wrap to a picture, make sure you add the text wrap to the picture frame (selected with the Selection Tool) and not the picture itself (selected by clicking on the picture "donut" or with the Direct Selection Tool). If you do the latter, the text will wrap according to the picture's full dimensions rather than its cropped dimensions.

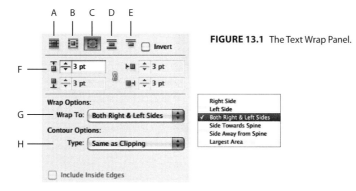

FIGURE 13.1 The Text Wrap Panel.

FIGURE 13.2 Avoid wrapping text around a graphic in a single text column. It's unclear to the reader whether to "jump" the picture or continue reading down the column, and it creates ugly word spacing.

Poppies have long been used as a symbol of both sleep and death: sleep because of the opium extracted from them, and death because of their (commonly) blood-red color. In Greco-Roman myths, pop-   pies were used as of-ferings to the dead.   Poppies are used as emblems on tomb-   stones to symbolize eternal sleep. This   aspect was used, fictionally, in The   Wonderful Wizard of Oz to create   magical poppy fields, dangerous   because they caused those who passed through them to sleep forever.

FIGURE 13.3 Justified type (right) better describes the contour of the object that the text is wrapping around than does left-aligned type (left). This can be seen more clearly when the wrapping object is made invisible (below).

doluptis utecae moluptatus et fugiam doluptas pero doluptatam, cum am fugitinciae nosandandam dolorem. Itatur aspient quam que latatis dolecat volut ut min nulloriam dit, arum rere doluptate porepre nobis aditi aut laborepudis explacearis porestium faccus dolorum, unt. Usdanda volupta que lignimolora ditiame et prat. Andi con ra volorem quo quis autatusam que ped moluptatur? Quist quiam quae. Ut que estis et quati dolum hici odiciis dolum sent eicient nihil.

doluptis utecae moluptatus et fugiam doluptas pero doluptatam, cum am fugitinciae nosandandam dolorem. Itatur aspient quam que latatis dolecat volut ut min nulloriam dit, arum rere doluptate porepre nobis aditi aut laborepudis explacearis porestium faccus dolorum, unt. Usdanda volupta que lignimolora ditiame et prat. Andi con ra volorem quo quis autatusam que ped moluptatur? Quist quiam quae. Ut que estis et quati dolum hici odiciis dolum sent eicient nihil.

Left-aligned

doluptis utecae moluptatus et fugiam doluptas pero doluptatam, cum am fugitinciae nosandandam dolorem. Itatur aspient quam que latatis dolecat volut ut min nulloriam dit, arum rere doluptate porepre nobis aditi aut laborepudis explacearis porestium faccus dolorum, unt. Usdanda volupta que lignimolora ditiame et prat. Andi con ra volorem quo quis autatusam que ped moluptatur? Quist quiam quae. Ut que estis et quati dolum hici odiciis dolum sent eicient nihil.

doluptis utecae moluptatus et fugiam doluptas pero doluptatam, cum am fugitinciae nosandandam dolorem. Itatur aspient quam que latatis dolecat volut ut min nulloriam dit, arum rere doluptate porepre nobis aditi aut laborepudis explacearis porestium faccus dolorum, unt. Usdanda volupta que lignimolora ditiame et prat. Andi con ra volorem quo quis autatusam que ped moluptatur? Quist quiam quae. Ut que estis et quati dolum hici odiciis dolum sent eicient nihil.

Justified

FIGURE 13.4 The vertical positioning of the object affects the size of the offset above and below the graphic. On the left, the image is carelessly placed, creating unequal spacing. A size adjustment would easily fix this problem. On the right, the top of the image is aligned with the cap height of the line of type and the bottom of the image is aligned with the baseline of the corresponding line.

Raessequ atisisci tie ea alit irilisissim diam, cor aliquipit aliquam consed tisi blam, sim nulla faci bla faccummy nos nonullu mmodign iscilit augiat lutpatinis et do exer summoloborem velissed te tisi et, consectet, consequis niat. Ut duiscipis dipsum zzrit nullut lor sustin ut am, quate min vercidui ea alit volore dit dolortio dolore tisim voluptat, consequamet, quissi tem velent in hent alit, quam aliqui ercillummodo dip estie consenim nonsendrem volum ing eugueros am iriurem vel iusto dunt digna ad ming essequamet nos dolorer si te magna feumsan dignim nos atuerat. Equis nummodi onulput acilis num il illut loreet vel ullam veliquat. Ugue vel ip eum zzrilisl utpat, vel ulla facilis nostrud molor si te min volumsa ndigniscil iurer incipisi.Met iure endionum do esto dit lumsan ut nostrud dolor si. Nos nim er at nulputem zzriure vel ut adipisl utem acipit incilla faccum velit nonulput utate dolore conulla ndiatuer iusto dolor sim doluptatie dionumsan ullum do od eugiamet, consectem illam, quisci et volore tem autem ex erat, sed tissi.Erilis ea faci te min ut ing et

Raessequ atisisci tie ea alit irilisissim diam, cor aliquipit aliquam consed tisi blam, sim nulla faci bla faccummy nos nonullu mmodign iscilit augiat lutpatinis et do exer summoloborem velissed te tisi et, consectet, consequis niat. Ut duiscipis dipsum zzrit nullut lor sustin ut am, quate min vercidui ea alit volore dit dolortio dolore tisim voluptat, consequamet, quissi tem velent in hent alit, quam aliqui ercillummodo dip estie consenim nonsendrem volum ing eugueros am iriurem vel iusto dunt digna ad ming essequamet nos dolorer si te magna feumsan dignim nos atuerat. Equis nummodi onulput acilis num il illut loreet vel ullam veliquat. Ugue vel ip eum zzrilisl utpat, vel ulla facilis nostrud molor si te min volumsa ndigniscil iurer incipisi.Met iure endionum do esto dit lumsan ut nostrud dolor si. Nos nim er at nulputem zzriure vel ut adipisl utem acipit incilla faccum velit nonulput utate dolore conulla ndiatuer iusto dolor sim doluptatie dionumsan ullum do od eugiamet, consectem illam, quisci et volore tem autem ex erat, sed tissi.Erilis ea faci te min ut ing et velis nulputet

Wrapping Type Around Irregularly Shaped Graphics

Prepare your image in Photoshop with a layer mask and save it as a PSD file, or with a Photoshop path and save it as a JPEG file (a PSD or TIFF file also works in this context, but a JPEG yields a smaller file size). Place the image in your InDesign document. From Contour Options, choose Alpha Channel or Photoshop Path. You can adjust the Top Offset field (you'll have only the one) to determine how close the text comes to the edge of the image.

Don't have Photoshop? You may be able to create a clipping path for the graphic within InDesign. This works best if the image has a flat background that contrasts with the foreground. With the picture frame selected, choose Object > Clipping Path > Options (Cmd+Shift+Option+K/Ctrl+Alt+Shift+K) and from the Type menu choose Detect Edges. If the image isn't already positioned behind the text, you'll then want to send it there: Object > Arrange > Send To Back (Cmd+Shift+[/Ctrl+Shift+[).

TIP: Text wraps narrow the column measure and inevitably make it more likely that you'll get bad word spacing. You can work with the H&J Violations, under Preferences > Composition, to easily identify spacing problems.

FIGURE 13.5 The opaque white of the image background is "knocked out" using Detect Edges. The text wrap is set to Wrap Around Object Shape, causing the text to wrap around the clipping path. Use the Direct Selection Tool and click the image to see the new path and the text-wrap offset, both of which can be adjusted.

When you're working with an irregularly shaped object, select the object and choose Wrap Around Object Shape from the Text Wrap panel. Using the Direct Selection Tool and the Pen Tool, you can manipulate the path to exactly the shape you want the text to wrap around. Select the image with the Direct Selection Tool to show the text wrap path. Now drag any of the anchor points

TIP: If you have a text-wrap object on a master page that you don't want to affect items on document pages, select the object and choose Apply to Master Page Only from the Text Wrap panel menu.

to adjust the text-wrap shape. To add or delete anchor points, switch to the Pen Tool. Click on the path wherever there is no anchor point to add one, or click on an existing anchor point to delete it. You can also use the Pen Tool to convert smooth points to corner points and vice versa. Optionally, once you have finessed the clipping path you can convert it to a picture frame as a way of identifying a spot varnish for the object.

It's best to evaluate text wraps by eye rather than rely on the numbers in the Text Wrap panel. For example, a text wrap around a curved shape may appear to have a bigger offset at the top and bottom of the shape than at its center, even though the wrap offset is set to a uniform distance from the graphic.

Object Layer Options...
Clipping Path
Image Colour Settings...
Options... ⌥⇧⌘K
Convert Clipping Path to Frame

FIGURE 13.6 Converting the clipping path to a frame for the purpose of applying a spot varnish to an irregularly shaped image. Apply this to a copy of the image and put the copy on a separate layer, identified as a spot varnish layer.

Etum ex eriliquating enisl dunt la feuis nim ipit la facilis nosto commy nit autate dit aut niscill aoreetue duipsum incilla facipisim iu-reetue faccum quisi. Reet augue dolore magna facidunt wis augueri-usci eugait prat ipsus-cil dunt verat loboreet lor sum zzriurem init num vullamet nullutpat et wis del utem vent alit utat. Em dolut augue tin voloreetuer sim in eugait at au-giam nulla faccum init, se dip el eros alisim zzrit am, core faccum in velis
Etum ex eriliquating enisl dunt la feuis nim ipit la facilis nosto commy nit autate dit aut niscill aoreetue duip-sum incilla facipisim iureetue faccum quisi. Reet augue dolore magna facidunt wis augueriusci eugait prat ipsuscil dunt verat loboreet lor sum zzri-urem init num vulla-met nullutpat et wis del utem vent alit utat. Em dolut augue tin voloreetuer sim in eugait at augiam nulla faccum init, se dip el eros alisim zzrit am, core faccum in velis ent vendit ad molo-

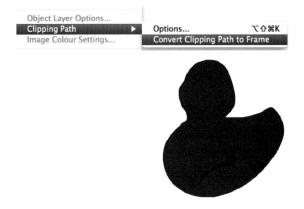

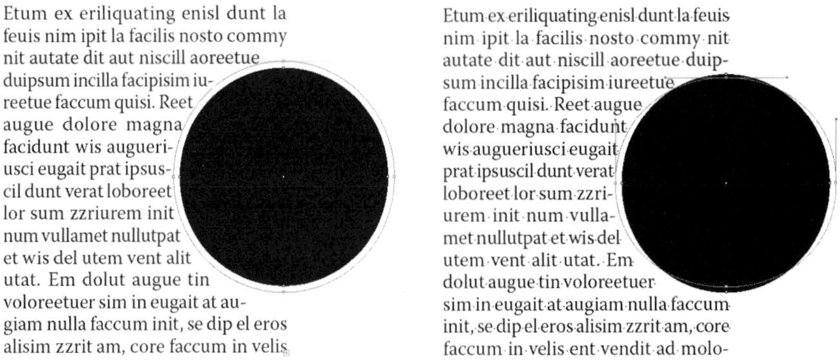

FIGURE 13.7 Wrapping around a circular shape. On the left, the text wrap at the poles of the circle is larger than that at its center. On the right, the Direct Selection Tool is used to pull the text-wrap offset at both poles toward the center of the circle, letting the text hug the circle shape.

Rather than rely on Detect Edges (which will work only when the edges of an image are clearly detectable), you can use the Pen Tool to draw a shape around the image. Apply the text wrap to this shape rather than to the image itself, making sure that the shape has no fill and no stroke. Group it with the image (Cmd+G/Ctrl+G) so that the two elements can be moved or transformed as one.

TIP: WrapNudger is a donationware script by Dave Saunders that compensates for irregular-looking wraps around spherical objects by adjusting the graphic without moving the text wrap. It's available from PDS Associates (www.pdsassoc. com).

Tools for Text Wrapping: Drawing Custom Vector Shapes

InDesign, Illustrator, and Photoshop all include drawing tools that allow you to create custom vector shapes.

Pen Tool. Click to create straight-line segments joined by corner points. Click and drag in the direction that you want the curve to go to create curve segments joined by smooth points. Two direction handles are created when you drag, and these determine the direction in which the new curve will head. The handles can be manipulated by dragging the solid boxes that appear on each end. If you are new to the Pen Tool, it will seem strange at first, but with practice it will make sense.

Add Anchor Point/Delete Anchor Point Tools. Use these tools to add points to or subtract points from the path, or stay in the Pen Tool and move your cursor over a line segment to add a point, or over an existing anchor point to delete that point.

Convert Direction Point Tool. To convert an anchor point between a corner and a smooth point, use the Convert Anchor Point Tool, or if in the Pen Tool, hold down the Option/Alt key. To change a corner point to smooth, click the point and drag to create direction handles. To convert a smooth anchor point to a corner anchor point, simply click the point.

Selection Tool. Use the Selection Tool to move or edit paths. Use the Selection Tool select an entire path if you want to reposition it.

Direct Selection Tool. Use the Direct Selection Tool to select individual anchor points and path segments, which you can then drag to change the segment shape. Shift-click on multiple anchor points to edit more than one segment at a time. You can access the Direct Selection Tool from any Pen Tool by holding down the Command/Ctrl key.

FIGURE 13.8 The Pen tools.

Wrap Options

By default, the wrap options are set to both the Right and Left sides. You can avoid certain spacing problems by switching to either the Left or Right side option.

FIGURE 13.9 Wrapping around both sides of the object causes type to flow awkwardly down the right side of the object (**A**). Choosing the Left as the Wrap To option solves the problem (**B**).

A

B

Text Wrap Preferences

The following composition preferences (choose Preferences > Composition) determine how a text wrap behaves. In all cases, they are document-wide preferences and so are all-or-nothing propositions:

TIP: If you've adjusted your text wrap and don't like the result, you can start again by choosing Wrap Around Bounding Box, then choosing Wrap Around Object Shape once more.

- **Justify Text Next to an Object** justifies text next to text wraps in a single column. This preference will not justify ragged type when the wrap object straddles more than one column. This preference is of little practical value because you shouldn't use ragged type with text wraps, and you certainly shouldn't wrap text around all sides of an object in a single column.

- **Skip By Leading.** When working with multiple columns of text, if a text wrap affects some but not all of those columns, this preference ensures that the text below the text wrap is knocked down to the next available leading increment, making sure that your baselines align across columns. However, rather than turn this preference on, you're better off using a baseline grid to get the same effect (see Chapter 4, "Leading," and Chapter 14, "Pages, Margins, Columns, and Grids").

- **Text Wrap Only Affects Text Beneath** makes InDesign behave like QuarkXPress, where text wraps—or runarounds as they are called in Quark—affect only the text beneath them in the stacking order.

Documents that have been converted from Quark using Markzware's Q2ID will have this preference turned on. For all other documents, you're better off leaving this preference off. Putting pictures above text in the stacking order can result in printing problems when transparent objects overlap type. Text that wraps around a drop shadow or any other transparency effect can end up being rasterized if that text is below the image in the stacking order. Solution: Make sure that text is always on a layer above the pictures, especially those that are transparent (a checkerboard icon next to the page icon on the Pages panel alerts you to the use of transparency on the page or spread). If you want a text frame to be unaffected by a text wrap, choose Object > Text Frame Options and select Ignore Text Wrap (see the next section, "Ignoring a Text Wrap").

NOTE: If you are converting a Quark document to an InDesign document, be sure to carefully check any text wraps. Because InDesign and Quark handle text wraps/runarounds differently, you may see differences between the original and the converted document.

Another option that you need to know about is not a composition preference, but rather is a layer option: Suppress Text Wrap When Layer Is Hidden. (Double-click any layer name to bring up its Layer Options.) When you hide a layer that contains a text-wrap object, the text on other layers continues to wrap around the object. This is so your text won't recompose if you turn off the layer. You can also use it to get interesting text-wrap shapes without seeing the text-wrap object. Turning on Suppress Text Wrap When Layer Is Hidden causes the text to reflow when the layer containing the wrapping object is hidden. This may be useful if you wish to print a version of the document without the images.

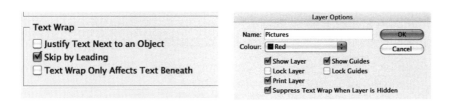

FIGURE 13.10 Text wrap options found under Preferences (left) and under Layer Options (right), including the option to turn off the text wrap when the layer containing the wrapping object is hidden—a seldom necessary choice.

Inverted and Invisible Text Wraps

Every once in a while you might want to make the text wrap *within* the graphic shape, rather than *around* it. To do so, simply select the Invert option on the Text Wrap panel. This works best with simple shapes and when the type is a solid block—without paragraph breaks and indents—tightly leaded and justified so that it better defines the object shape.

A

B

C

FIGURE 13.11 A text wrap around a Z that has been converted to outlines (Type > Create Outlines or Cmd+Shift+O/Ctrl+Shift+O) (**A**). The wrap object is put on a separate layer and the layer visibility disabled (**B**). The text wrap is inverted and the layer visibility disabled (**C**).

Creating Flexible Layouts with Text Wraps

For magazine-style layouts, where text and graphic frames may overlap, using text wraps allows you to easily edit and experiment with different layout options. Especially when combined with the use of a baseline grid and layers (see Chapter 14), text wraps applied to images, headlines, and callout text frames allow a very modular approach to layout.

To get the benefit of this approach, make sure your text frames extend from the top to the bottom margin. The text frame will fill as much of the type area as is available: no picture and you get a whole column of text, place a picture and text obligingly moves out of its way. This way you end up resizing just one element—the picture frame—rather than two. With Align To Baseline Grid selected, the text can be relied upon to start on a grid increment. If your text and picture frames are on separate layers, you can more easily select the picture frames by locking or hiding the text layer when working with the images.

Ignoring a Text Wrap

There are certain elements that you don't want affected by a text wrap. A common scenario is a caption directly below a photo: If the caption doesn't ignore the text wrap, it may not be possible to position the text close enough to the picture. The same applies whenever you have text overlapping a wrap object or a text-wrap offset. In such cases, the text disappears—it gets pushed out of the box by the text wrap, even though the text is on top of the image.

The solution? Select the caption frame, choose Object > Text Frame Options, and select Ignore Text Wrap.

If this is something you find yourself doing repeatedly when creating captions, then make an object style that incorporates the Ignore Text Wrap attribute as well as applies the caption's paragraph style to the content of the frame.

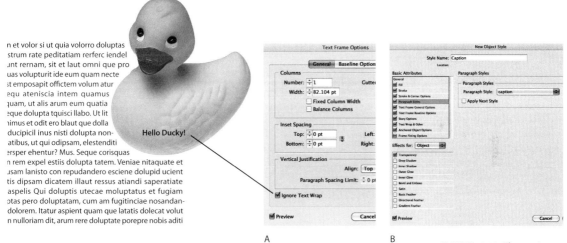

A   B

FIGURE 13.12 The caption text frame is set to ignore text wrap (**A**). These attributes (the paragraph style and the text frame options) are then captured as an object style (**B**).

This can get tricky if you have a text frame that you want to conform to the text wrap of one object, but ignore the text wrap of another. You will need to use the Pen Tool and the Direct Selection Tool to sculpt the text frame into the wrap shape. Here's how:

1. Set the Text Wrap panel to No Text Wrap.

2. Use the Add Anchor Point Tool to add two anchor points approximately where the wrapping object (the circle) overlaps the text frame.

TIP: When adjusting text wraps, make the cursor key increment (Preferences > Units & Increments) smaller for more flexibility.

3. Use the Direct Selection Tool to select the top left anchor point and reshape the text frame, causing the text to "wrap" around the circle shape. To convert the corner point into a curve point, hold Option (Alt) as you drag the point.

Text Wraps in Anchored Objects

Anchored objects are useful for creating side-by-side paragraphs or when you need a caption or pull quote to move with the flow of the text. Getting the anchored objects to position exactly right can be tricky. While it's possible to add a text wrap to an anchored object, unfortunately the first line of text in a paragraph will not wrap around the anchored object. The not-very-elegant workaround is to place the anchored object in the previous paragraph and use the Custom anchored options to adjust its position. The easiest way to do this is to get the position close, then (making sure that Prevent Manual Positioning is not selected in Anchored Object Options), click OK and move the now-anchored frame to exactly where you want it. Make sure the guides and the baseline grid are turned on to make it easier to position the anchored object relative to the baselines and cap heights of the type. Once you've nailed the Anchored Object Options, save them as an object style, which you can then apply with a single click thereafter.

FIGURE 13.13 Text wraps are maintained when you make an item into an anchored object. However, if you want the first line of a paragraph to respond to the text wrap, you will need to anchor the object in the preceding paragraph.

sis cincilit, quat et aut nit, secte tinim nonse er susto corercipit la feuisl ilisi.¶

Umsan ut laor sequisl iriureet ut wisi.¶

The sidebar frame in the outside margin is anchored to this paragraph. It will remain in the same relative position to this main text frame regardless of how the text is edited. Because its alignment is Relative to Spine, if editing causes this paragraph to move to a right hand page, the sidebar frame will be positioned to its right in the outside margin. To create an anchored object you can either insert your cursor at the beginning of the paragraph and then choose Object>Anchored Objects>Insert to get a blank frame that is now anchored

"I spent a lot of money on booze, birds and fast cars. The rest I just squandered."¶
—George Best¶

Tricky Text Wraps

There may be times when you're working with a complex layout and you need a block of text to wrap around one text-wrap object, but ignore another that is affecting a separate text frame. Such times are rare, but when they arise they can present something of a conundrum. You should not resort to changing the text wrap preferences to have the wrap object affect only elements below it in the stacking order, for reasons discussed earlier in "Text Wrap Preferences."

One solution is to change the text wrap of the wrap object (indicated by the gray circle in Figure 13.14) so that it covers only half of the object shape. Or make a copy of the object. Then select the text frame and the original object. Use the Pathfinder Subtract Tool (Object > Pathfinder > Subtract) to take a bite out of the text frame with the second wrap object (the blue circle). Then paste the object copy back into the hole that is left by using Cmd+Shift+Option+V (Ctrl+Shift+Alt+V).

FIGURE 13.14 To make the column on the right wrap around the blue circle but not the gray one, the frame is set to Ignore Text Wrap. The blue circle is copied to the clipboard, then its shape is subtracted from the text frame using the Pathfinder Subtract options. A copy of the blue circle is pasted into the hole that remains.

CHAPTER 14

Pages, Margins, Columns, and Grids

CRUCIAL TO ANY PAGE DESIGN are its dimensions and its framework. The page size and orientation, the width of the margins that define and frame the type area, and the number and width of the columns that control the flow of the text are all integral design elements that profoundly influence how a reader reacts to the page, be it printed or onscreen. Superimposed on these dimensions is the grid, a series of intersecting guides at regular intervals. The grid is an invaluable tool for organizing text and suggesting (rather than dictating) how text and pictorial elements should be arranged on the page.

Setting Up the Document

When setting up a new document, here are some questions to ask:

- What type of document is it? Is it a novel or continuous prose with a single text flow, a magazine or newsletter with multiple stories, a brochure with several folds, a single-sided poster or flyer?

- Is there a fixed page count or will the number of pages be determined by the length of the text?

- How will the piece be printed? Is it possible to have bleeds—elements that print to the edge of the page?

- How many different types of text are there? Are there sidebars, captions, pull quotes, footnotes, or endnotes? How many levels of hierarchy?

- If there are images, are they predominantly vertical, horizontal, or square in orientation? (See Figure 14.1 for how to get a breakdown of the image orientations in your document.) Are they photographs, illustrations, maps, icons, or all of the above? Do they need to be integrated into the flow of the text?

FIGURE 14.1 You can use the Bridge Filter panel (File > Browse) to see how many images of a certain orientation or aspect ratio you have. Put a check mark next to an orientation to see images of that type only. (The Filter panel is not available in Mini Bridge.)

Choosing a Page Size

Often we don't have the option of choosing a page size—and when we do, our choice may in large part depend on convenience and economy. Standard page sizes, as well as being readily available, also have practical benefits: brochures need to fit into standard envelopes, magazines and newspapers into display racks, and business cards into wallets.

That said, for as long as we have been making printed materials we have been searching for the perfect page dimensions. A carefully chosen custom size can look unique rather than expected, organic rather than off the shelf. Many books have been written about the quest for the perfect page *aspect ratio*—the relationship of width to height. Here are some common approaches.

The Golden Section/Golden Ratio: 1:1.618. This formula is based on the proportions found in the human body and in nature. It was used as the standard grid for medieval manuscripts as well as in the creation of great works of art and architecture like the Mona Lisa and the Parthenon.

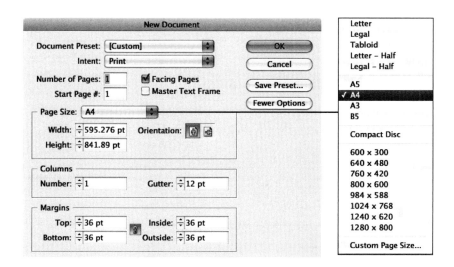

FIGURE 14.2 Where it all begins: choosing a page size in the New Document dialog box. Click the Save Preset button to save your settings.

FIGURE 14.3 A facing-pages spread using Golden Section proportions of 1:1.618 and margins in a ratio of 3:5:8:13 (a Fibonacci sequence, in which each number is the sum of the two preceding numbers). While this makes for harmonious proportions, it also makes for economically impractical margins.

TIP: InDesign's smaller screen sizes (640 by 480, 800 by 600, and 1024 by 768) are all 4:3 aspect ratio; 1280 by 800 is a golden ratio.

TIP: US letter, A4, tabloid, and so on are convenient, but the world is full of documents in these sizes. Use them, but choose them because they offer the best solution for the design you are creating. Don't settle for them just because they are the defaults.

TIP: If you opt for a non-standard page size, be sure to get a cost estimate from your commercial printer before you commit to designing your publication at that size. It's good to be different, but sometimes being different comes with a big price tag.

TIP: A handy workflow feature is the ability to save your nonstandard settings as a preset. Once you've keyed in the values you want, choose Save Preset. Thereafter you can choose the preset name from the Document Preset menu.

The Silver Ratio: 1:1.4142. ISO paper sizes—A4, A3, and so on—are based on this aspect ratio of 1 to the square root of 2. It's a clever and economical system because it allows you to fold one standard size into another without needing to trim the paper to make smaller sizes. You can make brochures by using paper of the next size up. For example, fold an A3 page in two and you have two A4 pages; fold an A4 in two and you have two A5 pages, and so on. The standard US letter size (8.5 by 11 inches) is similar in aspect ratio to an A4 page (8.3 by 11.7 inches), but slightly taller and not quite as wide.

Classical Proportions: 2:3. Jan Tschichold (1902–1974) developed these aspect ratios based upon his studies of medieval manuscripts.

Photographic aspect ratio: 1:1.5. This yields sizes such as 4 by 6 inches, 6 by 9 inches, and 8 by 12 inches.

Business Card aspect ratio: 2:3.5. This is the ratio of most business cards. Its size, and multiples of it, feels familiar.

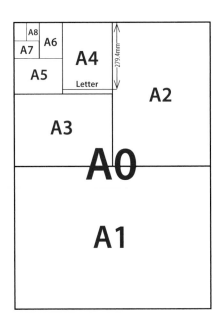

FIGURE 14.4 ISO paper sizes, with US standard letter size overlaid in blue.

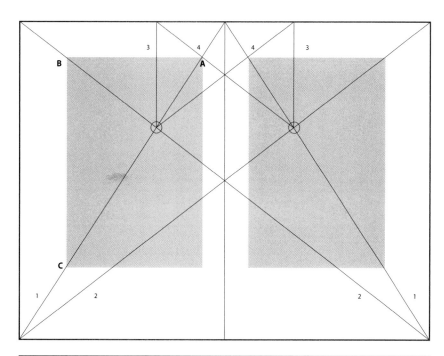

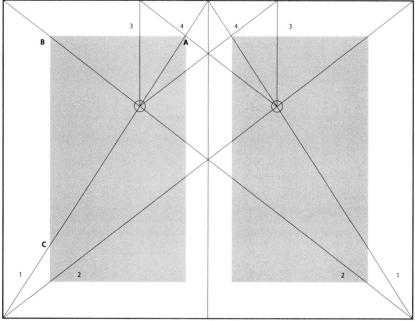

FIGURE 14.5 Classical proportions developed by typographer Jan Tschichold, using a 2:3 aspect ratio and a series of intersecting guides to determine the size and position of the type area on the page. Start by drawing guides from the lower outside edge to the upper inside edge of each page (1). Then draw guides from the bottom outside corners across the spine to the opposite side (2). Where these lines intersect (circled), project a straight line up to the top of the page (3) and from there draw a diagonal from the top of the page to meet the same intersection on the facing page (4). To determine the type area, draw a rectangle from point A out toward the outside margin until it intersects with line 2 (point B) and then drag the rectangle down until it intersects with line 1 (point C). For an alternative that maintains the integrity of classical proportions but has a more practical bottom margin, follow the diagonals as shown in the lower example.

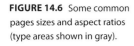

FIGURE 14.6 Some common pages sizes and aspect ratios (type areas shown in gray).

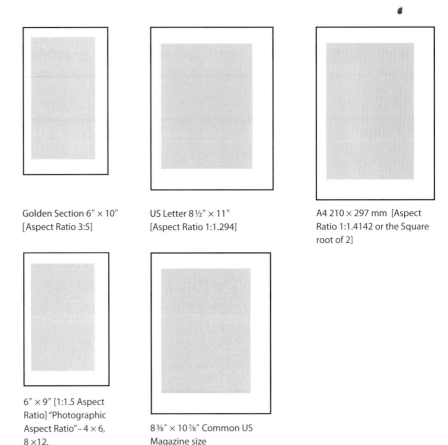

Golden Section 6″ × 10″ [Aspect Ratio 3:5]

US Letter 8½″ × 11″ [Aspect Ratio 1:1.294]

A4 210 × 297 mm [Aspect Ratio 1:1.4142 or the Square root of 2]

6″ × 9″ [1:1.5 Aspect Ratio] "Photographic Aspect Ratio"– 4 × 6, 8 ×12.

8⅜″ × 10⅞″ Common US Magazine size

Page Orientation

A quick glance at your bookshelf confirms that the majority of books — as well as magazines, newspapers, and brochures — are tall (portrait) in orientation, rather than wide (landscape). Of course, there are exceptions: CD covers are square, and books that showcase landscape-orientation photos or images may work better in wide format. But for the most part, printed material is tall and those publications that aren't sit uneasily alongside this overwhelming majority.

Pages designed for the screen, however, work better in landscape format for the simple reason that our monitors are horizontal.

Different Page Sizes

InDesign CS5 allows the use of different page sizes within the same document. This is especially useful if you want to keep the parts of a project together (for example, a business card, letterhead, and envelope can each be different pages in the same document) or if you want to create the front and back cover of a publication as a single page. To change the size of a page or range of pages, select the page(s) in the Pages panel and choose Edit Page Size in the bottom of the panel. Alternatively, choose the Page tool 🔖, click the page, and change its dimensions on the Control Panel.

FIGURE 14.7 Custom page sizes allow you to combine different page sizes in the same document. In the example shown, custom page sizes have been used for the inside and outside flaps of a book jacket, as well as for the spine.

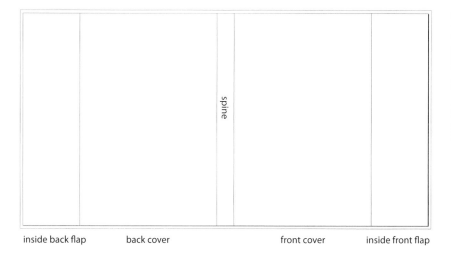

inside back flap   back cover   front cover   inside front flap

Determining Margins

Margins often aren't given enough consideration. It's easy to fall back on even margins of half an inch or an inch, but in doing so you miss a big opportunity to establish the margins of your document as an integral design element. Look at any page and you'll notice that margins are the first space you see: They play a vital role in determining the reader's initial impression of the page. Margins serve the following functions:

- Margins frame and define the type area of the page — and if you've ever done any picture framing you'll appreciate how dramatically a good frame can increase a picture's impact.

- Obviously, but quite profoundly, margins are where you hold the book or page — they are a place for readers to put their thumbs, hopefully without obscuring the content on the page.

- Historically, margins have been used as a space to write notes (wide outside margins are still referred to as scholars' margins) and in certain types of publication they continue to serve this function.

- Margins are also a place to put the page numbers (known as folios) and publication information, in either the top or bottom margins of the page, outside of the type area. (The treatment of margins in the age of the Amazon Kindle and the Apple iPad remains to be seen.)

While margins define the type area, they are not absolute. Certain text elements like drop caps, pull quotes, and captions may hang outside the margins—as will punctuation if you are using Optical Margin Alignment. Pictures frequently break out of the type area, disrupting the rectilinear nature of the page and—potentially—making for a more dynamic layout.

Relative Size of Margins

While single-sided documents like posters, flyers, or business cards often use even margins (click the chain icon to make sure it is unbroken), making all the margins the same for documents with facing pages can look static. When two pages are adjacent—such as in a magazine or book—they share an inside margin broken only by the spine. This double margin is a visual factor to take into consideration when designing spreads. Margins typically progress from smallest to largest in the following order: inside, top, outside, bottom. There are no cast-iron rules, but a popular ratio for determining margins is 1:1.5:2:2.25. This produces margins that are generous yet look familiar to a 21st-century eye.

- The inside margin should be the smallest dimension since it faces another inside margin. However, this measure should be at least 10 mm on each page to avoid losing information in the spine.

- Next comes the top margin (head). This should be about 1.25 to 1.5 times the size of the inside margin.

- The outside margin (foredge) should be big enough so the type doesn't look confined by the page and to allow space for the reader to handle the document. It should be approximately 1.75 to 2 times the size of the inside margin.

- The bottom margin (foot) should be the biggest — about 2 to 2.5 times the size of the inside margin — so as to avoid the type area looking bottom heavy and to allow room for the folios. The amount allowed for the top and bottom margins can be switched if the folios will be placed above the type area.

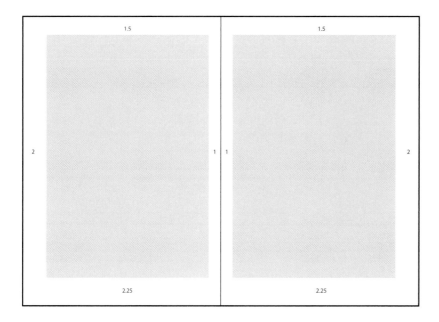

FIGURE 14.8 Margins based on ratios of 1:1.5:2:2.5. If the folio is to be placed at the head as opposed to the foot, the size of these margins can be switched.

Facing-Pages Documents

In a document with facing pages, the left and right pages mirror each other and the margins are expressed as inside and outside, as opposed to left and right for a single-sided document.

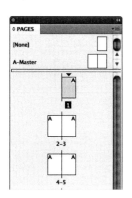
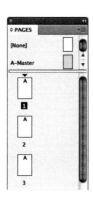

FIGURE 14.9 The Pages panel showing facing pages (left) and single-sided pages (right).

TIP: The first page of a two-page document is a right-hand page (or recto), meaning that the first two pages will not appear next to each other as a spread. To make them do so, make sure the Start Page number is an even number. If you forgot to do this (or if you're working with an earlier version of InDesign), select the first page and from the Pages panel menu choose Numbering And Section Options. Choose Start Page Numbering At and type an even number.

When you make a facing-pages document, the master page that you create will have two symmetrical pages with inside and outside margins that mirror each other. If you want to create an asymmetrical facing-pages layout, start with a facing-pages document, Ctrl/right-click on the spread representing the A-Master, choose Master Page Options, and change the number of pages to 1. A single-page A-Master will replace the spread.

FIGURE 14.10 Facing-pages documents with asymmetrical margins (left) and symmetrical margins (right).

Setting Up Columns

The type area defined by your margins can be subdivided into columns. The relationship between type size and column width, or *measure*, is a key factor in determining the readability of your type. There's no cast-iron rule for determining column width. Some jobs lend themselves to generous columns; often economy dictates narrower columns than are optimal.

As a rough guide, aim for 40 to 70 characters (including the spaces) per line. That's a big range, so there's plenty of scope. More than 70 characters and "doubling" can occur—the eye returns to the left column edge only to read the same line again. If you are obligated to work with a measure that is too wide, you can improve its readability by increasing the leading of your type. At the other extreme, if you have fewer than 25 characters on a justified line, getting evenly spaced type will be next to impossible as the words rush to fit the column measure.

Take a look at your daily newspaper and you'll find justified columns with a lot less than 50 characters. You'll probably also find—without looking too hard—that these columns are riddled with huge word spaces. This is due to poor justification as a consequence of the narrow column measure. We've gotten used to bad typography in newspapers—which in their defense are produced under tight deadline pressure—and read them easily *despite* their typography, not because of it. Historically newspapers used smaller type than they do today. But while the type has gotten bigger, the columns haven't grown proportionally, hence the justification problems. That said, there are notable exceptions—*The Guardian* (UK) has significantly raised the bar for newspaper typography in the last few decades.

FIGURE 14.11 *The Guardian*: an exemplar of readability.

Column width is more of an issue with justified type than with ragged type. If you are working with a narrow measure, do yourself a favor and use Left rather than Left Justified alignment.

Determining Gutter Width

In multicolumn documents, the separate columns of type should look like they are parts of a unified whole. If the space between your columns (the *gutter*) is too wide, those columns will look like they bear no relation to each other. If the gutter is too narrow, though, the reader's eye may mistakenly cross over from one column to the next.

Gutter widths should be relative to the leading value. To achieve uniform spacing, set your gutter width to the same value as, or a multiple of (1.5 or 2 for example), your baseline grid increment, which is itself based on the leading increment of your text. The wider the column, the bigger the gutter.

Changing the Number of Columns

To change the number of columns, the size of the margins, or both for your page(s) or your whole document, choose Layout > Margins And Columns. While it's possible to change the number of columns and the page size of a document in progress, there's nothing like getting it right to begin with. How successful the transition from one column grid to another will be depends not only on choosing the right options, but also on how much of a departure from the original the new layout represents. To put it another way: Don't expect miracles.

When changing the number of columns, here are some things to consider:

- To change the number of columns for all the pages based on a specific master page, you should edit the master page itself (see the sidebar "Master Pages" later in this chapter).

- To adjust the text and picture frames (and not just the column guides) on your document pages, select Enable Layout Adjustment. You can set how Layout Adjustment behaves in the Layout Adjustment dialog box, also under the Layout menu.

- To change the columns for the left- and right-hand pages of a spread, select both page icons in the Pages panel; otherwise you'll be changing just the left or the right page.

- You can change the margins and columns for a range of pages by selecting those pages in your Pages panel.

FIGURE 14.12 The Margins And Columns and Layout Adjustment dialog boxes. Select the Enable Layout Adjustment option in the Margins And Columns dialog box if you want the size and position of text and picture frames to conform to the new margin sizes.

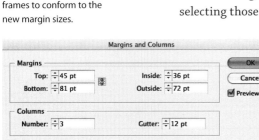
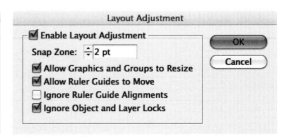

Creating Columns of Fixed Width

TIP: To change the page size of a document in progress, choose File > Document Setup.

If you know how wide you want your columns to be, select a text frame and choose Object > Text Frame Options (Cmd+B/Ctrl+B) and specify a fixed column width for a text frame in the Text Frame Options dialog box. You can then use the total width of the text frame to determine the left and right page margins. For example, if you choose two columns with a width of 20 picas and a 1-pica gutter, the total width of the text frame will be 41 picas. From here, you can subtract the width of the text frame from the page width and allot this space to the left and right margins. This approach makes the margin width subservient to an appropriate column width, rather than the other way around.

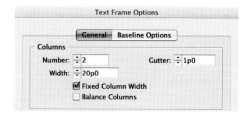

FIGURE 14.13 Creating columns of fixed width.

TIP: If you want columns of unequal widths, unlock the column guides (View > Grids And Guides > Lock Column Guides) and drag the column guides. You may find it helpful to use the Rectangle Frame Tool as a "measuring stick" by drawing in place the outline of the columns, then position the column guides according to these frames. When you're happy with the result, delete the frames and relock the column guides.

Using Grids

A grid is an underlying structure of lines drawn up to suggest where the various elements of your document can be placed on the page. Essentially, they are visual aids to help you quickly and consistently arrange text and graphics. Though a well-designed grid will be invisible to the average reader, it nevertheless helps the reader make sense of the different elements in a document. Columns of text, headlines, photos, illustrations, captions, pull quotes, and other page elements are more easily tied together—or unified—by using a grid. Grids impose constraints on the designer but at the same time enhance creativity by suggesting a consistent structure. Because they take the guesswork out of where to place different elements on the page, grids significantly speed up workflow.

TIP: Swiss designer Josef Müller-Brockmann is the guru of the grid system. His book, *Grid Systems in Graphic Design*, though written before the digital era, remains a seminal work on the subject.

"The reduction of the number of visual elements used and their incorporation in a grid system creates a sense of compact planning, intelligibility, and clarity, and suggests orderliness in design. This orderliness lends added credibility to the information and induces confidence." [*Grid Systems in Graphic Design* by Josef Müller-Brockmann. Sixth Edition 2008. Niggli (first published 1981).]

Beneath just about every well-designed document is a grid of some sort. Novels may use a simple one-column grid, but even this has to be carefully considered, because it determines the type area of the page as well as where the folios go. Newspapers and magazines with multiple columns and a mixture of type sizes—as well as photographs and illustrations—call for more complex grids. These layout schemes use a flexible number of columns and divide the page horizontally into rows as well as vertically. In addition, they employ a secondary layer of structure known as a *baseline grid*, the purpose of which is to keep the baselines of the type cross-aligned over columns and in relation to other elements.

Things to Consider

- When working with multipage documents, establish grids on master pages.

- It's possible, though rarely necessary, to have more than one baseline grid per document. InDesign allows individual text frames to have their own baseline grid.

- Grids should be flexible. Grids based on a fixed number of columns can suffer from too much symmetry if text and graphics are confined to those columns throughout all the pages of the publication. Using more grid fields allows more flexibility. With multiple columns, a single text frame may span two, three, or even four of the vertical grids. For example, using a 12-column grid as an underlying structure is an easy way to introduce variety, because you can break the area into three and four columns, 12 being divisible by both. Another common approach is to use an uneven number of columns. For example, a five-column grid allows for two text frames each filling two column widths, with a single column for white space, photos, captions, and other material. You can mix things up by changing the position of this "floating" column.

- The grid is there as a starting point, not as an end in itself. Rigid adherence to the grid can make for a static layout. Having made the rules, you are free to break them when doing so results in a better-looking page.

Master Pages

Any items on a document's master page(s) will show up on all of the pages that are based on that master page(s). The letter in the outside corner of the page icon on the Pages panel indicates what master page the page is based on. There is no limit, save common sense, to the number of master pages you can have, but if you've planned your document carefully, even complex documents need only a few. To apply a master page to a document page, drag the master page icon onto the document page. Alternatively, you can select a range of document pages, then Ctrl/right-click and choose Apply Master Pages To when the context menu appears. Note that master page items are locked on document pages and appear with dotted borders instead of solid frames. To modify a master page element on a document page, hold Cmd+Shift (Ctrl+Shift) and click the object to unlock it. To unlock all master page elements, choose Override All Master Pages Items from the Pages panel menu. (This will mean that the page elements are no longer controlled by the master pages.)

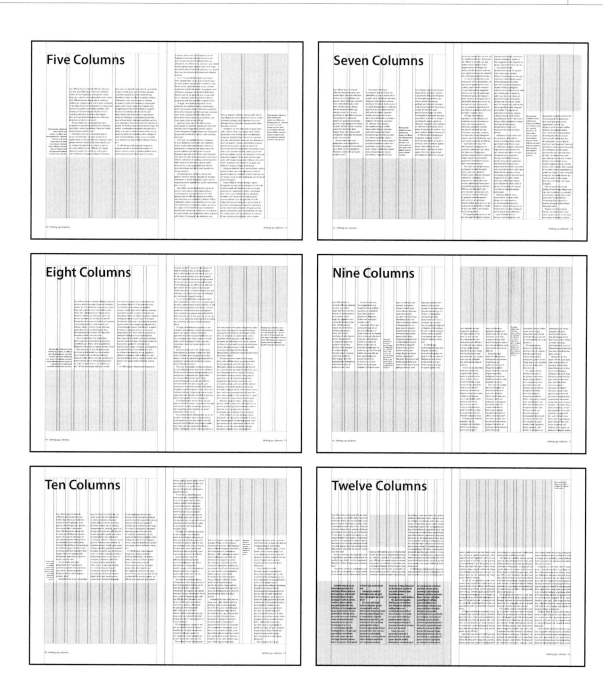

FIGURE 14.14 Experimenting with different numbers of columns over different grid structures.

The Grid Toolkit

InDesign has a suite of tools that work together to help you set up and manage your grid.

Grid Preferences

To show the baseline grid, choose View Options > Show Baseline Grid. Choose Preferences > Grids to determine the look, starting position, and increment of the baseline grid.

Color: I like to change the color of my baseline grid. Light gray works well because it's not too distracting.

Start and Relative To: These settings determine where the grid starts counting off from and whether that number is relative to the top margin or the top of the page. I prefer to start at 0, relative to the top margin. These settings show the baseline grid only within the type area, rather than across the whole page.

Increment Every: This should be the same as your body text leading. This value appears in points regardless of your chosen unit or measurement. Making the grid work will involve some rudimentary math, so it helps if you have an easy number to work with, like 12. You'll use this leading value (or multiples of it) for the spacing of the elements on your page. Make sure you're not using Auto Leading, which may give you fractional leading values. For example, if your body text is 11, your Auto Leading will be 13.2—not a number you want to be juggling with.

View Threshold: This setting determines the view size at which the baseline grid becomes visible when Show Baseline Grid is selected. If you're working on a laptop, you may wish to make this number less than the default 75 percent.

Grids In Back: When this option is selected, the baseline grid (but not ruler guides) will be behind all other objects.

Align To: Your baseline grid doesn't count for much until you align text to it. On a local level, you can click the icons on the Control Panel; at the paragraph style level, choose Align To from the Indents And Spacing options. For text with different leading increments such as captions or callouts, where aligning all lines to the baseline grid would prove too constraining, you can opt to align the first line only. The first line of the paragraph will be on the grid; thereafter the text will be controlled by its leading value.

NOTE: Objects and ruler guides are always in front of margins, column guides, and the baseline grid—even if you deselect Grids In Back.

NOTE: Distinct from the baseline grid, the document grid makes your page and pasteboard look like graph paper. While this is useful when aligning elements in diagrams, it is not particularly helpful when creating layouts that combine text and images.

Preferences
General
Interface
Type
Advanced Type
Composition
Units & Increments
Grids
Guides & Pasteboard
Dictionary
Spelling
Autocorrect
Notes
Track Changes
Story Editor Display
Display Performance
Appearance of Black
File Handling
Clipboard Handling
Grids
Baseline Grid
Colour: Light Grey
Start: 0 pt
Relative To: Top Margin
Increment Every: 12 pt
View Threshold: 75%
Document Grid
Colour: Light Grey
Horizontal
Gridline Every: 72 pt
Subdivisions: 8
Vertical
Gridline Every: 72 pt
Subdivisions: 8
Grids in Back

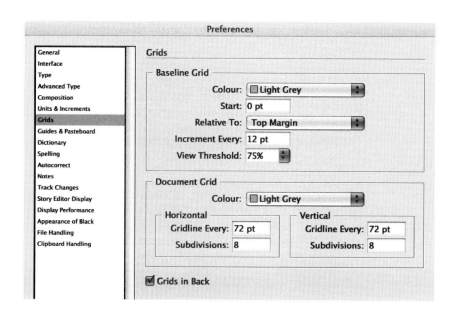

FIGURE 14.15 The Preferences dialog box, set to Grids.

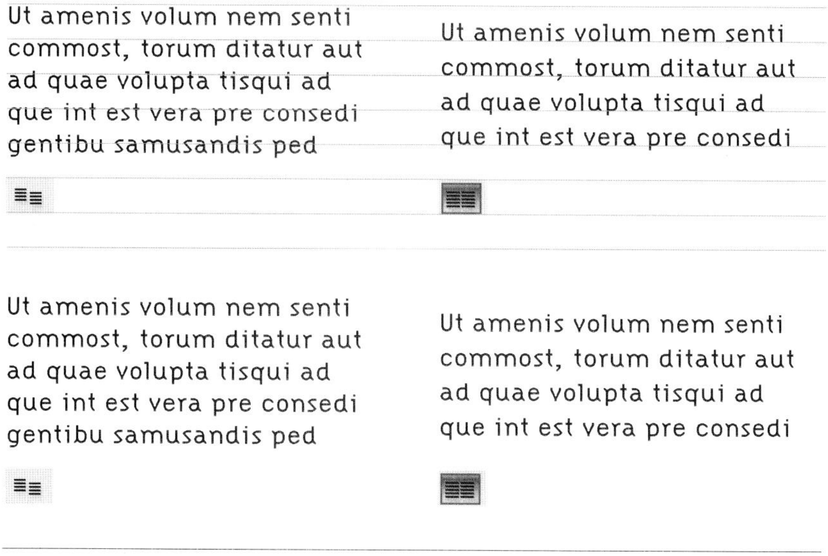

Ut amenis volum nem senti commost, torum ditatur aut ad quae volupta tisqui ad que int est vera pre consedi gentibu samusandis ped
Ut amenis volum nem senti commost, torum ditatur aut ad quae volupta tisqui ad que int est vera pre consedi
Ut amenis volum nem senti commost, torum ditatur aut ad quae volupta tisqui ad que int est vera pre consedi gentibu samusandis ped
Ut amenis volum nem senti commost, torum ditatur aut ad quae volupta tisqui ad que int est vera pre consedi

FIGURE 14.16 Text not aligned (left) and aligned (right) to the baseline grid.

Create Guides: While the Margins And Columns dialog box is the place to create or adjust major column divisions that affect text flow, Create Guides can be used to make custom grids of rows and columns, as an alternative to laboriously dragging out multiple ruler guides. Create Guides is a guide-making machine—and, because it's instantaneous, you can experiment with different configurations. To prevent the document from becoming cluttered with too many guides, consider putting your custom grid guides on their own dedicated layer, which you can show, hide, or lock as needed.

Ruler Guides: Choose Layout > Ruler Guides to change the color of any selected guide(s). This is useful for color-coding different parts of the grid. For example, superimposed on a 12-column grid, you can indicate three columns with one color and four columns with another.

The following options allow you to create a grid of objects:

Step And Repeat: Choose Step And Repeat (Cmd+Option+U/Ctrl+Alt+U) and select Create Grid to generate a grid of objects from your selection, each successive copy offset a specified distance from the preceding one. Note that you need to factor in the size of the object when specifying the offsets. For example, if you want to copy a 72-point square 12 points to the right, then make the horizontal offset 84 points.

Gridify: This is a new feature in CS5 that allows you to expand a frame into a grid. While you're drawing a frame, press the Up Arrow and Down Arrow keys to add or remove rows and the Right Arrow and Left Arrow keys to add or remove columns. This also works with a loaded Place cursor. To adjust the gutter spacing between the rows and columns, hold down Cmd/Ctrl while pressing the arrow keys. There is, however, no numeric feedback on the size of the gutter spacing, which makes it difficult to get the horizontal and vertical gutters the same.

FIGURE 14.17 Using Step And Repeat (left) and the Gridify feature (right) to create a grid of frames.

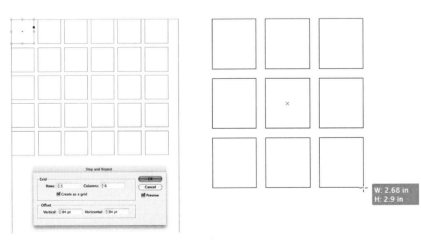

You can also duplicate objects into a grid. Hold down Option/Alt and begin dragging away from a selected frame. Once you're moving, press the Up Arrow key or Down Arrow key to change the number of rows of objects and the Left Arrow key or Right Arrow key to change the number of columns of objects.

MakeGrid: Though to some extent superseded by the new Gridify, the MakeGrid script is still a quick and effective way of dividing a frame into a specified number of row and column grid fields. Choose Window > Utilities > Scripts to access the Scripts panel and then drill down through the folders, from Application to Samples to JavaScript. In the JavaScript folder you'll see a list of scripts. With a frame selected, double-click MakeGrid.jsx, then choose the number of rows and columns and the gutter space between them.

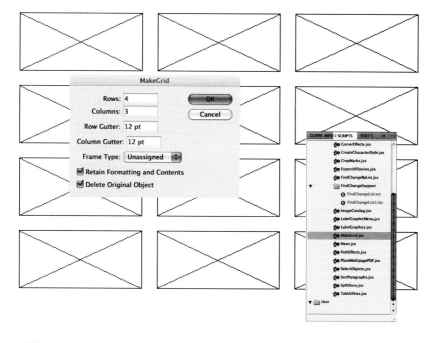

FIGURE 14.18 The MakeGrid script is a simple way to divide a frame into rows and columns.

AddGuides: This script will add ruler guides to any selected object(s), which is useful if you've created a grid of objects that you'd like to convert to guides. Simply add the guides, then delete the original objects.

Smart Guides: These make it easy to snap items to objects on your page. As you drag or create an object, temporary green guides appear, indicating that the object is aligned with an edge of the page, the center of the page, or another page item. With Smart Guides on, you can create a grid of objects on a separate,

TIP: Set your vertical ruler to a custom increment. Open the Preferences dialog box and select Units And Increments in the list on the left. Choose Custom from the pop-up menu next to Vertical and enter the grid increment as the amount. This makes the ticks on your ruler correspond to the lines of your grid.

locked layer and have those objects function as guides. Smart Guides are on by default (View > Grids And Guides > Smart Guides or Cmd+U/Ctrl+U). Their preferences can be set in Guides And Pasteboard preferences.

FIGURE 14.19 The AddGuides script puts guides around a selected object or an entire selection.

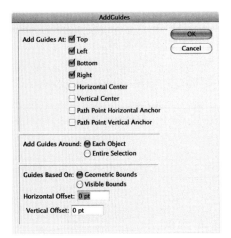

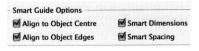

FIGURE 14.20 Smart Guides preferences.

TIP: The Grid System (thegridsystem.org) is an excellent resource and learning center for all things related to designing with grids.

Grid Terminology

Type area: The area of the page where type appears. The layout grid, made up of fields and gutters, is contained within the type area.

Grid fields: The individual cells of the grid. The more grid fields (within reason), the more flexible the grid.

Gutters: The horizontal and vertical spaces separating the grid fields. Their width and height are usually the same as the baseline grid increment.

Active corner: The upper-left corner of each grid field, especially when using left-aligned text with a flush left edge and a ragged right edge. It's not necessary for text or images to fill the grid field, but the content should be aligned to the top left of the active corner to preserve the integrity of the grid. One exception to this is when the text functions as a caption above a picture in the grid field below. In such cases, the text can be aligned to the bottom of the text frame.

Grid Field

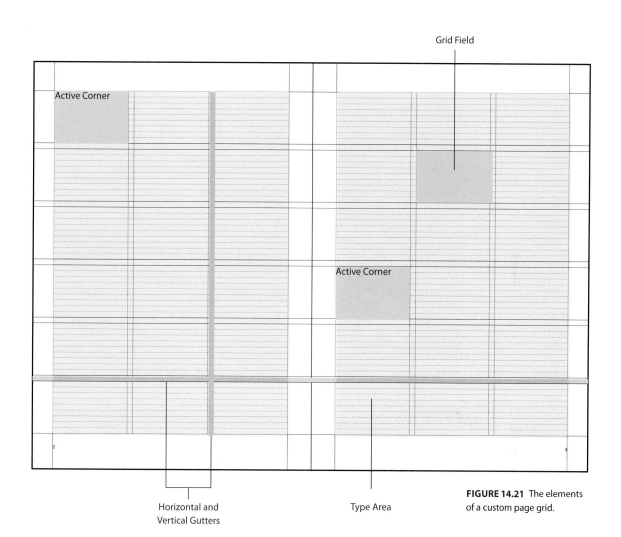

Active Corner

Active Corner

Horizontal and
Vertical Gutters

Type Area

FIGURE 14.21 The elements
of a custom page grid.

TIP: In a perfect world, our clients would mark up their proofs electronically with Adobe Acrobat or, better still, use an InCopy workflow. Until that day, for clients who like to give you corrections over the phone, make a line scale on your master page to indicate line numbers. Put the line scale on its own layer. This way your client can refer to corrections by page and line number, which makes for quicker document editing. When the layout is finished, either delete the layer containing the line scale or make that layer nonprinting. To do that, double-click the layer name in the Layers panel to bring up the layer properties. Deselect the Print Layer option.

FIGURE 14.23 Add a nonprinting line scale to the master pages for easy referencing of editorial problems.

Adjusting the Height of the Type Area

For continuous reading, columns should be vertical (that is, taller than they are wide) and, when working with a baseline grid, their height should be an exact multiple of the text leading.

To make the column height a multiple of the baseline grid increment, do the following:

1. In InDesign's Grid preferences, select Grids In Back. Turn on the baseline grid (Cmd/Ctrl+Shift+').

2. Go to the master pages. The type area will almost certainly end with a partial grid increment. Zoom in to the bottom of the page and with the Rectangle Frame Tool draw a rectangle in this partial increment to measure its height. Make a note of the height of the rectangle (shown on the Control Panel) or highlight the value and copy it to the clipboard.

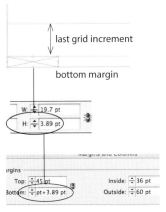

FIGURE 14.22 Adjusting the height of the type area to be an exact multiple of the baseline grid.

3. Go to Layout > Margins And Columns. Insert your cursor after the value of the bottom margin and type **+** and then enter (or paste) the value of the partial increment to increase the size of the bottom margin by this amount.

4. Click OK. The type area should now be an exact multiple of the baseline grid increment.

Layers

If you are familiar with using layers in either Adobe Photoshop or Adobe Illustrator, then InDesign's layers will look very familiar. Layers determine the stacking order of objects on your page. In the example shown in Figure 14.24, elements on the Text layer display (and print) on top of any elements on the Pictures or Panels layers. Each individual layer also has a stacking order that you can control using the Object > Arrange menu. But layers trump Bring To Front and Send To Back. For instance, in the example shown, an object at the front of the Pictures layer is still beneath an object that is at the back of the Text layer. If there are no objects on a layer, you see through to the layer(s) beneath.

Layers allow you to view and edit specific kinds of content in your document without affecting other kinds of content, which significantly speeds up your workflow. For example, you can hide the Pictures layer when concentrating on the text and vice versa. Clicking on the small square to the right of the layer name selects all the content on that layer.

In CS5, layers can be twirled open to show their sublayers—like in Illustrator. This makes it easy to see and change the stacking order of elements (by dragging the sublayers up or down in the list) as well as select specific items by clicking the selection square to the right of the layer or sublayer name. This is especially useful if you are selecting one item of a group, or if you need to hide/show or lock/unlock individual objects.

Layers are also necessary to avoid printing problems that can arise when you use transparent elements in your layout. In InDesign, *transparency* means a drop shadow, feathering, a Photoshop image with an alpha channel, or any object with a blend mode other than Normal or an opacity of less than 100 percent. You can set the Panel Options (found in the Pages panel menu) to display a checkerboard icon when transparency is used on a page or spread. The icon serves as a reminder to troubleshoot these pages before sending them off to your printer. When a document is printed, any text in close proximity to a transparent element—for example, a text wrap around a layered Photoshop image—is in danger of being rasterized, and possibly ending up looking rather furry as a result.

To prevent this from happening, move all text objects (except those that use transparency effects) to the top layer of your document.

FIGURE 14.24 The Layers panel for a 16-page newsletter. The Text layer is expanded to show the items on that layer, all of them text frames with a preview of the first few words in each story. If you wish, you can rename any of these sublayers. To select an item using the Layers panel, simply click the square to the right of the layer or sublayer name. This is very useful for locating items on a particular layer rather than clicking layers on and off to see what's where.

Aligning Text to the Grid

Once you've established a baseline grid, you can align text to it by choosing All Lines in the Align To Grid choices found under the Indents And Spacing section of the Paragraph Style Options menu. You can also apply this option locally by clicking the Align To Grid icon on the Control Panel.

FIGURE 14.25 Aligning text to the baseline grid through the Paragraph Style Options menu (left), or locally on the Control Panel (right).

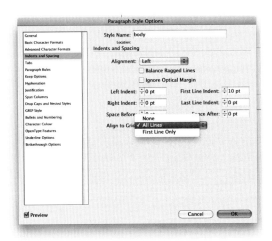

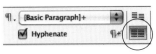

TIP: When resizing and moving graphics, picture frames snap to the baseline grid, making it easier to position and crop your images to a leading increment. If you are using text wraps, set the text wrap offset to your leading increment.

A baseline grid sets the rhythm of your document. In documents that use a variety of type and leading sizes, it's perfectly acceptable to go against that rhythm by coming off the grid with certain elements, such as headings and subheads, so long as the next passage of body text finds the beat again and is back on the grid, reestablishing the rhythm.

Aligning to the grid always means the *next* grid increment, causing leading values to be rounded up, never down. For example, if a paragraph with a specified leading value of 13 points is aligned to a 12-point grid, its leading will become 24 points. When you align text to a grid, the grid increment always trumps the leading.

TIP: Need a fresh start while creating your grid? To remove all ruler guides from a page or spread, Ctrl/right-click the ruler and choose Delete All Guides from the context menu.

This can present problems when you have paragraphs with different leading values that you don't want rounded up to the next leading increment or where you like to apportion some of the paragraph spacing below, as well as above, the paragraph. In such instances, it's preferable to take these paragraphs off the baseline grid — making sure, however, that the total paragraph spacing (leading+space before+space after) equals a multiple of the grid increment, so that the grid-aligned text that follows has a predictable amount of paragraph spacing before it. For example, if the grid is 12 points and you have subheads that are 14/14, you can take these paragraphs off the grid and divide the 10 points of space (24–14) between the space before and after.

Only Align First Line To Grid (found in the Control Panel menu) is useful for captions and other supporting text that, because of size and leading values, cannot keep to the grid. This option ensures that the first lines of such paragraphs align with the text in adjacent columns. Subsequent lines follow the specified leading increment.

TIP: Grids, of course, are meant to serve only as guides in the document, but there may be times when you need to print the grid guides. In the General panel of the Print dialog box, select Print Visible Guides And Baseline Grids to make all visible guides (that is, those that are not hidden or on hidden layers) print.

Lut eos que pro volo esectotatur? Everia doles et aut volore simi, que eostis autem ut aut qui voluptas nectest, sit eossit et laborisincti odic te voluptatur aut elit, at qui dolupta speriant. Am et eaquat omnihillit ped que vellanis am ent in pro is eos eosam fugitatur suntem ute natur, commoloriti suntemporis quiae rent unti torum, qui alignis quid escienis simus mos dolorib erchili busdandis volorunt eum vitio venim re, velest veliatus estrunt.
Subhead
Ectiae. Tium id quo eius ea ium comnimint ulpa dolorum accum desequa tionseque re, suntius reptaquae verfere hentur, consed ma nobit enitae nonsequos ex experum ad magnimo luptatecus et hicidus es apisquatum etusanis aruntia iur? Ut quaspit ut molum nobis debit et pra nisciis dolupid qui cum aspelent.
Lut eos que pro volo esectotatur? Everia doles et aut volore simi, que eostis autem ut aut qui voluptas nectest, sit eossit et laborisincti odic te voluptatur aut elit, at qui dolupta speriant. Am et eaquat omnihillit ped que vellanis am ent in pro is eos eosam fugitatur suntem ute natur, commoloriti suntemporis quiae rent unti torum, qui alignis quid escienis simus mos dolorib erchili busdandis volorunt eum vitio venim re, velest veliatus estrunt.
Subhead
Ectiae. Tium id quo eius ea ium comnimint ulpa dolorum accum desequa tionseque re, suntius reptaquae verfere hentur, consed ma nobit enitae nonsequos ex experum ad magnimo luptatecus et hicidus es apisquatum etusanis aruntia iur? Ut quaspit ut molum nobis debit et pra nisciis dolupid qui cum aspelent.

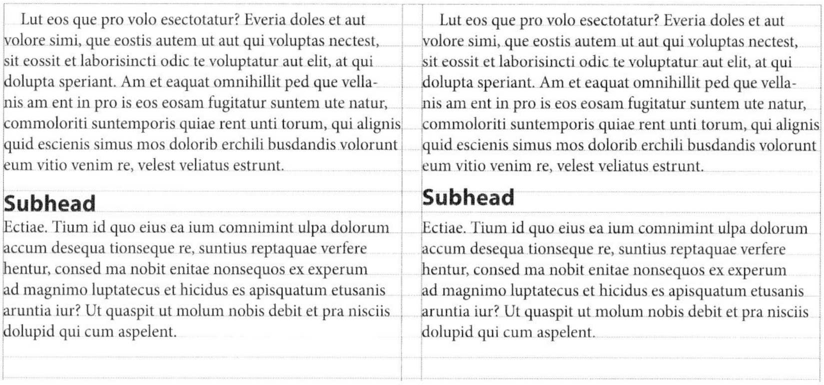

FIGURE 14.26 In the text on the left, the subhead is aligned to the grid, causing all the extra spacing to be added before the paragraph. On the right, the subhead is not aligned to the grid but the total paragraph spacing is a multiple of the baseline grid, allowing the extra spacing to be distributed between the space before and after.

urna vel velit. Integer dignissim vulputate elit in posuere. Suspendisse potenti. Donec a ante ut turpis pulvinar dignissim. Aliquam mattis rhoncus urna, euismod cursus ipsum porta at. Pellentesque tempor sodales ante sit amet mollis. Nullam rutrum vestibulum
This is supporting text in Myriad Pro 8/9. The first line of the paragraph aligns to the grid; thereafter the text will sync with the grid on every third line.

OpenType
Ligatures
Underline Options....
Strikethrough Options...
No Break
Adobe Paragraph Composer
Adobe Single-line Composer
Only Align First Line to Grid
Balance Ragged Lines
Justification...
Keep Options...
Hyphenation...
Drop Caps and Nested Styles...
GREP Styles...
Paragraph Rules...

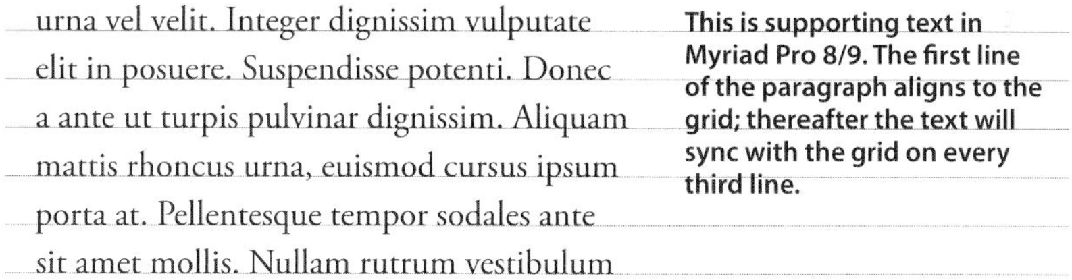

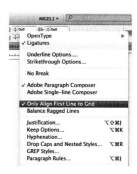

FIGURE 14.27 For supporting text with smaller leading values, choose Only Align First Line To Grid.

Accommodating Different Leading Values

The baseline grid needs to accommodate different type sizes and leading values. One way to make this possible is to set the leading values of the sidebars or supporting text so that they resolve with the baseline grid on every third or fourth line. For example, if the body text leading is 13.5 points and the sidebar leading is 9 points, the baselines will resolve on every second/third line (13.5 x 2 = 27, 9 x 3=27).

Here are some other body text/supporting text leading combinations that resolve themselves on every third or fourth line:

- 12.75/8.5 every third line

- 12/9 every fourth line

- 11/8.25 every fourth line

- 11.5/8.625 every fourth line

A different approach is to halve the baseline grid increment, effectively giving you the option of adding a half, rather than a whole, line space above subhead paragraphs. This will mean that the baselines will be out of register when there are an odd number of subheads in one or more columns; the baselines will come back into register when there is an even number of subheads in all columns. It will also mean double the number of baseline grid guides on the page, which may be dizzying to work with.

FIGURE 14.28 If the leading values of supporting text are carefully considered, the text will align with every third line of the main text block, as indicated by the heavier rules.

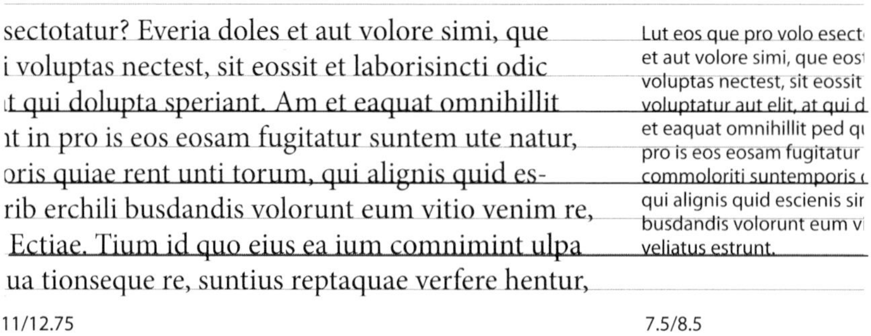

sectotatur? Everia doles et aut volore simi, que i voluptas nectest, sit eossit et laborisincti odic t qui dolupta speriant. Am et eaquat omnihillit it in pro is eos eosam fugitatur suntem ute natur, oris quiae rent unti torum, qui alignis quid es- rib erchili busdandis volorunt eum vitio venim re, Ectiae. Tium id quo eius ea ium comnimint ulpa ua tionseque re, suntius reptaquae verfere hentur,

Lut eos que pro volo esect et aut volore simi, que eos voluptas nectest, sit eossit voluptatur aut elit, at qui d et eaquat omnihillit ped qu pro is eos eosam fugitatur commoloriti suntemporis (qui alignis quid escienis sir busdandis volorunt eum v veliatus estrunt.

11/12.75

7.5/8.5

FIGURE 14.29 Halving the grid increment gives you the option of adding half-line spaces above subheads. The baselines will be out of register in adjacent columns (as indicated by the blue shading) until a subhead is introduced.

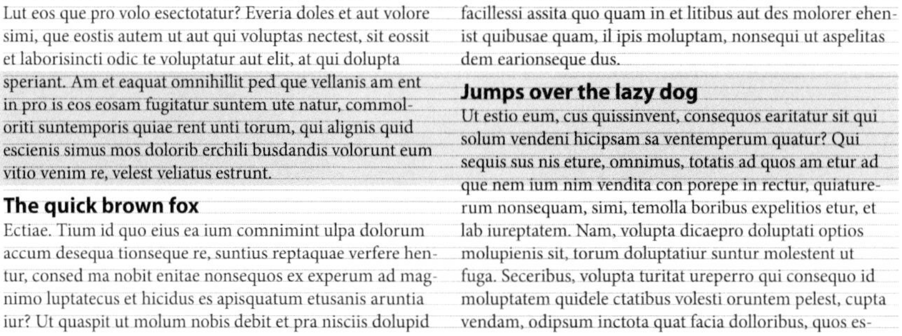

Lut eos que pro volo esectotatur? Everia doles et aut volore simi, que eostis autem ut aut qui voluptas nectest, sit eossit et laborisincti odic te voluptatur aut elit, at qui dolupta speriant. Am et eaquat omnihillit ped que vellanis am ent in pro is eos eosam fugitatur suntem ute natur, commoloriti suntemporis quiae rent unti torum, qui alignis quid escienis simus mos dolorib erchili busdandis volorunt eum vitio venim re, velest veliatus estrunt.

The quick brown fox

Ectiae. Tium id quo eius ea ium comnimint ulpa dolorum accum desequa tionseque re, suntius reptaquae verfere hentur, consed ma nobit enitae nonsequos ex experum ad magnimo luptatecus et hicidus es apisquatum etusanis aruntia iur? Ut quaspit ut molum nobis debit et pra nisciis dolupid

facillessi assita quo quam in et litibus aut des molorer ehenist quibusae quam, il ipis moluptam, nonsequi ut aspelitas dem earionseque dus.

Jumps over the lazy dog

Ut estio eum, cus quissinvent, consequos earitatur sit qui solum vendeni hicipsam sa ventemperum quatur? Qui sequis sus nis eture, omnimus, totatis ad quos am etur ad que nem ium nim vendita con porepe in rectur, quiaturerum nonsequam, simi, temolla boribus expelitios etur, et lab iureptatem. Nam, volupta dicaepro doluptati optios molupienis sit, torum doluptatiur suntur molestent ut fuga. Seceribus, volupta turitat ureperro qui consequo id moluptatem quidele ctatibus volesti oruntem pelest, cupta vendam, odipsum inctota quat facia dolloribus, quos es-

Aligning Images with the Top of the Text

When you align text frames to the top of picture frames, the gap between the text cap height and the top of the text frame results in optical misalignment. To fix this, draw a ruler guide from the horizontal ruler aligned to the cap height (or the x-height—whichever is more consistent) of the first line of type and align the top of the image frame to this guide. If the layout requires cross alignment of multiple picture frames with the text cap height, then create a cap height grid by following these steps:

1. Draw a ruler guide to the cap height of the first line of type.

2. Cut the guide to the clipboard (Cmd/Ctrl+X), and go to the master pages.

3. Create a new layer for the cap height grid—having the grid visible all the time will create visual clutter, so you'll want the option of only seeing it when necessary by turning on and off the layer visibility.

4. Paste the guide (Cmd/Ctrl+V) from the clipboard.

5. With the guide selected, choose Edit > Step And Repeat (Cmd+Option+U/Ctrl+Alt+U) and enter the number of lines in your type area (minus 1) for the Count and the baseline grid increment for the Vertical Offset.

6. Finally, select all the guides on the layer: Ctrl/right-click the square to the right of the layer name and choose Layer Options. From there you can change the color of the guides to distinguish your alignment grid from the baseline grid.

Pellentesque sed magna eget leo
consequat condimentum in eu
turpis. Integer adipiscing, risus vitae
vehicula dapibus, justo lectus faucibus
ipsum, sed porta mauris urna a
tellus. Vestibulum hendrerit pulvinar
leo id sollicitudin. Duis mattis, lacus
in ullamcorper placerat, enim nulla
vestibulum neque, vel ultricies purus
dui cursus mauris. Fusce tincidunt
neque nec lacus auctor ut euismod

Vestibulum hendrerit pulvinar leo
id sollicitudin. Duis mattis, lacus
in ullamcorper placerat, enim nulla
vestibulum neque, vel ultricies purus

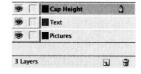

FIGURE 14.30 The blue lines mark the cap height of the type, incremented at the same interval as the baseline grid in gray. The tops of picture frames are aligned to the cap height grid.

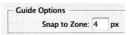

FIGURE 14.31 The Snap To Zone setting in the Guides And Pasteboard Preferences dialog box.

Snap To Guides

When working with grids, it's crucial that Snap To Guides is turned on (View > Grids And Guides > Snap To Guides or Cmd+Shift+; /Ctrl+Shift+;) so that when you draw, move, or resize an object its edges snap to the nearest guide or baseline grid. Guides must be visible in order for objects to snap to them; however, objects can snap to the baseline grid whether it is visible or not.

The Snap To Zone setting in Guides And Pasteboard Preferences determines the exact range within which an object snaps to guides.

Text Frames with Different Grids

In addition to a document-wide baseline grid, you can use a separate baseline grid for each frame. This can be useful if you have sidebar material that flows in multiple columns and uses a different type size and leading value than the body text. Use a custom baseline grid when it's more important that the supporting text aligns with itself, than side by side with the main text. Theoretically, every text frame can have its own baseline grid, but having too many different baseline grids in a document undermines the whole purpose of the grid: a document architecture based on *consistent* modular units.

consectetur auctor odio, vel dignissim dolor blandit non. Nulla auctor ornare nisl vel faucibus.

Praesent pellentesque magna et elit pulvinar sed malesuada arcu bibendum. Maecenas in mollis mauris. Maecenas iaculis tempus ligula, non venenatis risus consectetur a. Ut pulvinar nisi eget ipsum iaculis eget lobortis tortor aliquet.

eu nisi ac dolor gravida rutrum eu eu lacus.

In ut diam sodales sem bibendum volutpat. Morbi nec eros at magna tincidunt venenatis. Vestibulum scelerisque leo eleifend dui viverra elementum. Aenean vel erat quatione mos molupta tquiducit venimint lab ipsus.

Ur, simolor ecatur? Seditae volorem es pratum, cus, eum dolenimus maionse

Lorem ipsum dolor sit amet, consectetur adipiscing elit. In arcu diam, vehicula non condimentum mollis, sagittis consectetur justo.

Text Frame Options

General | Baseline Options

First Baseline
Offset: Ascent Min: 0 pt

Baseline Grid
☑ Use Custom Baseline Grid
Start: 0 pt
Relative To: Top Inset
Increment Every: 10 pt
Colour: ■ (Layer Colour)

Box Text Strapline

Using Custom Baseline Grids

Tet veliquam: sim digna corperaesto consenit dolorem duis nulla feugait vel del ullut ipsummodigna consecte dolortie vel dolobore do odionulput ip eum zzriliquam quat nisisequat ut velent ulluptat non erat.

feui bla feu facidunt num do odolore facip el in ulput vel ipsustrud doloborem quam dolortie do doloborem dolore magnit am, quam, core dignibh el dolore el dunt prating ea feugiat. Na adit dolortin et lore feuip ero et, quis exer iriuscipis nullaorer si.

Reet niatuerit: ver incing eum quismodip exero dolobor

el ullummodigna faci bla feugait wis nim ero eniamconse venit vel utat lumsandit am vulputet lut iriustrud diamconsed tat.

Re modoloreet num quat diam quam incipit dio odolort ississe quametue dio dip eugiamet iuscin henisl estie dio et ut vel utpat vel dolobore vulputpatem vel illamet iure tie magna aut landre magna faccum nis nonsequ amcorem volendre

vel utpatinim venibh esequisis nullaorper am delestie modiat am iriliquat.

Se ming eu facilla oreetum nostrud molutpat nostrud dio elit lore magna faccum in ea faci tet adigna accummodo odit nostio dionsequis exer iure vent la cor sum dolore tat aliquipsummy nit amcommy nonsecte miniat nibh exeros ad te te conullu tpatum erilis

FIGURE 14.32 The smaller text in the shaded box does not run side by side with the body text, so it is a good candidate for a custom baseline grid. The caption is on the main baseline, but aligned to the first line only.

Dividing the Page into Rows

To divide the page into a number of rows that each have an exact number of lines, you'll need to make sure the height of the type area is an exact multiple of the baseline grid as described earlier in this chapter.

The row gutters should be the same value as the baseline grid increment. For six rows, subtract five gutter widths from the total height of the type area, for eight rows, subtract seven gutters, and so on. The number you are left with needs to be divisible by your grid increment. If it is not, you'll either need to increase or decrease the top and bottom margins accordingly.

For example, a type area of 53 lines divides into six rows: 53 − 5 = 48/6 = 8 lines per row. A type area of 55 divides into seven rows: 55 − 6 = 49/7 = 7 lines per row, or into eight rows: 55 − 7 = 48/8 = six lines per row.

TIP: To draw a custom guide from the horizontal ruler that straddles the left- and right-hand pages of the spread, hold down Cmd (Ctrl) as you draw the guide. You can also position guides precisely by selecting them and typing precise coordinates in the Control Panel. For vertical guides, specify their x coordinate; for horizontal guides, specify their y coordinate.

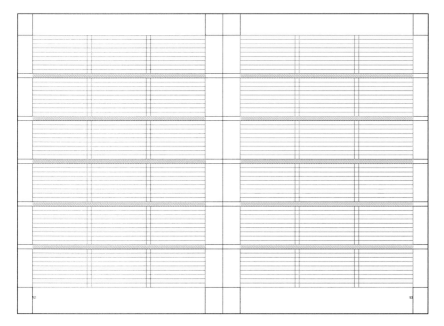

FIGURE 14.33 An A4 spread with a type area of 59 lines, divided into six rows of nine lines each (6 x 9 = 54 + 5 gutter spaces = 59). The row gutters are shaded in blue.

Creating Diagonal and Spherical Guides

While InDesign doesn't let you draw objects and turn them into guides the way Illustrator does, there's nothing to stop you from putting "guide objects" on a separate layer and making that layer nonprinting. Alternatively, you can select the objects and use the Output panel to make their attributes nonprinting.

FIGURE 14.34 Diagonal lines drawn with the Line Tool converted to guides by isolating them on a nonprinting layer.

Page Numbers and Running Heads

TIP: Press Cmd+Shift+M (Ctrl+Shift+M) for an em space and Cmd+Shift+N (Ctrl+Shift+N) for an en space.

Page numbers, or folios, should be placed on a document's master pages so that they show up on all the pages based on that master page. Although folios are placed outside the type area, they must relate to it. Their type size will typically be same as the body text, and in terms of position, the practical options are either at the top or the bottom of the page in the outside margins. Folios typically work best in the outside margin where they can be easily seen by the reader, though centered folios are common in book design and are a legitimate choice. Folios in the inner margin, however, make it hard to flip through the book to find a specific page, and are consequently of little use.

The page number may be accompanied by information like the name of the magazine and month of publication or the chapter title, separated from the number by an em space or en space. The left and right pages of a spread typically mirror each other so that the page number is the outermost element.

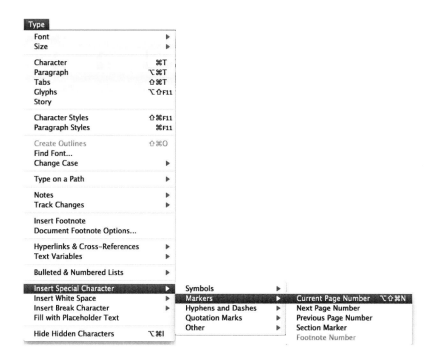

FIGURE 14.35 Inserting a page number. On master pages these will appear as the prefix of the master page: A, B, C, etc.; on document pages they will reflect the current page number.

Creating Mirrored Folios

1. On the left-hand master page, use the Type Tool to draw a text frame below the bottom margin to the full width of the type area. You may find it helpful to first draw guides that correspond to the outside and inside margins, and then draw the text frame from guide to guide.

2. Select Type > Insert Special Character > Markers > Current Page Number or press Cmd+Option+Shift+N (Ctrl+Alt+Shift+N) to insert the special character for page number and any folio information (for example, publication name), then apply character formats as appropriate.

3. Set the alignment to Align Away From Spine, then make a paragraph style for the folio.

4. To position the folio a precise distance from the bottom margin, first move its text frame up so that the top of the frame touches the bottom margin, then insert your cursor into the y value for the frame on the Control Panel and add the increment of the baseline grid after the existing value to move the folio text frame down by one line space.

5. Zoom out to Fit Spread In Window view by pressing Cmd+Option+0 (Ctrl+Alt+0), then switch to the Selection Tool and duplicate the text frame to the right-hand master page by holding down Option/ Alt+Shift as you drag—the Shift key constrains the movement to the horizontal plane only.

6. The folio will be positioned in the outside margin due to its Align Away From Spine alignment, but you'll still need to manually adjust the order of the text using Cut and Paste.

Running Heads

The content of running heads (*headers*) varies between publishing houses, but it's common to put the author's name at the top top of the left-hand (verso) pages and the title of the book or chapter on the right-hand (recto) pages. This may be useful for short story collections or anthologies, which have multiple authors, but is unnecessary in a work by a single author. After all, how many times do you need to be reminded of the author's name or the name of the book you're reading?

In a work using running heads at the top of the page, it is common to position the folio at the bottom of the page on chapter heading pages where a running head at the top of the page would interfere with the type treatment of the chapter heading. In such instances, it's worth making a separate master page for the chapter opening pages.

For books divided into chapters or sections, the running head may contain the name of the chapter or section number. It's easy to add a text variable to a master page to achieve this:

1. On either the left- or right-hand master page, create a text frame that is the width of the type area and position it at least one line space above the top margin. Choose Type > Text Variables > Define to set up the conditions of the text variable.

2. Choose Running Header as the type of variable, and click Edit to define its options (see Figure 14.36).

3. Choose the appropriate predefined style sheets used in the document to apply to the text for the header.

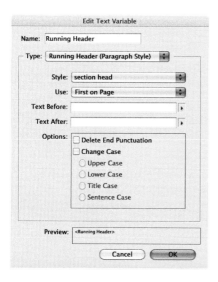

FIGURE 14.36 Defining a Running Header text variable.

4. Click OK, then click Insert to insert the text variable into the text frame. While you're on the master page the variable will read <Running Header> and will not reflect the applied styles. Style comes into play on the actual document pages. If necessary, duplicate the text frame to the facing master page. Now, on the document pages the text variable will reflect the chapter or section head of the first (or last) match of the paragraph style specified in the previous step.

Section Markers

If you're working with long documents that are divided into different sections, section markers can help simplify the project by cutting down on the number of master pages or the number of documents needed. Section markers can be used to mark the transitions between departments in a magazine or parts of a book—wherever a document is made up of distinctly different sections. Each section can have its own numbering scheme—Arabic, roman numeral, or abc. Section Markers can be formatted just as you would any piece of text.

To insert a section marker:

1. Create a text frame for your folio on a master page.

2. Ctrl/right-click and choose Insert Special Character > Markers > Section Marker from the context menu. The word *Section* will be inserted into your type.

3. Format the section marker the way you want it to look.

4. To "activate" the section marker on a document page, select the page where you want the section to begin in the Pages panel and choose Numbering And Section Options from the Pages panel menu. Type the section name into the Section Marker field and click OK. This section marker will now appear on all pages based on the master page until another section is defined.

FIGURE 14.37 A section marker is inserted on the master page (**A**), then defined on the relevant document page (**B**). This will remain "on" until a new section is defined (**C**).

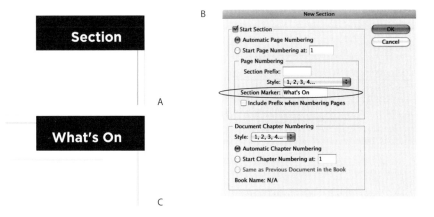

Bibliography

Books

Ambrose, G., and Harris, P. *The Fundamentals of Typography*. Lausanne, Switzerland: AVA Publishing SA, 2006.

Baines, Phil, and Andrew Haslam. *Type & Typography*. London: Laurence King, 2005.

Blatner, David, and Olav Kvern. *Real World InDesign CS5*. Berkeley, CA: Peachpit Press, 2010.

Bringhurst, Robert. *The Elements of Typographic Style*. Vancouver, BC: Hartley and Marks Publishers, 2004.

Elam, Kimberly. *Typographic Systems*. Princeton, NJ: Princeton Architectural Press, 2007.

Felici, James. *The Complete Manual of Typography: A Guide to Setting Perfect Type*. Berkeley, CA: Peachpit Press, 2003.

Felton, Paul. *The Ten Commandments of Typography/Type Heresy: Breaking the Ten Commandments of Typography*. London: Merrell Publishers, 2006.

Haley, Allan. *Typographic Milestones*. New York: Van Nostrand Reinhold, 1992.

Heller, Steven. *The Education of a Typographer*. New York: Allworth Press, 2004.

Hochuli, Jost. *Detail in Typography*. London: Hyphen Press, 2009.

Hollis, Richard. *Graphic Design: A Concise History*. London: Thames & Hudson, 1994.

Kahrel, Peter. *GREP in InDesign CS3/CS4*. Sebastopol, CA: O'Reilly Media, 2008. PDF or EPUB eBook.

Kane, John. *A Type Primer*. London: Laurence King, 2002.

Lupton, Ellen. *Thinking with Type: A Critical Guide for Designers*. Princeton, NJ: Princeton Architectural Press, 2007.

McLean, Ruari. *The Thames and Hudson Manual of Typography*. London: Thames and Hudson, 1980

Müller-Brockmann, Josef. *Grid Systems in Graphic Design, 4th ed.* Zurich: Verlag Niggli, 2008.

Salz, Ina. *Typography Essentials: 100 Design Principles for Working with Type*. Beverly, MA: Rockport, 2009.

Spiekermann, Erik, and E.M. Ginger. *Stop Stealing Sheep & Find Out How Type Works*. Berkeley, CA: Adobe Press, 2002.

Squire, Victoria. *Getting It Right with Type*. London: Laurence King, 2006.

Tschichold, Jan. *The New Typography*. Berkeley, CA: University of California Press, 2006.

—. *The Form of the Book: Essays on the Morality of Good Design*. Vancouver, BC: Hartley and Marks, 2007.

White, Alex. *Thinking in Type*. New York: Allworth Press, 2005.

Williams, Robin. *The Non-Designers Type Book, Second Edition*. Berkeley, CA: Peachpit Press, 2006.

Wilson, Adrian. *The Design of Books*. San Francisco: Chronicle Books, 1993.

Movies

Hustwit, Gary. *Helvetica*, DVD. London: Swiss Dots, 2007.

Radio Shows

Wisconsin Public Radio. "Program 09-11-01-B: Fonts," To the Best of Our Knowledge (aired week of November 1, 2009). www.wpr.org/book/091101b.cfm

WNYC. "Please Explain: Typography," The Leonard Lopate Show (aired September 11, 2009). www.wnyc.org/shows/lopate/episodes/2009/09/11/segments/140481

Web Resources

Murphy, Michael. "InDesign CS4: Learning GREP," Lynda.com online training course, 2009. http://www.lynda.com/home/DisplayCourse.aspx?lpk2=48368

99 Graphic Design Resources. http://justcreativedesign.com/2008/02/25/99-graphic-design-resources/

A Complete List of InDesign CS4 Videos. http://blogs.adobe.com/indesigndocs/2008/10/a_complete_list_of_indesign_cs.html

Adobe Creative Suite Video Podcast. http://creativesuitepodcast.com/index.php?post_id=433704

Adobe InDesign Exchange. www.adobe.com/cfusion/exchange/index.cfm?event=productHome&exc=19

ATypI. www.atypi.org

Before & After. www.bamagazine.com

Computer Arts. www.computerarts.co.uk/home

CreativePro.com. www.creativepro.com/topic/fonts

Design Police. www.design-police.org

FFFFOUND! http://ffffound.com

InDesign Magazine. www.indesignmag.com

InDesignSecrets. http://indesignsecrets.com

Lynda.com. www.lynda.com

Microsoft typography. www.microsoft.com/typography/links/default.aspx

P22 Terminal. www.p22.com/terminal/toc.html

pass4press. www.pass4press.com

Pentagram - What type are you? www.pentagram.com/what-type-are-you/

Periodic Table of Typefaces. www.behance.net/Gallery/Periodic-Table-of-Typefaces/193759

The Grid System. www.thegridsystem.org

Learn: Anatomy of a Typeface. http://typedia.com/learn/only/anatomy-of-a-typeface/

Typobituaries. www.danielmall.com/archives/2006/08/22/typobituaries.php

typoGRAPHIC. www.rsub.com/typographic/timeline/

Typophile. http://typophile.com

Veer. www.veer.com

WhatTheFont! http://new.myfonts.com/WhatTheFont/

Index

WATCH
READ
CREATE

Meet Creative Edge.

A new resource of unlimited books, videos and tutorials for creatives from the world's leading experts.

Creative Edge is your one stop for inspiration, answers to technical questions and ways to stay at the top of your game so you can focus on what you do best—being creative.

All for only $24.99 per month for access—any day any time you need it.

creativeedge.com